PROUST, BECKETT, AND NARRATION

This is the first book-length comparison of the narrative techniques of two of the twentieth century's most important writers of prose. Using a combination of theoretical analysis and close readings of Proust's *A la recherche du temps perdu* and Beckett's trilogy of novels, *Molloy, Malone Dies*, and *The Unnamable*, James H. Reid compares the two novelists' use of first-person narration in constructing and demystifying fictions of consciousness. Reid focuses on the narrator's searches to represent and erase a voice that speaks the novel; searches, he argues, that structure first-person narration in the works of both novelists. He examines in detail the significant impact of Proust's writing on Beckett's own work as well as Beckett's subtle reworkings of Proust's themes and strategies. This study is an important contribution to critical literature, and offers fresh perspectives on the crucial importance of the *Recherche* and the trilogy in the context of the twentieth-century novel.

JAMES H. REID is Associate Professor of French Literature at Illinois State University. He is the author of *Narration and Description in the French Realist Novel* (Cambridge, 1993) and of numerous articles.

PROUST, BECKETT, AND NARRATION

JAMES H. REID

PUBLISHED BY THE PRESS SYNDICATE OF THE UNIVERSITY OF CAMBRIDGE
The Pitt Building, Trumpington Street, Cambridge CB2 IRP, United Kingdom

CAMBRIDGE UNIVERSITY PRESS
The Edinburgh Building, Cambridge, CB2 2RU, UK
40 West 20th Street, New York, NY 10011–4211, USA
477 Williamstown Road, Port Melbourne, VIC 3207, Australia
Ruiz de Alarcón 13, 28014 Madrid, Spain
Dock House, The Waterfront, Cape Town 8001, South Africa

http://www.cambridge.org

© James H. Reid 2003

This book is in copyright. Subject to statutory exception
and to the provisions of relevant collective licensing agreements,
no reproduction of any part may take place without
the written permission of Cambridge University Press.

First published 2003

Printed in the United Kingdom at the University Press, Cambridge

Typeface Adobe Garamond 11/12.5 pt.   *System* LATEX 2$_\varepsilon$ [TB]

A catalogue record for this book is available from the British Library

ISBN 0 521 82847 3 hardback

The publisher has used its best endeavors to ensure that URLs for external websites referred to in this book are correct and active at the time of going to press. However, the publisher has no responsibility for the websites and can make no guarantee that a site will remain live or that the content is or will remain appropriate.

For Barbara

Contents

List of abbreviations		*page* viii
	Introduction	1
1	Remembering forgetting: *Le Drame du coucher*	13
2	Impressions, the instant of artistic consciousness, and social history	26
3	Lying, irony, and power: Proust's deceptive allegories	46
4	Proust's forgetful ironies	69
5	Molloy's Way: The parody of allegory	79
6	Moran's Way: The forgetful spiral of irony	99
7	*Malone Dies* and the impossibility of not saying I	117
8	*The Unnamable*: The death of the ironical self and the return of history	138
Notes		156
Bibliography		185
Index		193

Abbreviations

R   Marcel Proust. *A la recherche du temps perdu*. Bibliothèque de la Pléiade. 3 vols. Paris: Gallimard, 1954.

TN   Samuel Beckett. *Three Novels by Samuel Beckett: Molloy, Malone Dies, and The Unnamable*. New York: Grove Press, 1958.

Introduction

Marcel Proust's *A la recherche du temps perdu* had a substantial impact on Beckett's dramatization of his first-person narrators' search for self in his trilogy of novels, *Molloy, Malone Dies,* and *The Unnamable*. Numerous studies have cited, as evidence of this influence, not only Beckett's discussion in his early essay *Proust* of the search for self in Proust's *Recherche*, but also his own narrators' Proustian concern with whether or not their words express a self.[1] However, despite the critical importance of the *Recherche* and the trilogy for the twentieth-century novel, and despite the significant impact of the Proustian search for self on Beckett's trilogy, there has been no rigorous comparison of the two novelists' use of first-person narration to construct the fiction of consciousness, or of the critical theme of self-consciousness which structures the search for, and demystification of, self in both their novels.

The present study seeks to fill this gap in the critical literature by exploring the different ways in which first-person narration structures the search for self-consciousness in both the *Recherche* and the trilogy. I will argue that, in these texts, first-person narration takes the form of an interplay between the tropes of allegory and irony as they are defined by Paul de Man.[2] The difference between irony and allegory is succinctly expressed by Beckett. In *The Unnamable*, he speaks of irony as "affirmations and negations invalidated as uttered, or sooner..." He speaks of allegory as "affirmations and negations invalidated...later" (*TN*, 291).[3] Irony presents signs of the subject of discourse as always already negated in the present of narration.

For de Man, allegory and irony are different modes of disclosing, behind signs of the individual difference of a subject, a repetition of the same temporal or spatial structures.[4] In other words, they are different modes of foregrounding the split nature of the subject of first-person narration. Allegory tends to take the form of a linear, narrative process of asserting and putting into question, over time, the story of the subject's search for an original self.[5] This putting into question of the search for self temporalizes the split subject of first-person narration by recounting the subject's discovery that it is always too early or too late to represent or remember a present or past self. By contrast, irony is a repeated, simultaneous assertion and negation of self-representation.[6] Irony repeatedly spatializes the split subject of first-person narration by giving it the form of the coincidence in a single instant of an assertion and a negation of self. Irony marks words as saying both too much and too little about a self.[7]

I will propose that in both Proust and Beckett the allegorical development of the subject as split in time gives way to an ironical constitution of the subject as split in space, but that this ironically split subject eventually gives way to the allegorically split subject. It is as if Proust's and Beckett's novels repeatedly pointed towards the necessary return of allegory.

Besides exploring the interplay between allegory and irony in the *Recherche* and the trilogy, I will investigate the roles of repetition and differentiation which structure the literary historical relationship between the trilogy's and the *Recherche*'s first-person narrators.[8] Beckett places allusions to the *Recherche* into his first-person narrators' discourses in order to set up multiple literary historical relationships with Proust's narrator, relationships that are shifting, dynamic, and deceptive. Although the trilogy's first-person narrators frequently establish seemingly clear resemblances with and differences from Proust's first-person narrator, sooner or later their discourses put into question the possibility of such clear relationships. The challenge for the reader of these shifting literary historical relationships between the trilogy and the *Recherche* is to document the signs of historical similarity and difference that Beckett's narrators seem to posit, to tease out the multiple ways in which similarities with Proust become differences and differences become similarities, and to interpret this interplay.

Critics, especially Beckett critics, have tended to posit clear-cut historical relationships between the two authors' narrators.[9] Some have viewed the *Recherche* through the lens of Beckett's early thematic essay, *Proust*, arguing that the essay makes an unambiguous historical distinction between Proust and Beckett.[10] Of the few articles and one book that study the trilogy's relationship to the *Recherche*, most have constructed this relationship as a clear and distinct historical change from a Proustian narration based on the overcoming of forgetting and the recovering of lost memories of self to a Beckettian narration based on the failure of memory and the absence of self.[11] According to Nicholas Zurbrugg, the narrators in Beckett's trilogy use "systematically anti-Proustian imagery" and "excremental rhetoric" to deny the Proustian narrator's claim to remember past selves. In his view, the trilogy produces a "nihilistic," "existential vision" of the world.[12] Similarly,

Introduction 3

James Acheson asserts that the narrator of *Molloy* illustrates Beckett's theory that "the modern artist has 'nothing to express...'."[13] For both Zurbrugg and Acheson, the literary historical relationship between Proust and Beckett takes the form of a linear transformation of the Proustian first-person narrator, who says he has a self to express, into the Beckettian narrator, who says that he has no self to express. The "Beckettian" narrator in this formulation tells stories about himself as a means of diverting himself from the painful knowledge of the absence of a self.[14]

This critical story of literary historical transformation oversimplifies the functioning of the first-person narrators in the *Recherche* and the trilogy. It elides the full interplay between the differentiation of a self and the repetition of conventional signs of self, which structures not only the narrators' discourses in the trilogy and the *Recherche*, but also the dynamic literary historical relationships between them.

In order to explore fully the complex literary historical interplay between first-person narration in the *Recherche* and the trilogy, it is necessary to describe and interpret the interplay between repetition and difference within each of the first-person discourses of Proust's or Beckett's narrators. The best recent studies of repetition and difference in Proust's or in Beckett's first-person narration posit a split between an "I" who asserts the existence of a self and an "I" that negates this existence.[15] The first-person narrators' disclosure of their split nature puts into question whether they are expressing a real self or merely constructing a fictional self by telling a story and calling it theirs. David Ellison reads the *Recherche* as an allegory of the narrator's deconstruction over time of his own assertions that he is remembering or expressing a self. This deconstruction, Ellison argues, invites an ironical reading of the narrator's representations of his self and his own discourse. Thomas Trezise studies the temporal interplay between difference and repetition in the production of fictional consciousnesses within the discourses of the trilogy's split first-person narrators, touching repeatedly, if often indirectly, on allegorical and ironical structures.[16]

This study seeks to interpret the full interplay between allegory and irony within Proust and within Beckett. Not only does allegory in each of these novelists' texts undercut itself and produce irony; irony undercuts itself and produces allegory. The study will argue that Beckett's literary historical allusions to Proust are structured by an interplay between the ironical and allegorical relationships that they establish with Proust's first-person narrator. The first four chapters of this study will interpret the formal nature of the interplay between allegory and irony as that interplay structures the *Recherche*. They will focus on particular ways in which the

Recherche dramatizes this interplay. The last four chapters will explore not only the interplay between allegory and irony in Beckett's trilogy, but also the literary historical interplay between allegory and irony that Beckett's repetition and transformation of Proust creates.

The narrators of the *Recherche* and the trilogy rarely if ever use the terms "allegory" or "irony" to discuss the temporality of their first-person narration. However, they do comment in great depth upon the structures that these terms signify. They discuss allegory and irony indirectly by commenting upon the temporality of their forgetting and lying.[17] The split subject of first-person narration can claim to represent itself truthfully only by presupposing that it can remember itself objectively. But the forgetting and deceptiveness of signs of memory always put this self-representation into question.

Forgetting and lying are different ways in which Proust's and Beckett's narrators mark the split subject of their first-person narration. Forgetting is the erasure of a memory of the past from the present of consciousness. Occurrences of forgetting and commentaries on forgetting in the discourses of Proust's and Beckett's narrators are critical signs of their use of allegory, which, according to de Man, is a discursive mode of disclosing the subject's forgetting of its past and present selves.[18] Lying, in contrast to forgetting, is by definition the explicit assertion of a false truth in order to deceive a reader and the simultaneous negation of that false truth within the liar's mind. Lying, as Kierkegaard notes, has a critical relationship to irony, which, like lying, explicitly asserts and simultaneously negates a truth.[19] But, whereas lying hides this negation in order better to deceive the reader, irony includes irony signals that indirectly reveal this negation to the rhetorically aware reader.[20] Lying becomes irony when a deliberately false statement is accompanied by irony signals which reveal the fabrication and prevent readers from being deceived.[21] These indirect signs invite readers to share in the writer's misrepresentation and implicit negation of this misrepresentation. Of course the distinction between irony and lying becomes fuzzy when it is recognized that the ironical author and his ironically complicitous readers know that some readers will not see the irony signals and will be deceived.[22]

A major goal of this study is to extend the de Manian analysis of the figures of allegory and irony to the literary historical interplay between repetition and difference in Beckett's allusions to Proust. If there is a fundamental distinction between Proust's and the trilogy's dramatizations of the interplay between allegory and irony, then the literary historical relationship between the *Recherche* and the trilogy will take the form of an historical

Introduction 5

allegory that discloses this temporal difference. Historical allegory is constituted by the opening up of temporal and historical difference. Beckett's allusions to Proust function to construct just such an historical allegory of the differentiation of his narrators' discourses from Proust's. But these allusions also undercut this historical allegory ironically and "demonstrat[e]," in de Man's terms, "the impossibility of our being historical."[23]

The result of this allegorical assertion and ironical denial of literary history is a dynamic interplay between allegory and irony in the reading of the trilogy. The interplay can best be illustrated by an analysis of consciousness and first-person narration in those passages of the trilogy that allude to the beginning and end of *Combray*, the first volume of the *Recherche*. At the beginning of *Combray*, Proust's narrator appears to constitute the temporality of his remembering and writing by dramatizing his slow awakening from sleep to consciousness during a recent period of his life. He interprets this process of awakening to consciousness as his mind's act of reconstructing a seemingly objective consciousness of the bedroom in which he fell asleep and the self who fell asleep there.[24] The narrator recounts how he became aware of this process of reconstruction when he would sometimes wake up in the middle of the night in his pitch-dark bedroom of his mother's apartment after falling asleep in an unaccustomed position. As he awakened, he would have difficulty remembering where, when, and who he was. He would see a myriad of imaginary and remembered bedrooms in which he imagined he had fallen asleep or in which he actually had fallen asleep sometime in the past. His memories of past bedrooms, the narrator tells us, were not objective memories of actual past bedrooms, but only memories of his past perceptions of these bedrooms. In order to awaken fully, the narrator had to decide which of the many remembered and imagined perceptions of past bedrooms flowing through his slowly awakening mind coincided with the perceptions he had had of his present bedroom before he had fallen asleep. The narrator would eventually choose what he believed to be the correct memory of his last perceptions of his bedroom in order to construct a consciousness of his present bedroom. Consciousness of a present world and self, for Proust, is thus the remembering of a past consciousness and the erasure of other possible past consciousnesses.

This awakening to consciousness of what I will call Proust's "remembering narrator" took the form of an act of mental construction. His mind constructed his consciousness of space, indirectly identified the time of life in which he was waking, and interpreted this consciousness as a metaphor of his present self. The narrator's consciousness at this moment of his life is thus constructed by his memory of where, when, and who he was when he awakened and by his certainty that this memory is accurate: "Certes, j'étais bien éveillé maintenant... et le bon ange de la certitude avait tout arrêté autour de moi, m'avait couché sous mes couvertures..." (*R*, 1: 8).[25] His remembered perceptions of other past bedrooms also theoretically marked the time in which he had had those perceptions and the different selves who had had those perceptions. By becoming conscious of where and when he is, he becomes conscious of who he is, as defined by the different manner of perceiving the world that distinguishes his present self from past and future selves.

Waking at the beginning of *Combray* appears to produce a full, non-split subject in the form of a fictional consciousness, which can correctly identify the subject's place in space and time and the self to which this subject refers. Until the remembering narrator achieves self-consciousness, his mind remains split between a subject that desires consciousness of a single self and a myriad of mental objects that raise questions about the existence of such a self. The narrator fully awakens only when this "kaleidoscope" of remembered and imaginary bedrooms gives way to the consciousness of a single bedroom, after he chooses a particular memory to represent where, when, and who he is now and where he was when he fell asleep. On those nights when he fell asleep in an unaccustomed position, however, this process of awakening and remembering was deferred by the persistence of the narrator's forgetting who he was when he fell asleep. This persistent forgetting temporarily prevents him from deciding with certainty which of the remembered and imaginary images of bedrooms represents his self and which misrepresents it, which constitutes an objective self-consciousness and which a subjective self-deception. This forgetting and indecision induces his mind to create and recreate a multiplicity of remembered bedrooms in order to find the one that will allow him to wake up. It jogs his memory of large parts of his past, which is why, even after he has chosen which memory represents where, when, and who he now is, he spends the rest of the night exploring memories of his past, all of which are associated with his perceptions of bedrooms other than the one in which he is now sleeping. This conceit appears to explain the "remembering narrator's" entire narrative of his past throughout the novel.

However, Proust's remembering narrator, who theoretically remembers everything recounted in the *Recherche*, is himself remembered. His thoughts are recounted in past tenses by what I will call Proust's writing narrator: "Longtemps, je me suis couché de bonne heure. Parfois, à peine ma bougie éteinte, mes yeux se fermaient si vite que je n'avais pas le temps de me dire: 'Je m'endors.' Et, une demi-heure après, la pensée qu'il était temps de chercher le sommeil m'éveillait..." (*R*, 1: 3). It is Proust's writing narrator who reconstructs his past remembering of past perceptions of bedrooms and who puts these past remembrances in a more or less chronological, narrative order. This narrative is structured by the protagonist's lifelong search to overcome his forgetting of his past perceptions in order to remember his past and write a novel about it. The *Recherche* thus structures the narrator's life as an initial falling asleep to the temporal diversity of his past and present selves as the growing man forgets his past perceptions of world and self, and a subsequent awakening to conscious memory of these past selves through involuntary memories when he is much older. This awakening appears to culminate in the writing of the story of the narrator's forgetting of his past and subsequent awakening to conscious memory. The writing narrator thus seems to be born when the protagonist in the last pages of *Le Temps retrouvé* and of the novel begins to write the story of his past life and to create the autobiography we appear to be reading. Writing narrator, remembering narrator, and remembered past perceiving selves, all would coincide in the consciousness of a unified, fully awake subject called "Proust," who speaks every moment of his first-person narration.

But Proust's writing narrator never achieves this unified, fully awake consciousness of his life.[26] He must put off indefinitely the moment when his past self, the protagonist, becomes a present self, the writing narrator. Throughout the opening passage of the *Recherche*, there are strong signs that the remembering narrator is "recomposing," rather than accurately remembering, his past and present perceptions of the world. His repeated expressions of certainty that he has become fully conscious of his present self and bedroom are in fact attempts to convince himself that he can remember and represent himself objectively (*R*, 1: 6).[27] These indirect signs of the remembering narrator's error are confirmed at the end of *Combray*, where the writing narrator ceases recounting the story of his childhood summers in the village of Combray and returns to the more recent period, in which he would repeatedly wake up in the middle of the night and remember his past. The writing narrator recounts how, after his long night of remembering his past, the sun would come up and reveal that he was not in the bedroom he had thought he was in. He would discover that he had identified himself with the wrong remembered bedroom and thus with the wrong past or imaginary bedroom and self. When he thought he had become conscious of his present bedroom, he had not overcome his forgetting of who he was nor his indecision over which of his diverse memories of past selves represented him. Rather, he had constructed a deceptive consciousness of world and self and convinced himself that it was objective.

This revelation of the subject's split between, on the one hand, a remembering narrator who repeatedly deceives himself into believing that he can represent his past and present selves objectively and, on the other hand, an older writing narrator who knows that he was deceiving himself, brings to the fore how allegory and irony constitute Proustian first-person narration. In the writing narrator's discourse, the story of the protagonist's search to wake up and remember his past takes the form of an allegory of the transformation of a remembering narrator, who believes that he can remember his past and present selves, into a writing narrator, who knows that he cannot. This allegorical transformation recounts the protagonist's discovery that his memories of his past and present selves cannot fully escape his waking mind's indecision over whether he is remembering his past or forgetting and inventing it. The protagonist's search to recapture his different past ways of seeing the world is thus always too late to arrive at self-representation – he has forgotten the past – and too early to arrive at remembering his past. Narrator and protagonist can never coincide in a "here and now."[28] Proust's writing will always be too early and too late to be autobiographical.

Alongside this allegorical writing narrator there is an ironical writing narrator whose existence is revealed by the end of *Combray*. When the writing narrator informs his readers that his remembered representations of his past selves were misrepresentations, he reveals that, at the beginning of *Combray*, he knowingly created the illusion that he was accurately remembering his past selves. This deliberate deception transforms the writing narrator's discourse into an ironical juxtaposition of the remembering narrator's assertion and the writing narrator's negation of the autobiographical objectivity of his self-representations. By revealing this sleight-of-hand at the end of *Combray*, the writing narrator invites readers to reread the entirety of *Combray* ironically, to be accomplices in the narrator's self-misrepresentation and its simultaneous demystification.

The coincidence of allegory and irony in Proust's first-person narrator's discourse splits the narrator, not only between asserting and negating his different manners of perceiving world and self, but also between incompatible modes of relating assertion to negation: an allegorical mode that seeks to narrate the temporal difference between spatial representations of past and present selves, but whose negations put this narrative off indefinitely; and an ironical mode that repeats in time the assertion and simultaneous negation of such a narrative of temporal difference and constitutes the narrator's discourse spatially. These different modes of relating the assertion and the negation of self cannot culminate in the narrator's conclusion that his discourse is a transtemporal repetition of the same conventional signs and structures of self. They cannot culminate in the rebirth of the narrator's past in the present. Rather, they produce indecision over whether or not his discourse can capture or establish the temporal difference between selves that theoretically constitutes his life, a difference that the conventions of narrative form require him to repeatedly reassert.

This critical Proustian meditation on the temporality of self-remembering and first-person writing, I will argue, takes on a literary historical dimension in Beckett's rewriting of the meditation in his trilogy. Beckett's allusions to Proust's meditation are conspicuous. Three of the trilogy's narrators – Molloy, Moran, and Malone – write in their respective bedrooms and two write in bed, the privileged places of Proust's narrator's meditation on first-person narration. The narrator of the last volume, *The Unnamable*, speaks from a linguistic refuge, the pronoun "I," that tries to close itself off from any representation of a real world or self, just as Proust tried to close off his bedroom with cork from the world outside it. One narrator, Molloy, writes in a bedroom of his mother's house, as does Proust's narrator when he begins writing at the end of the *Recherche*. Ironically, Molloy even writes in his mother's bed.[29] The trilogy's narrators are increasingly ill and nearing death, as is Proust's writing narrator.[30]

The writing situations of Beckett's narrators are, like Proust's, metaphors for the acts of thinking and writing. Just as Proust's waking narrator reconstructs his consciousness of bedroom and self, so too do the trilogy's narrators. Hence the beginning of *The Unnamable*, where the narrator repeats the three questions that are central to Proust's waking narrator: "Where now? Who now? When now?" (*TN*, 291).

The trilogy's methodical repetition of Proust's real and fictional writing situation is striking. So too are the ways in which Beckett's narrators transform this writing situation, seemingly differentiating their narration from Proust's. Beckett's narrators remind us, much more frequently than Proust's, that they are reconstructing an artificial consciousness of world and self. They do so not only during the process of waking, but throughout their discourses.[31] Indeed, the trilogy's narrators often seem to be caught in that moment of waking when Proust's narrator is split and cannot yet tell whether he is remembering his present bedroom or dreaming about other remembered and imagined bedrooms. At one point Molloy says ironically that he is "virtually bereft...of consciousness" (*TN*, 54). Even at moments when the trilogy's narrators act as if they have arrived at a complete consciousness of world and self, they quickly remember their indecision over whether or not they are or can be conscious: "A and C I never saw again. But perhaps I shall see them again. But shall I be able to recognize them? And am I sure I never saw them again? And what do I mean by seeing and seeing again?" (*TN*, 15). At times, the trilogy's narrators create the false impression that they have achieved consciousness, while fully knowing that their consciousness of world and self is an uncertain construction of conventional thoughts and words. Sometimes they say they lie:

And every time I say, I said this, or I said that, or speak of a voice saying...a fine phrase more or less clear and simple, or find myself compelled to attribute to others intelligible words, or hear my own voice uttering to others more or less articulate sounds, I am merely complying with the convention that demands you either lie or hold your peace. (*TN*, 88)

The trilogy's narrators' reminders that consciousness is a misrepresentation transforms these lies into irony. Proust's allegory of an endless search for difference, which seems to drown out his irony, thus seems to give way in literary history to Beckett's irony, which repeatedly subordinates allegory to irony. The trilogy thus appears to establish a clear literary historical distinction between its and Proust's self-reflective narrators.

But temporal difference in the trilogy as well as the historical repetition and transformation of the Proustian scene of remembrance are always falling back into repetition, as if narration and literary history were caught between difference and repetition. Irony, the apparent mark of Beckett's literary historical difference, is thus paradoxically also a denial of historical difference: "I say years, though here there are no years. What matter how long?...A short time, a long time, it's all the same" (*TN*, 309). The trilogy's irony becomes an indirect sign of both the presence and the absence of literary historical difference between Proust's and Beckett's writing. Ironical repetition transforms parts of the trilogy into a parody of the temporal difference that Proust's remembering narrator posits between the different moments of his life – each supposedly distinguished from the others by its distinct manner of painting the world "de couleurs si différentes de celles qui maintenant revêtent pour moi le monde..." – and between his works and the works of precursors (*R*, 1: 48; 3: 159–60, 248–61). The trilogy's narrators parody the multicolored, historical kaleidoscope of past selves seen by Proust's waking mind by transforming all sensations – past, present, or future – into a uniform gray. This gray world suggests that what we call a consciousness of self is never more than a shutting out of the confused blur of pre-conscious perceptions.[32]

Beckett dramatizes this mental loss of the ability to perceive or represent temporal or historical difference as the gradual handicapping and decomposing of his narrators' bodies. The process of mental decomposition motivates his narrators to take refuge in language, particularly in the first-person pronoun, which conventionally acts as if it refers to a self who speaks the text. But mental and physical decomposition handicaps the first-person pronoun as well. In *The Unnamable*, the first-person narrator seems to have lost the ability to escape from a spatial present of narration: "I have been here, ever since I began to be, my appearances elsewhere having been put in by other parties" (*TN*, 293). This pure present invites an ironical reading of the subject pronoun's own inevitable references beyond the present of narration to something outside it, not only to a spatial outside, but a temporal outside: "Past happiness in any case has clean gone from my memory... Nothing has ever changed since I have been here" (*TN*, 293). It is as if the narrator has been reduced to a pure, first-person pronoun that can only refer to the present of narration. In this purely linguistic present, the text retrospectively creates the fictional voice that seems to precede it and narrate it, the text masks this voice as human and attributes this voice to the sign "I." The text speaks the "I," rather than being spoken by a preceding, human, narrating voice: "I seem to speak, it is not I, about me, it is not about me" (*TN*, 291); "There are no humans here" (*TN*, 293). Within the bedroom of a purely linguistic "here" and "now," all "human" representations of time and space as relations to the "then" and the "there" become ironical: "This voice that speaks, knowing that it lies, indifferent to what it says..." (*TN*, 307). It is this ironical, linguistic present that appears to obliterate time and the human in the trilogy, as well as create what appears to be an observable, literary historical difference with Proust's narrator.[33] But Beckett's narrators always fail to represent themselves as the atemporal, spatial inside of a first-person pronoun that is cut off from the outside of reference.

Irony never succeeds in constituting Beckett's narrator as an ironical voice. It always gives way to allegory as that which must try and fail to represent the narrator's life according to the conventional terms of narrative difference. This study will explore the drives towards irony in the trilogy and allegory in the *Recherche*, as well as the ways in which these drives fail to arrive at their goal and fall back into a gap between irony and allegory. Beckett's unnamable narrator in *The Unnamable* repeatedly questions its ability to imprison itself in an ironical present in which all voices are fictional: "The fact would seem to be, if in my situation one may speak of facts,... that I shall have to speak of things of which I cannot speak" (*TN*, 301).

The different ways in which the *Recherche* and the trilogy dramatize the interplay between the allegorical and ironical appearances of their first-person narration could be called their different "styles." The trilogy's drive towards an ironical present constitutes its narrators' discourse and its place in literary history as a repeated attempt and failure to obliterate allegory's search for, and deferral of, past and present. Conversely, the *Recherche*'s drive towards allegory constitutes its narrator's discourse and its place in literary history as a repeated attempt and failure to subordinate his ironical negation of self to the allegory of his search for, and deferral of, his past. But both authors, I will argue, associate the act of writing, and action in general, with the incomplete but necessary passage from irony, which negates all difference, to allegory, which vainly asserts it.[34]

The literary historical relationship between the first-person narrators of the *Recherche* and the trilogy can thus be studied in terms of the trilogy's allusions to Proust. Beckett's allusions establish a complex literary historical relationship that is defined by the temporal interplay between allegory and irony. The trilogy's allusions to the *Recherche* alternate between constructing an allegorical discourse that seeks to differentiate the trilogy's narrators from Proust's, and constructing an ironical discourse that negates the possibility of literary historical difference, where ironical parody of Proust seems to be both a mark of Beckett's difference and a denial of any such difference.[35] By undercutting its irony, Beckett's allusions bring to the fore the ways in which the trilogy, like the *Recherche*, opens its narrators' discourses up to questions not only of temporal and literary historical difference, but also, I will argue, of social history.[36]

I will be comparing the French text of the *Recherche* to the English version of the trilogy. Although Beckett originally wrote the trilogy in French, his English rewriting is in my opinion a richer version of the novels. Nevertheless, when his translation eliminates relevant aspects of the French version, I will quote the original version in the text or the notes.

My thanks to Christopher Breu, Thomas Trezise, and Barbara Kurtz for their critical comments on parts of this manuscript.

CHAPTER I

Remembering forgetting: Le Drame du coucher

> For the important thing for the author is not what he experienced, but the weaving of his memory, the Penelope work of recollection. Or should one call it, rather, a Penelope work of forgetting? Is not the involuntary recollection, Proust's *mémoire involontaire*, much closer to forgetting than what is usually called memory?
>
> Walter Benjamin[1]

Literary history has tended to memorialize Proust's novel as a monument to memory, a *Remembrance of Things Past* (as the English translation is titled), rather than a monument to time or forgetting, a *Recherche du temps perdu* (as the French novel is titled). Proust's first-person narrator seems at first glance to support this reading. Over the course of the novel, he appears to tell the story of how he overcame forgetting and wrote a novel of memory. As a child he began to repress memories of his past. He later conquered this forgetting when, as an adult, he discovered the power of involuntary memories, which are produced by chance associations rather than conscious will. Finally, he began to write an autobiographical novel that was built upon his involuntary memories of his past and recounted his lifelong search for these memories.

If we were to assume that this traditional story of Proust's triumphant resurrection of memory is the central story in the *Recherche*, we would incorrectly conclude that the first-person narrator is a realist narrator who accurately represents past things through his memory. But, for Proust's narrator, realist representations of things are produced by what he calls "voluntary memories," which have nothing to do with the past. What the narrator does claim to narrate sometimes is involuntary remembrances of his past. Involuntary memories recreate not past things but the narrator's past mental impressions of things. These impressions theoretically express, in a present instant that is outside time, his unique past ways of seeing the world and the essence of his past selves. The famous madeleine passage in *Combray* and the repetition of similar experiences of involuntary memory in *Le Temps retrouvé*, the last volume of the *Recherche*, reinforce, thematically and structurally, this "impressionist" reading of the *Recherche* as a novel written with, and about, involuntary memories of past impressions, past ways of seeing the world and past selves. According to Proust's impressionist reading, the end of the *Recherche* represents the moment when the protagonist, the narrator's past self, finally understands that only his involuntary memories can truly resurrect his past impressions of things. He rejects his past error of relying on voluntary memories and writes an autobiographical novel based on involuntary memories. It is this hypothetical autobiographical novel of involuntary memory that Beckett faithfully and sometimes ironically describes in his essay, *Proust*.

But Proust in fact builds his literary cathedral of memory on the quicksand of what Richard Terdiman calls a "massive disruption of traditional forms of memory" in nineteenth-century discourse, a disruption that Foucault associates with society's increasing awareness of time as change.[2] This is the century that gave us Nietzsche's essay on the advantages of forgetting history and the beginnings of Freud's writings on how forgetting functions as both a negative means of repression and a positive means of sublimation.[3] Proust's narrator's story of his past loss and involuntary rediscovery of memories of past impressions is in fact part of another story of how the protagonist discovered "[l']heureux oubli," which necessarily takes place in time (*R*, 3: 1040). Involuntary memory, Walter Benjamin pointed out, is "much closer to forgetting than what is usually called memory." For Proust, involuntary memory and an impressionist autobiography based on it are an "infaillible proportion...de souvenir et d'oubli" (*R*, 3: 879), an interplay between a remembering "I" and a forgetting "I." *A la recherche du temps perdu* splits its first-person narrator's desires between a desire to remember and a desire to forget the past. Only in Beckett's novel trilogy will Beckett delve into the functioning of this forgetting narrator. The narrator's split between remembering and forgetting foreshadows the narrator, Molloy, in Beckett's trilogy, who writes the story of his past relation with his mother even as he forgets his mother's address, her name, his own name, and most words.[4]

The protagonist's search to write an impressionist autobiography based on involuntary memories is part of the story of how he learned that involuntary memories not only remember his past selves, they forget and reconstruct these memories. "Chercher? pas seulement: créer," the narrator says in the madeleine episode, as he tries to bring an involuntary memory to consciousness (*R*, 1: 48). The past vision of the world that arises out of the protagonist's taste of a cup of tea and madeleine – "tout cela qui prend forme et solidité" (*R*, 1: 48) – is thus an artificial construction of the novel's forgetting and writing narrator, the "I" who knows that the act of remembering the past is an active rewriting and transformation of the past. Whereas involuntary memory is theoretically outside time, this act of reconstructing past selves takes place in time. *A la recherche du temps perdu* asks whether the protagonist who ultimately decides to write a novel – the "Marcel" who finally comprehends the error of voluntary memory and the truth of involuntary memory – coincides with the writing narrator, and thus the author, Marcel Proust, who reinvents this past self. Is the *Recherche* autobiographical or fictional? Proust's narrator, who is split between a remembering and a forgetting "I," puts into question the very possibility of an historical discourse that not only recreates the historical past, but also accurately represents the temporal relation between its present of remembering/reconstruction and the historical past.

Proust's story of how his protagonist came to write a novel based on involuntary memories recounts the latter's search to comprehend the temporality of the narrative act of reconstructing the past. The narrative act is always already an interplay between losing and recapturing, forgetting and remembering the past. My emphasis on forgetting in this chapter is thus a strategic means of breaking down the conventional reading of Proust's narrator as a remembering narrator and opening reading up to the interplay between the voices of Proust's remembering and forgetting narrators. This interplay takes place within the words of a first-person writing narrator who never knows whether his words are linking him to, or cutting him off from, the past.

The "beginning" of the narrator's story of his search for his past – the "drame du coucher" – marks his apprenticeship in forgetting the past.[5] The protagonist's obsession with forgetting arises out of an evening when his strict yet loving mother – against her strict principles – passed an entire night in her young son's bedroom in order to calm his nerves and satisfy her husband's apparent desire to sleep in peace. After this evening, the narrator tells us, he became obsessed with the memory of that moment, which recalled both his fear of going to bed without his mother's goodnight kiss – "le drame de mon déshabillage" – and his desire for his mother: "C'est ainsi que, pendant longtemps, quand, réveillé la nuit, je me ressouvenais de Combray, je n'en revis jamais que...le décor strictement nécessaire...au drame de mon déshabillage..." (*R*, 1: 43–44). The protagonist's memory became fixated on the moment of hope and fear when he waited for his mother on the stairway that fateful night, on the moment of a desire that seemed to have once, if only once, been satisfied.

The satisfaction that the young Marcel felt he received during that one night was produced by his mother's mode of reading a novel by Georges Sand. She read it in a manner that, according to him, recreated and preserved the author's self.[6] "[L]ectrice admirable," Marcel's mother spent the night reading Sand's romantic novel, *François le Champi*, to her anxious and sleepless child. This novel tells the story of a love affair between a woman and the orphan boy she adopts. It thus indirectly refers to the incestuous relation between the protagonist and his mother. Because of the mother's principles, which prohibit incest, she deliberately skips any passages that make explicit the incestuous implications of the mother/son relationship that the novel unfolds. However, by choosing to read this particular novel to her son, while skipping the passages on incest, she indirectly alludes to the relation that she is helping set up with her son, even as she hides it from him and from herself.

Marcel's mother indirectly expresses her ambivalence, not only in reading a novel about incest, but in the relation that she establishes, as reader, with the author, Sand. Although his mother is not faithful to all that Sand says, she is faithful, the narrator says, to the peculiar "accent" that distinguishes Sand's unique style. She reads with an extraordinary sensitivity to the author's distinct identity which, according to Proust's narrator, is expressed not by what Sand says or represents but by the way she writes: "Elle retrouvait pour les attaquer dans le ton qu'il faut, l'accent cordial qui leur préexiste et les dicta, mais que les mots n'indiquent pas" (*R*, 1: 42).[7] Marcel's mother reads Sand with the same empathy for the author's emotions that she shows to her frightened son by holding his hands while he cries and allowing him to see her own desire to cry in the face of his pain. To read Sand's words and her son's tears in this way is, theoretically, to constitute herself as the receptacle of their unique selves, which are communicated, not by the content of their words, but by their manner of expressing this content.[8] She is the ideal reader of autobiographical signs, who resurrects the author's selves, preserves them, and renders them timeless.

Such an ideal reading of Marcel's actions was the type of reading that he had hoped to procure when, earlier in the evening, in what Samuel Weber calls his "premier acte littéraire" (*R*, 1: 41), he had written his mother a message pleading for a goodnight kiss and had asked the maid Françoise to give her this message at the dinner table. The son's "demande de lecture," which Ross Chambers has taught us to read as a "demande d'amour," like the son's tears later on that evening, asked his mother for a reading that was sensitive to the anguish that his letter expressed and that would motivate her to leave her guests and come to console him.[9] The very hope of such a loving reading, however, depended upon his lying to Françoise: "[J]e n'hésitais pas à mentir et à lui dire que ce n'était pas du tout moi qui avais voulu écrire à maman, mais que c'était maman qui, en me quittant, m'avait recommandé de ne pas oublier de lui envoyer une réponse relativement à un objet qu'elle m'avait prié de chercher" (*R*, 1: 29).¹⁰ The child's lie is not only a means of convincing the family servant to carry his words to his mother; it is also an act of self-deception by which he recreates his fantasy of an impossible writing and reading situation, one in which his mother, the ideal reader, gives herself totally to the emotions expressed by her son's, the author's, written words. He asks his mother to confirm the reality of this fantasized situation by leaving her guests and giving him a goodnight kiss. In this fictional writing and reading situation, his ideal reader, he deceitfully says, has already enjoined him to write to her about an "objet qu'elle m'avait prié de chercher." The act of writing to his mother becomes an act of trying to satisfy what he believes to be her desire that he express in writing his emotions and desires, his self. This fantasized, openly incestuous motherly reader indirectly represents the remembering narrator's ideal reader, the one whose desire to know Marcel is satisfied by the latter's writing of remembrances expressing the essence of his self. The child's demand for a loving reader maintains his self-deception about the possibility of such a reading, but his mother reveals this self-deception by rejecting his request when she tells the maid to tell him: "Il n'y a pas de réponse." She leaves Marcel only with his ignorance about what she, his reader, really desires, motivating him to put off to a future moment any satisfaction of his desire to see that he is desired by his ideal reader (*R*, 1: 32).

This self-deception of autobiographical writing, along with reading's demystification and deferral of the writer's satisfaction of his autobiographical desire to be desired, precede and structure the later scene, in which the mother comes to his bedroom, shares his emotions, and spends the night, at his father's behest. Marcel can never truly feel that he possesses his mother through her goodnight kiss, because her presence reminds him of her imminent departure. Its act of self-confirmation is a promise of a future end to this self-confirmation, which he fears as a death (*R*, 1: 13). Her calming stay in his bedroom this one time thus increases his anguished knowledge that she will never do it again. Her desires are in fact split. She wants to satisfy his desire for her to console him by means of her presence, but she also wants to strengthen his independence and ability to desire for himself by teaching him that he will not die in her absence. This desire to strengthen her son's will is reinforced by her strong principles, which forbid the incestuous satisfaction of her son's desires and which her husband has forced her to break. From Marcel's perspective, he has achieved the presence of his compassionate mother only at the expense of rendering the rule-giving mother (who plays the role of the symbolic rule-giving father) absent. He thus imagines that his demand for her love has traced a "première ride dans son âme" and "fai[t] apparaître un premier cheveu blanc" (*R*, 1: 39). The result of this evening will be Marcel's daily alternation between his forgetting of his fear of death every morning in his search for his compassionate mother's presence and the remembering of this fear of death every evening, when the rule-bound mother refuses to stay in his bedroom and rejects his illusion that he can possess her. "Désormais," Samuel Weber says, "ce désir sera condamné à osciller entre deux pôles également intolérables: l'absence (maternelle), qu'il ne peut supporter, et la présence (maternelle) qu'il désire mais qui est sa destruction."[11]

During the one night when Marcel's mother reads Georges Sands's incestuous novel to him in the bedroom, she displaces his dependence on signs of her love from her physical presence to an ideal, motherly reading, thus reinforcing his desire to write an autobiographical novel for her. The mother's contradictory responses to her son's demand to be loved – her satisfaction of this demand through her reading and her physical rejection of this demand – situates her son's autobiographical desire between conflicting and irreconcilable readings: on the one hand, he desires to write about his self, to be read autobiographically, and to be remembered by a compassionate motherly reader; on other hand, he desires to do penance for breaking his mother's rules against incest by putting off involuntary remembering and by forgetting and demystifying self-representation. As a result, any act of inscribing signs of self becomes a self-misrepresentation that is too early or too late to recapture the self. Self-writing takes on the form of allegory, which situates discourse in a temporal gap between a lost past self and an always-deferred future expression of a self. Proust, as we know, wrote the first drafts of the *Recherche* in *Contre Sainte-Beuve* as if he were speaking to his deceased mother. It was as if the writing son and the reading mother would forever be alone in the same room, he expressing his self through writing, she expressing her desire to find her son's self in his writing. But Proust replaced this fictional frame with the scene of waking to consciousness at the beginning of *Combray* and the demystification of this consciousness at the end, which I discussed in the Introduction. Proust thus reminds his readers that his narrator's apparent representations of past or present selves are always artificial reconstructions that necessarily lose these selves or defer their representation into an indefinite future.

Proust's "drame du coucher" suggests that his remembering "I" is an ambiguous sign that always also signifies forgetting as well. The narrator's story of remembering past selves turns out to be an allegory of how forgetting erases his past selves from consciousness and defers their expression into an indefinite future. This forgetting is rendered necessary by the split nature of both the narrator as subject and the reader as ideal object of the narrator's love. The narrator calms his and his reader's fears that his narrative has forgotten his past – he seduces himself and the reader into thinking that he is remembering his past – by erasing signs of the artificiality of his signs. This erasure produces a forgetting of the narrator's and reader's contradictory desires and creates the illusion of a single, shared desire for the presence of the author's past and present selves. It thus removes signs of the narrator's absence and creates the illusion of an escape from temporal difference, an escape from forgetting, in the absolute coincidence of the narrator's past with the present of his remembering discourse.

It is Marcel's drive to obsessively forget his forgetting of his rule-giving mother that motivates him to put off writing. For writing is associated with his mother's refusal to respond to his deceitful message. It is a reminder that his self-representation is a self-misrepresentation and that this misrepresentation defers, rather than ensures, his mother's confirmation of his self.[12] And yet there are everyday moments that repeatedly remind him that his memories are also signs of the death of self, of forgetting, such as Marcel's fear of dying when he falls asleep or his erasure of past selves from consciousness by fixating on a voluntary memory. Writing has in fact always already taken place, as he will later discover when, at the end of the novel, he speaks of the "livre intérieur de signes inconnus" that structures his mind's memories of his past and that consciousness can only "translate" (*R*, 3: 879).

Writing's reminder that Marcel forgets as well as remembers his self, along with his periodic alternation between remembering and forgetting, opens up the question of the moral and ethical status of writing, a question that, at first glance, seems to be absent from the *Recherche*.[13] Marcel's desire to express himself in writing, I have argued, implies a desire to erase, symbolically to kill off, a self, alongside a desire to resurrect a self. This suicidal desire is mediated in the "drame du coucher" by his wish symbolically to kill off the mother who enforces the law against incest and who confuses a mother's goodnight kiss with a lover's promise. The son's anxiety before going to bed is not only anxiety about dying; it is also guilt over wanting to eliminate his rule-giving mother, who stands in for the absent father, who conventionally represents the law prohibiting incest. This anxiety conveys a fear of being punished for expressing his incestuous desire: "on ne me laisserait plus rester à la maison, on me mettrait au collège le lendemain, c'était certain" (*R*, 1: 33). To separate Marcel from his mother would be to separate him from himself, the self he finds in his mother's compassion. It would be to punish him with death for the capital sin of compulsively trying to possess the compassionate mother: "Mais dans l'éducation qu'on me donnait, l'ordre des fautes n'était pas le même que dans l'éducation des autres enfants, et on m'avait habitué à placer avant toutes les autres (parce que sans doute il n'y en avait pas contre lesquelles j'eusse besoin d'être plus soigneusement gardé) celles dont je comprends maintenant que leur caractère commun est qu'on y tombe en cédant à une impulsion nerveuse" (*R*, 1: 33).

According to the author, Proust, guilt for killing mother long preceded his incestuous relation with his mother. It coincided with his birth, for it is birth that generates the mother's worries. Hence Beckett's quotation in *Proust* of Calderón, as cited by Schopenhauer, where Beckett attributes sin in the *Recherche* to the son's sin of being born: "'Pues el delito mayor/Del hombre es haber nacido.'"[14] Soon after Proust's mother died, his recent acquaintance, Henri von Blarenbergh, murdered his mother, then committed suicide. In response to this event, Proust wrote: "[N]ous tuons tout ce qui nous aime par les soucis que nous lui donnons." The son's demands for motherly love transform her love into a "douloureuse tendresse." From birth, it is the son's responsibility that the mother's "cheveux longtemps restés indomptablement noirs" are "ensuite vaincus comme le reste et blanchissants."[15] But, as the "drame du coucher" makes clear, this guilt is also linked to the fundamentally incestuous nature of the mother/son relationship, which is accompanied by a desire to kill off the representative of the law, in Proust's case the rule-giving mother, in order to possess the mother who is concerned for him.

The "drame du coucher," however, puts into question the moral issue of whether Marcel can make reparation for his guilt of trying to kill off his rule-giving mother.[16] Marcel tries to make reparation for his obsessive demands for his compassionate mother by repressing his past and destroying his will to write. But this repression only repeats his sense of guilt by erasing from consciousness the compassionate mother, who wants him to write. He thus must make reparation for this repression by resurrecting a self.[17] To make reparation for guilt is to repeat the guilt otherwise, as Macmann discovers in *Malone Dies*. Marcel finds himself in a moral abyss: his obsessive attempts and failures to do penance for his desire to kill off his rule-giving mother by killing off his compassionate mother, for which he must then do penance by bringing the compassionate mother back alive (as with involuntary memory), itself producing guilt for incest, *ad infinitum*. Marcel's compulsive drive to make reparation turns out to be a drive to eliminate the very possibility of distinguishing a guilty act from an act of reparation, and thus the possibility of making moral distinctions. The goal of Marcel's drive to make reparation is the destruction of the moral question itself and thus of guilt, but the drive only repeats this question over and over.

Only by learning to accept his compulsive drive to eliminate the moral question, which repeats this question, can Marcel gain a measure of freedom to choose what he does, to will, to act ethically. Recognizing the rule, while accepting the prohibited drive, makes possible a measure of freedom to choose between his compulsive drive and his love of the law, which, together, constitute his split self.[18] Marcel's mother's attempt to give him freedom from his drive only reinforces his imprisonment within it, precisely because she forbids identification with his drive. Only when she signals her acceptance of his drive, when she gives him some madeleines later in life and evokes his involuntary memories, does she give him the possibility of freedom.

Throughout the *Recherche*, the narrator develops the relation between autobiography and the ethical and psychological questions posed by his drive to kill off the moral question. At the end of the novel, when he finally finds the will to write, the narrator comes back to the question of guilt and reparation by expressing his guilt for having symbolically killed all those who have loved him, most notably his motherly grandmother, and hoping that his writing will make reparation for his guilt (*R*, 3: 1037–38): "[J]e me demandais si tout de même une oeuvre d'art dont elles ne seraient pas conscientes serait pour elles, pour le destin de ces pauvres mortes, un accomplissement. Ma grand'mère que j'avais, avec tant d'indifférence, vue agoniser et mourir près de moi!" (*R*, 3: 902). Marcel associates writing itself, which theoretically resurrects his past impressions and past selves, with the guilty act of erasing others, who are associated with his mother – his grandmother and Albertine – and with erasing his own past, which he sought in their compassion. The proper names of the lost souls that will appear in his novel "ne sont plus pour nous qu'un mot incompris." Even these words become "mots oubliés" (*R*, 3: 903). Writing is thus always already a symbolic form of Blarenberg's murder/suicide, which obsessively reproduces the moral question and the question of self, even as it repeatedly breaks down the distinction between remembering and forgetting, and moral distinctions.[19]

But writing also becomes a step away from Marcel's dependence upon this obsessive repetition and towards a modicum of free will and ethical choice. For he concludes that he cannot write a novel based only upon his compulsive desire to recapture a past that has been irredeemably forgotten, or redeem the present that has forgotten it. He ends the novel by redefining the goal of his novel to dramatize time, in other words, the purely formal temporality of the interplay between allegory and irony that structures the interplay between remembering and forgetting, guilt and reparation, in the narrator's first-person discourse (*R*, 3: 902–3). This step involves the author's ethical sacrifice of the search for self and redemption, for self-expression to readers, and a transformation of writing into a gift to readers, such as Beckett:

En réalité, chaque lecteur est, quand il lit, le propre lecteur de soi-même. La reconnaissance en soi-même, par le lecteur, de ce que dit le livre, est la preuve de la vérité de celui-ci, et *vice-versa*, au moins dans une certaine mesure, la différence entre les deux textes pouvant être souvent imputée non à l'auteur mais au lecteur. De plus, le livre peut être trop savant, trop obscur pour le lecteur naïf, et ne lui présenter ainsi qu'un verre trouble avec lequel il ne pourra pas lire. Mais d'autres particularités (comme l'inversion) peuvent faire que le lecteur a besoin de lire d'une certaine façon pour bien lire; l'auteur n'a pas à s'en offenser, mais au contraire à laisser la plus grande liberté au lecteur en lui disant: "Regardez vous-même si vous voyez mieux avec ce verre-ci, avec celui-là, avec cet autre." (*R*, 3: 911)

Whether or not one reads the "drame du coucher" as an ontological discourse on the remembering and forgetting of the self, a moral discourse on sin and atonement, or a psychological discourse on guilt and reparation, the passage unfolds the subordination of these discourses to an allegorical search to write the temporal interplay between them. Allegory in the *Recherche* always puts into question its own adequacy. It seems to give first-person narration the form of a linear search to reconcile self-memory with self-forgetting. However, this search repeatedly discloses the truth of its own falling into error, its temporal "errance." First-person allegory thus becomes the search for an indefinitely deferred understanding, not of self, but of what language is doing. This deferral of language's self-representation deconstructs the narrative nature of autobiographical discourse. Allegory puts off indefinitely the moment when first-person narration will arrive at its end, which theoretically reveals its beginning, the author's origins. Allegory is thus never more than "the tendency of the language toward narrative," towards having a distinct beginning and end. But then allegory cannot even identify itself as the origin or destination of first-person discourse. It necessarily discloses that first-person discourse is always too early or too late to identify itself as allegory. There is always an excess of the text for which allegory can never account, an excess of negation, which cannot be controlled by the ethical rules of the return to allegory and which reintroduces the question of what, if anything, writing is doing.

By deconstructing itself, first-person allegory in the "drame du coucher" can either continue to chase its fleeting tail or give way to an apparent "uniform subcurrent of irony," as argued by Ellison: the virtually simultaneous negation of what the narrator says.[20] The disclosure of the indefinite deferral of self-memory which structures the temporality of Marcel's desires invites an ironical reading of the first-person narrator's discourse as an ironical simultaneity, in space, of signs of memory and signs of forgetting. Allegory's revelation of its inability to be allegorical thus takes on the structure of the unhappy consciousness of Hegel's slave, a self-consciousness that condemns the slave to the ironical knowledge that his words are always doing the opposite of what they say they are doing. Consequently, allegory produces the possibility of a non-allegorical, ironical rereading of the "drame du coucher." We could thus read the mother's act of obeying the law against incest by skipping over the semi-incestuous passages in Sand's novel as an ironical act of revealing her incestuous desire to give herself to her son as an ideal reader if he becomes a writer.

Irony in the *Recherche* is most frequently associated with Marcel's father as a failed representative of the law. The father's act of forgetting the law against incest, when he tells his wife to spend the night in their son's bedroom, ironically produces a reminder of the law. Immediately after the father tells the mother to spend the night in the son's bedroom, he says: "Il ne s'agit pas d'habituer... Allons, bonsoir, moi qui ne suis pas si nerveux que vous, je vais me coucher... Il était encore devant nous, grand, dans sa robe de nuit blanche sous le cachemire de l'Inde violet et rose qu'il nouait autour de sa tête depuis qu'il avait des névralgies, avec le geste d'Abraham dans la gravure d'après Benozzo Gozzoli que m'avait donnée M. Swann, disant à Sarah qu'elle a à se départir du côté d'Isaac" (*R*, 1: 36–37). The father's supposedly non-neurotic erasure of the law, whose neurotic nature is ironically suggested by his tying of a scarf around his head for his neuralgia, is itself ironically negated by the allusion of this gesture to Abraham's gesture of enforcing the law. Unlike Marcel's father, who forgets the law when he gives the mother to her son, Abraham, like Marcel's mother, remembers and obeys the law of the Father by taking his son away from his mother and offering to sacrifice him, in blind obedience to the strict, Jewish, Old Testament God's arbitrary command.

The assertion that the father's action resembles Abraham's redefines the first-person allegory of the son's search for self as a series of endless ironies. The narrator's analogy between his father's act of giving life to his son and Abraham's act of sacrificing his son ironically undercuts the apparent nature of the father's act. The ironic analogy suggests that the father's compassionate gift of life to the son in disobedience of the law is actually a cruel gift of death: the first wrinkle and gray hair in the mother's soul, and Marcel's atoning for his disobedience to the law by forgetting his past and present selves.[21]

But this ironical negation of the father's apparent gift of life is in turn ironically negated by Abraham's sacrifice, which results of course in God's giving life back to his son. Similarly, Marcel's long sacrifice of self-memory to making reparation through forgetting ultimately culminates in his apparent return to self-remembering through involuntary remembering, which is ironically made possible by the long forgetting that he owes to his father's actions. The narrator's ironical negation of the father's gift of life, and ultimate ironical negation of this negation, does not culminate in self-memory. Rather, it negates any possibility of saying what the father was doing. Irony of irony thus replaces the temporal difference that allegory establishes between the too-earliness and too-lateness of meaning with a repeated attempt and failure, in time, to constitute language as the atemporal co-existence of assertion and negation of meaning. Irony tends towards, but never arrives at, an ahistorical confusion of contraries that dissolves differences between memory and forgetting, self and non-self.

First-person narration in the "drame du coucher" thus seems, at first glance, to be an allegory of the first-person narrator's search for past selves. This allegory takes on the temporal form of an interplay between remembering and forgetting, where remembering is always too early or too late to recapture the real past selves that Marcel first seeks in his mother's presence. But allegory ultimately defers and puts into question any certainty of its own allegorical nature. It thus opens up the possibility that the first-person narrator is only positing the allegory of his search for self in an ironical mode, fully knowing that this allegory is deceptive. Hence the narrator's ironical comparison of his father's gift of life with Abraham's gift of death, a comparison that ultimately breaks down any distinction between life and death, self and non-self. By negating allegory in the very act of affirming it, irony redefines first-person narration as a tendency, not towards narrative, but towards the simultaneous, the atemporal, and the ahistorical.

Can irony in the *Recherche* truly collapse the first-person narrator's allegory into a repetition of ironical moments? Why then, in the very act of collapsing time and history in his ironical comparison of his father to Abraham, does the narrator reach out to Judeo-Christian history and his partially Jewish biography?

CHAPTER 2

Impressions, the instant of artistic consciousness, and social history

Proust's allegory of forgetting structures the *Recherche* as a series of stories about the interplay, in the first-person narrator's discourse, between remembering and forgetting representations of self. In the "drame du coucher" passage, the first-person narrator's search to remember past selves became an allegory of his forgetting. The very existence of a Proustian art of remembering depends upon the possibility of reversing this process, so that forgetting brings back remembering in the form of a repetition of that which has been erased.

The first-person narrator of the *Recherche* recounts Marcel's discovery of two modes of resurrecting his forgotten past: involuntary memory and art. Forgetting, Beckett points out, preserves memory in Proust.[1] This preservational forgetting is brought about by habit, fear, and guilt. Habit, fear, and guilt erase unfamiliar and uncomfortable representations of the world from our mind. They replace these representations with familiar and non-threatening ones by constituting our consciousness in a socially acceptable manner. It is these habitual representations that the deliberate attempt to remember, "la mémoire volontaire," recreates. But forgetting also preserves the memories that habit, fear, and guilt repress beneath our conscious representations, and these repressed memories can be reawakened in the form of involuntary memories. An involuntary memory takes place when a chance encounter with an object produces an unexpected sensation that recalls a past sensation, one to which our mind has associated repressed memories. The result of this chance repetition is, of course, illustrated by the madeleine passage, which takes place at that moment when a much older protagonist has ceased to feel guilty about his incestuous desires, has given up trying to voluntarily remember his past, and has achieved a relative indifference to this past. Marcel's mother, who has stopped refusing her affection to him, which she had hoped would force him to overcome his neurotic attachment to her, gives him a mixture of madeleine cake and tea. The taste of this mixture motivates his mind to recreate the past impressions he had when, as a child, he spent his summer vacations in the village of Combray and was served a similar mixture by his Tante Léonie.

But, as Beckett notes, there are only eleven involuntary memories recounted in the *Recherche*. These are too few to be of use in writing an autobiography. They simply cannot account for his future writing of an entire autobiography based on past impressions. Indeed, Proust's narrator posits a second mode of producing involuntary memories, one based on a deliberate, artistic forgetting of one's voluntary memories. This deliberate forgetting motivates the artist's mind to recreate past impressions.[2] Only such an indirect, voluntary means of producing involuntary remembering, which is generated by the will to forget the past, can make possible autobiographical discourse as an allegorical difference between past impressions and the present repetition of these impressions. It also makes possible a literary historical relation between the *Recherche* and its repetition in Beckett's trilogy.

The very attempt, by Proust's allegory of artistic forgetting, to account for personal autobiography and literary history raises a number of questions, however. By deliberately erasing the conventional signs with which language and society structure conscious representations, Proust's artist and writer decenter the ways in which they structure personal time and history. They subordinate language and society to an autonomous, personal mode of representation, as if personal art and the repetition of previous works of personal art were independent of the impersonal forces of language and social history.[3] Is personal difference really retained in the novel? Can Proust's assertion of a repetition of the past that arises out of the deliberate forgetting of conventional signs of the past escape an ironical reading in which forgetting only creates an illusion of resurrecting the past?[4]

The key to Proust's theory of autobiographical and literary historical repetition is the particular past that involuntary memory and artistic forgetting recreate: past personal impressions. Involuntary memories are grounded in repetitions of past sensations: "[L]a meilleure part de notre mémoire est hors de nous, dans un souffle pluvieux, dans l'odeur de renfermé d'une chambre ou dans l'odeur d'une première flambée, partout où nous retrouvons de nous-mêmes ce que notre intelligence, n'en ayant pas l'emploi, avait dédaigné, la dernière réserve du passé..." (*R*, 1: 643). Sensations only appear to resurrect memories of real past persons, places, or things, that is, memories of objects external to consciousness: "Il est clair que la vérité que je cherche n'est pas en [la madeleine], mais en moi" (*R*, 1: 45).[5]

Involuntary memories in fact recreate a particular past state of consciousness, impressions of the world, which communicate "l'être que nous fûmes" (*R*, 1: 643).[6] The past self is contained in the particular way in which the mind transformed a sensation into an impression, our past "manière de voir" (*R*, 2: 419). The past impression is "remembered" when the mind repeats in the present its past transformation of a sensation into an impression.[7]

As the madeleine passage makes clear, involuntary memory is not a passive repetition of a past impression. Rather, it is an active recreation of this impression in the present, which involves the will. As George Poulet remarks, Marcel must make a substantial effort to recreate the images associated with his strange sensation of tea and cake: "Mais si tout dépend d'abord de cette miraculeuse contingence, si c'est elle originellement qui est cause première, elle n'est pas cause unique, elle appelle notre collaboration, elle exige de nous le maximum d'effort".[8] Marcel must try over and over to bring to consciousness the past impression to which his present sensation seems to refer: "Certes, ce qui palpite ainsi au fond de moi, ce doit être l'image, le souvenir visuel, qui, lié à cette saveur, tente de la suivre jusqu'à moi" (*R*, 1: 46). The attempt to find this past memory transforms it into something else: "Chercher? pas seulement: créer" (*R*, 1: 45).[9] Past impressions cannot be remembered exactly for Proust. The mind retains them only in the form of a network of signs, a "livre intérieur de signes inconnus" (*R*, 3: 879). The Proustian unconscious is a text made up of unreadable signs of past impressions. The deliberate act of reawakening past impressions in the present, of aiding their rebirth in the present, replaces the unreadable signs of these past impressions with different signs. It "translates" them into a new, and necessarily different text, which constitutes the present impression (*R*, 3: 887, 80). Hence Gilles Deleuze's characterization of the *Recherche* as the protagonist's active apprenticeship of reading and writing signs.[10] Because involuntary remembering is a repetition that takes place only through differentiation, it does not recapture the particularities of the past impression. All it recreates, according to the narrator, is the essence of the past impression: the past self.[11]

Since involuntary memory is the repetition of an act of transformation, it is constituted by an "infaillible proportion... de souvenir et d'oubli" (*R*, 3: 879).[12] Involuntary memory can remember the essence of a past impression only by erasing the impression itself, in the process of translating it. This repeated forgetting structures the temporality of involuntary remembering in terms of the "no longer" and "not yet" of allegory. Involuntary memory's forgetful and creative repetition of past impressions is always no longer and not yet a sign of the essence of the past impression.

Artistic forgetting is the artist's attempt to provoke the repetition of a past impression by deliberately seeking out similar sensations and by forgetting the habitual signs that constitute his everyday memories of the past.[13] Marcel learns the voluntary art of forgetting from his fictional painter of impressions, Elstir: "[A]vant de peindre [Elstir] se faisait ignorant, oubliait tout par probité" (R, 1: 840).[14] Proust's painter can recreate his past impressions on a canvas, he can remember their essence in paint, only by deliberately erasing the conventional signs that constitute his consciousness of the world and thus his "mémoires volontaires" or "mémoires habituelles" of his past impressions of the world.[15] This process of erasure is illustrated by the narrator's dramatization, at the beginning of the *Recherche*, of the narrator's awakening in the middle of the night after falling into a "sommeil... profond... [qui] détendît entièrement mon esprit." Deep sleep produces in Marcel's waking mind a "bouleversement" of its habitual understanding of the "ordre des années et des mondes" (R, 1: 5). It erases his power to remember where he is, and thus when and who he is. This deliberate erasure liberates his mind from the constraints of habitual thought, enabling it to reconstruct a myriad of past bedrooms and selves. Even when he finally identifies where, when, and who he believes he is, his memory and imagination have been sufficiently freed up for him to spend the rest of the night remembering his past, as it is associated with the different bedrooms in which he has slept during his life:[16] "Proust could not get his fill of emptying the dummy, his self, at one stroke in order to keep garnering that third thing, the image which satisfied his curiosity – indeed, assuaged his homesickness."[17] It is sleep's erasure of conventional signs of consciousness that artistic forgetting sets out to intentionally repeat. Just as Schopenhauer's artist "neutralis[e] des catégories de la conscience collective" in order to liberate the "*individualité* du peintre," so Elstir erases conscious signs of the past in order better to translate the unconscious traces of his past impressions and unique past selves into a tissue of present pictorial signs.[18]

This deliberate erasure of conscious signs of present and past is produced in writing by a methodical deconstruction of their conventional nature: "[L]'art défera... le travail que, à chaque minute, quand nous vivons detournés de nous-même, l'amour-propre, la passion, l'intelligence, et l'habitude accomplissent en nous, quand elles amassent au-dessus de nos impressions vraies, pour nous les cacher entièrement, les nomenclatures..." (R, 3: 896).[19]

The allegory of forgetting that was discussed in Chapter 1 must now be redefined as an allegory of the deconstruction of the conventional signs with which the mind constructs our consciousness of past and present, a deconstruction that "dissou[d] cet agrégat de raisonnements que nous appelons vision" (*R*, 2: 419). Deconstruction of signs of consciousness opens up the writer's mind to memories of past impressions, which are repressed by our habitual way of seeing the world, since impressions always construct the world differently. It frees the writer's mind to reinvent these past impressions in the present, in order to communicate to the reader "cette essence qualitative des sensations d'un autre."

The essence of the writer's past self can only take the form of a difference: the different manner in which the writer differentiates the essence of his impressions from the conventional signs of consciousness, which are always too late or too early to capture this essence. This personal act of differentiation produces a "[d]iversité double": a "diversité au sein de l'oeuvre," constituted by differences between the narrator's past and present selves; and a diversity between works, constituted by differences between all of the author's works and by differences between his works and the works of literary precursors and followers (*R*, 3: 159). Proust's allegory of deconstruction thus establishes the literary historical individuality of his own work within the temporal differences between literary precursors like Flaubert and followers like Beckett.[20]

Proust's novel can thus be read as Marcel's apprenticeship in the deliberate artistic deconstruction and forgetting of conventional signs that produces involuntary memories of past impressions and that recreates these past impressions anew.[21] The novel can also be read as an apprenticeship in reading. The translation of involuntary remembering into writing requires that the narrator teach readers to deconstruct and erase the conventional meanings attached to the signs in the narrator's discourse, such as "ma mère," "Combray," "la pluie," "je," or "Marcel." Only if readers learn that the signs of the protagonist, like "je" and "Marcel," are too early and signs of the present narrator, like "je," are too late to represent the essence of the author's self, can they learn to read, like Marcel's ideal mother, the unique authorial accent, "Proust," that lies hidden in the differences between signs of past and present selves.

Involuntary remembering can become the writing of an impressionist autobiography, therefore, only when Marcel finds the will to give back to his mother, not only the gift of the self that her compassion appeared to mirror, but also the gift of the will to write that she most wanted him to recapture. The will to write can only come about when she and he accept, rather than condemn, his incestuous desire for her, so that he can overcome his need to do penance for this desire by forgetting his past. This means harnessing this forgetting, and the process of deconstruction that brings it about, to a rewriting of the past that "remembers" the core of his past selves.

The success of the narrator's strategy of transforming Marcel's story of forgetting into an autobiographical recreation of the past depends upon a reading of Proust's allegory of deconstructing conventional signs of past impressions, according to which the process of deconstructing these signs repeats the essence of the original impressions that they fail to represent. Proust's narrator tries to constitute the writing of an impression as a deconstruction of representations of the instant of consciousness in which an impression takes place, a deconstruction that repeats the self that the painting's conventional signs misrepresent. This instant would at once be an empty moment of time, "un peu de temps à l'état pur" (*R*, 3: 872) and an essence of self outside time, a "fragmen[t] d'existence soustrai[t] au temps" (*R*, 3: 875).[22]

In a critical passage of the *Recherche*, Proust's narrator describes two periods of Elstir paintings, which represent two "aspect[s], tout autre[s] il est vrai, de ce qu'est l'Instant" (*R*, 2: 421). Each of these aspects of the Instant constitutes a different side of the temporality of first-person narration for Proust, one allegorical, the other ironical, both of which negate the power of conventional signs to represent a self. For Proust's autobiographical strategy to work, the two empty forms of temporality must indirectly affirm what they deny to conventional signs: the existence of a self outside time. *A la recherche du temps perdu* would gradually disclose, over the time of reading, the two ways in which time's negations deconstruct signs of self, while indirectly expressing a self by means of these negations. The end of the *Recherche* would constitute a synthesis of the two aspects of the Instant. However, the novel puts the very possibility of such a synthesis into question.

The narrator's discussion of the two aspects of the Instant of first-person narration, which he finds painted in some of Elstir's paintings, foregrounds an impersonal, rhetorical structure of language which creates an interplay between signs of the author's unique self and socially conventional signs that obliterate these signs of self. The narrator's discussion takes place when Marcel first arrives for dinner at the home of the Duc de Guermantes. Before meeting the elite aristocratic guests, Marcel asks the Duke to leave him alone for a time in the salon where the Duke's Elstir paintings are hanging. Once alone, he meditates upon the two aspects of the Instant depicted in the paintings and on their revelation of the artist's unique manner of seeing the world. Marcel's experience of this artistic revelation is made possible by his forgetting of the guests and their conventional social representations of art and the world: "j'oubliai tout à fait l'heure du dîner" (*R*, 2: 419). But, as we shall see, Elstir's rhetoric of the Instant not only erases social signs of self, it also repeats them in a manner that inevitably forces Marcel to reconsider the role that society's impersonal structures play in constructing the individuality of the artist.[23]

Whereas consciousness of an impression, like the painting of an impression, theoretically exists only in the present, the painter or novelist can represent and interpret their consciousness of an impression only by mentally reconstructing this impression in their minds and works. Because every moment of consciousness partially reinvents the unreadable traces of the past impression, the narrator rejects society's illusion that "notre oeil est... un simple appareil enregistreur qui prend des instantanés." Society's habitual notion of consciousness as a snapshot repeats Lessing's reduction of the pictorial to an atemporal, describable space. It "méconna[ît] la façon dont se forment en nous les impressions artistiques" (*R*, 2: 524). As Beckett observes, "[t]he observer infects the observed with his own mobility."[24] For Proust, the space of a painting in consciousness must, like the words of a description, be "read" in time, sequentially, as determined by the formal structure of the painting's tropes.[25] Consciousness of impressions (and of paintings of impressions) is thus already a writing and reading. In Beckett's ironical words, "[t]he reality of a cloud reflected in the Vivonne is not expressed by 'Zut alors' but by the interpretation of that inspired criticism."[26]

Marcel discovers the temporality of the writing and reading of impressions in the allegorical aspect of one of Elstir's paintings hanging in the Guermantes salon. This painting depicts a "fête populaire au bord de l'eau" (*R*, 2: 420–21). Marcel's allegorical unfolding of this first aspect of the Instant is structured by the turning of the painting's tropes from literal to figurative meanings and from common figurative meanings to uncommon ones. This turning of tropes is the same movement that the child, Marcel, discovered during his walks on the Méséglise Way, when he sought to penetrate the surfaces of signs, such as flowers and little girls, in order to disclose the "secret" or "essence" that they hid (*R*, 1: 138, 140). The painting's rhetoric structures its own viewing as the construction and deconstruction of a series of interpretations of the painting. A similar allegory of the deconstruction of the realistic surface of the sign has been identified by contemporary art critics in nineteenth-century impressionist paintings.[27] This turning of tropes deconstructs and erases the conscious meanings that previous readings attached to signs and replaces them with new readings.

The painting of a working-class fête repeats and erases the "literal" meanings that society and the artistic community habitually associate with their consciousness of people, places, things, and moments. The painting initiates its story of deconstruction and forgetting by foregrounding a socially correct reading. The same "monsieur" is represented both in the "fête" painting of a working-class scene "où il n'avait évidemment que faire" and in a painting of an aristocratic "salon." This coincidence, the narrator states, "prouvait que pour Elstir [monsieur] n'était pas seulement un modèle habituel, mais un ami, peut-être un protecteur…" (*R*, 2: 420). This biographical reading of the repetition of the "monsieur" in the painting also alludes to a person within the novel, Charles Swann, an upper-class Jew who, before Marcel was born, penetrated into the highest of aristocratic society, urged the Guermantes to buy Elstir's paintings, and acted as the painter's patron (*R*, 2: 500).[28]

But the significance of the biographical allusion is negated by the next, impressionist reading. In representing the dilettante/patron, the fête painting evokes a contradiction between, on the one hand, the figurative connotations of class hierarchies that society commonly attaches to a dilettante and a working-class woman and, on the other hand, the painter's artistic impressions of both figures. The dilettante is a lover of art from the social elite who, like the painter, has an artistic impression of the working-class scene. This impression makes him temporarily forget the social incompatibility that society expects him to maintain between himself and a working-class woman. Similarly, Swann once fell in love with the cocotte, Odette, because he projected onto her a memory of the character Zephora from a Botticelli painting and erased her lack of social status (which, paradoxically, motivated this loving projection in the first place). Not only do the dilettante's aesthetic impressions erase society's signs of social difference, they make him forget the historical class transformations that are dramatized in the novel. These transformations are making possible the bourgeois Swann's presence in aristocratic society, but they are also gradually destroying aristocratic society's social hegemony.

Elstir's impressionist painting of a working-class scene produces an allegorical reading of the turning, as tropes, of the paintings representations from a biographical, social class reading to an artistic, impressionist reading. This allegorical transformation escapes the Duke who owns the painting, but not the present viewer of the painting, Marcel. The juxtaposition of the dilettante's clothing with the working-class scene that is transfixing his gaze does make Marcel remember the class distinctions that dictate the social difference of the dilettante, who, he says, "n'avait évidemment que faire" in the working-class scene. The same memory of social hierarchy also makes Marcel identify the other people and things represented in the painting, as if the painting were a collection of signs of real people and things gathered together during a marvelous afternoon. But Marcel also recognizes the turning of tropes in the dilettante's gaze from a social to an artistic reading, which is brought about by the similar reflections of sunlight off all the objects in the scene: "La rivière, les robes des femmes, les voiles des barques, les reflets innombrables des unes et des autres voisinaient parmi ce carré de peinture qu'Elstir avait découpé dans une merveilleuse après-midi" (*R*, 2: 420). Marcel's interpretation of the tableau is in turn transformed by the retrospective narrator into an allegory of the deliberate artistic acts of deconstructing and forgetting society's conventional signs of the real and of expressing an ineffable essence in late nineteenth-century art and poetry. This allegory is not unrelated to the contemporary socio-historical process in which upper-class bourgeois society was erasing the social differences posited by aristocratic society and redefining society on its own terms.[29]

But impressionist representations of similar reflections off the social objects in the fête painting encourage viewers to forget the social identities that the dilettante's presence evokes, and, with them, the socio-historical transformation to which Elstir's art may allude, in order to focus on the aesthetic effect that the painting is creating. Similarly, Marcel completely forgets where he is, at a dinner at the house of the elite Duchesse de Guermantes, whose guests are waiting for him, and he loses himself in reconstructing the turning of tropes and the deconstructive process that theoretically reproduce the painter's original impression (*R*, 2: 419).

The fête painting's tropes thus turn Marcel's full attention towards the similar, enchanting manner in which they represent the people and things in the painting:

Cette fête au bord de l'eau avait quelque chose d'enchanteur. Ce qui ravissait dans la robe d'une femme cessant un moment de danser à cause de la chaleur et de l'essoufflement, était chatoyant aussi, et de la même manière, dans la toile d'une voile arrêtée, dans l'eau du petit port, dans le ponton de bois, dans les feuillages et dans le ciel. (*R*, 2: 420–21)

By turning the interpreter's attention away from the socially defined, literal or figural, meanings of its conventional signs, the painting transforms these signs into metaphors – or rather catachreses – of something they do not normally signify. The same shimmering appearance now gives all represented things their only value within the impression. It transforms them into metaphors of the quality of the sunlight at this particular time of day and season. Similarly, nineteenth-century impressionist paintings, according to contemporary theory, tended to put an "equal emphasis" on different elements within pictures, by " de-emphasiz[ing] individual figures and... integrat[ing] figures and landscape."[30]

The shimmering appearance in Elstir's fête painting might appear to be, as Beckett suggests, a Shelling-like synthesis of object and subject, which reconciles the objects depicted with the shimmering reflections of the artist's manner of representing them. But the shimmering sunlight is a metaphor only for the subject, the particular quality of the inner "manière de voir personnelle de ce grand peintre et que ne traduisaient nullement ses paroles," not for the object (R, 2: 421, 419). The turning of tropes from the social meanings of things as signs to a subjective, artistic impression of them puts into question any value of the object, any literal reference of the signs. The painter's unique vision deconstructs the meanings that society attaches to exterior people and things and denies them value and existence:

Comme, dans un des tableaux que j'avais vus à Balbec, l'hôpital, aussi beau sous son ciel de lapis que la cathédrale elle-même, semblait, plus hardi qu'Elstir théoricien, qu'Elstir homme de goût et amoureux du Moyen Age, chanter: "Il n'y a pas de gothique, il n'y a pas de chef-d'oeuvre, l'hôpital sans style vaut le glorieux portail," de même j'entendais: "La dame un peu vulgaire qu'un dilettante en promenade éviterait de regarder, excepterait du tableau poétique que la nature compose devant lui, cette femme est belle aussi, sa robe reçoit la même lumière que la voile du bateau, il n'y a pas de choses plus ou moins précieuses, la robe commune et la voile en elle-même jolie sont deux miroirs du même reflet. Tout le prix est dans les regards du peintre." (R, 2: 421)

Whereas the dilettante imagines that the value of his impressions lies in an external, inherently aesthetic scene – just as Swann falls in love with Odette by confusing the value of his Botticelli impression with the real woman – the painter and his interpreter deny the existence of things, including the work of art. "Il n'y a pas de gothique, il n'y a pas de chef d'oeuvre" in the creative eyes of an artist. The identities of things are erased, forgotten. "Tout le prix" of the artistic cathedral now lies in the artist's transforming gaze, which is the real source of the special shimmering effects in the painting. The thing that provokes a visual sensation in the artist or the viewer, like the cake and tea that produce the taste of the madeleine, may be beautiful or ugly, good or evil. All that matters is that they occasion a sensation, new or repeated, that motivates the artist to transform the object in his unique way.

By questioning the existence of things, Elstir's art seeks to "dissoudre cet agrégat de raisonnements que nous appelons vision": to dissolve conscious representation of the external world (*R*, 2: 419). Artistic forgetting dissolves both visual and pictorial representations: "[L]e tableau consiste dans cette picturalité dont le critère de réussite est de se faire oublier comme telle – de n'être point perçue."[31] The painting erases visual and pictorial consciousness of things by deconstructing the very vocabulary and syntax with which language asserts their reality – not only names like "gothique," but also the verb "to be" and the descriptive syntax that makes possible the identification of things.[32] This deconstruction of descriptive syntax constitutes what Paul de Man calls the rhetorization of grammar.[33] Paradoxically, this rhetorization of grammar constructs the instant of Elstir's and Marcel's consciousness only by negating and erasing conscious representations of things: by dissolving vision. This is not a negation of the existence of a world outside our perceptions, but only of the outside world that society's conventional signs construct in constituting our consciousness.

But Proust's allegory of deconstruction has not reached its end. The resemblances created by the reflected sunlight repeat the error they deconstruct. They are conventional and deceptive metaphors, not for the object of representation, but for the subject, for the way in which the painter sees the world. The reflections of sunlight, the signs of the subject, are visible objects that, according to the deconstructive logic of the painting, exist no more than the working-class woman or a cathedral. Any vision, that is identification, of the subject, must also be deconstructed and dissolved. As a result, after the painting differentiates its signs of things from real things by redefining these signs as visible metaphors for the subject, the painting differentiates itself from these visible signs of the subject: "Or [le peintre] avait su immortellement arrêter le mouvement des heures à cet instant lumineux où la dame avait eu chaud et avait cessé de danser, où l'arbre était cerné d'un pourtour d'ombre, où les voiles semblaient glisser sur un vernis d'or" (*R*, 2: 421). The painting structures Marcel's interpretation as a movement away from visible metaphors for the subject and towards the "vernis d'or" on a "toile." These are signs of the material paint and canvas with which the painter artificially produces the illusions of a real woman or real reflections of sunlight. The painting thus now illuminates a "luminous instant" that is necessarily invisible: the instant of the mind's and art's acts of artificially transforming material signs into an impression. The materiality of signs necessarily erases the real movement of the dancer, reduces visible light to paint, which can only suggest movement and light. The pictorial representations of sunlight are thus as material as the non-representational frame, which surrounds them in the same way that a shadow surrounds the tree. The painter's unique gaze, as subject, is now represented as an act of

Impressions, artistic consciousness, and social history

transforming material signs into fictional metaphors of a gaze on things, as metaphors of a subject. To see artistically becomes an act of creating the illusion of vision as a consciousness of things and of self, of constructing fictions of object and subject.[34]

The painting thus represents the turning of its signs as tropes, first from literal signs of visible objects to visible metaphors of a viewing subject, then from visible metaphors of a viewing subject to invisible metaphors of a creative subject. This subject transforms material signs into fictional representations of the present, just as the subject of involuntary memory also creates, rather than just discovers, his past. But even the metaphor for the subject as a luminous instant of transforming material signs into illusions of representation is deceptive. The instant in which the mind creates this impression out of material signs is necessarily lost:

Mais justement parce que l'instant pesait sur nous avec tant de force, cette toile si fixée donnait l'impression la plus fugitive, on sentait que la dame allait bientôt s'en retourner, les bateaux disparaître, l'ombre changer de place, la nuit venir, que le plaisir finit, que la vie passe et que les instants, montrés à la fois par tant de lumières qui y voisinent ensemble, ne se retrouvent pas. (*R*, 2: 421).

The painting so emphasizes the represented instant of artistic creation that it marks the instant of the interpreter's retrospective recreation of this artistic act. It thus foregrounds the way in which the interpreter creates rather than discovers the painter's past, and consequently the flight of the past artistic instant from the present of interpretation: "[L]es instants... ne se retrouvent pas." What the transformation of material signs into impressions erases is the multiplicity of ways in which the painter's mind recreated the world ("tant de lumières") in the instant of his act of creation. By structuring the interpretation of the instant of artistic creation as a temporal flight of this instant from representation, Elstir's painting radically temporalizes the visible space of the Instant. The act of remembering the painter's creative act becomes a flight into the forgetting of this act, into the too-lateness and too-earliness of interpretation that defines allegory. This allegory of the deconstruction of the space of the present of consciousness is thus what Proust's narrator calls one of the two "aspect[s], tout autre[s] il est vrai, de ce qu'est l'Instant" (*R*, 2: 421).

Proust's dramatization of the allegorical aspect of the Instant marks the flight of the Instant from autobiographical signs of a past self. The "I," which according to Benveniste refers only to the present of its enunciation, marks, not the self, but the flight of the self from representation. The "I" seems to refer only to the act by which language constructs the fiction of a self. But the luminous instant of the act of construction is itself in flight, so that the narrator cannot say what this act is doing or whether it is doing anything at all.

The allegorical aspect of the Instant, its erasure of signs of self, puts the autobiographical narrator in an awkward position, to say the least. His theory tries to appropriate allegory's flight into forgetting by transforming it into an indirect means of producing memories of the artist's essence: the act of deconstructing signs of self repeats the unsignifiable essence of self. But the very presence of an autobiographical author in these impressions remains highly uncertain.

Such a solution to the forgetting that plagues Proust's autobiographical discourse would seem to make possible a moral resolution to Marcel's imaginary sin of desiring and symbolically killing his mother. By deliberately deconstructing and erasing all conscious representations of his past and present selves and desires, as he obsessively does before he discovers involuntary memory, he would punish himself and make reparation for his guilty act. But, as discussed in Chapter 1, this punishment repeats the guilty act by killing off the compassionate mother, who wants him to express his self, and the rule-giving mother, who wants him to write. However, if the obsessive and masochistic act of self-deconstruction produces a repetition of a positive essence of self in the spaces between its negations, then it no longer kills off the self and the compassionate mother. It only kills off signs of self.[35] The final sequence of involuntary memories at the end of the novel which motivates Marcel to write would thus be, in Beckett's words, both "an assumption and an annunciation," a (re)birth of mother and sacred child.[36] However, the autobiographical solution repeats the murder of the rule-giving mother, undercutting any solution to Marcel's moral dilemma.

Indeed, the narrator's allegorical reading of the "fête" painting states the failure of signs to illuminate the instant of what they are doing: to say whether they are remembering or forgetting an essence of the painter's or author's past impressions. Allegory in the fête painting breaks down the very remembering/forgetting difference that makes possible any certainty of the repetition of an essence of an author's self. It recounts the flight of the present of the autobiographical "I" into a temporal situation where it is always too late and too early to know whether the "I" remembers or forgets. It thus redefines the *A la recherche du temps perdu* as a search to represent time, rather than the self.

Allegory's disclosure of the flight from representations of what it is doing suggests that its attempts to distinguish between remembering and forgetting are vain. It thus brings to the fore the other aspect of Proust's Instant, the ironical aspect, which simultaneously asserts and negates allegory, involuntary memory, and history as fundamentally self-deceived modes of discourse. Elstir's early mythological watercolors dramatize the instant of first-person narration as a repeated ironical assertion and negation of the personal subject and redefine it as a product of social structure rather than individual vision. The ironical aspect of the Instant redefines Marcel's unique art as a deceptive product of social reality.[37] Proust's critique of his theory of individual expression prefigures Fredric Jameson's reading of Proust, whose work Jameson mistakenly reduces to the "modernist" vision in which "each consciousness is a closed world." As the interpretation of the mythological watercolors will show, however, Proust would not be totally uncomfortable with Jameson's reading of such modernism as the product of colonialism and monopoly capitalism, in which the subject of historical action always escapes individual experience.[38] However, he would point out that Jameson's ironical treatment of modernist illusion is itself subject to irony and that this irony of irony is only one aspect of time.

The ironical redefinition of the personal in terms of the social arises out of the nature of language itself. Elstir's mythological paintings turn tropes in the reverse direction from that found in the fête painting. The fête painting rhetoricizes grammar. Like a romantic poem, it turns the viewer's attention away from signs that conventionally identify an external world or a self observing that world, and towards metaphors of a unique manner of transforming this world. The painting's rhetoric thus dissolves the representational illusion that its own syntax creates: the illusion of a perceivable present of consciousness constituted by a distinct relation between an object and a subject. The mythological watercolors, by contrast, negate and turn attention away from all metaphors of the painter's personal self by treating this self as a pure fiction. The paintings do this by means of what de Man calls a grammatization of rhetoric: a turning of tropes away from metaphors of the subject and towards the conventional signs and linguistic syntax with which society constructs a conventional consciousness of a real world and a real self.[39] Rather than dissolve our vision of reality, the watercolors produce an "effet de réel." But they do so ironically, not as a reference to an historically identifiable world, but as a means of negating the romantic illusion of a real, unique self.[40]

The ironical aspect of the mythological paintings' realist representations repeats and negates the general attributes of individual expression found in the fête painting, revealing them to be a function of literary convention.

The interest of the mythological paintings, according to Proust's narrator, lies in "la sincérité avec laquelle le sujet avait été pensé."

What they sincerely "think out" is the conventionality of the romantic rhetoric of the sincere self:

[L]es Muses étaient représentées comme le seraient des êtres appartenant à une espèce fossile mais qu'il n'eût pas été rare, aux temps mythologiques, de voir passer le soir, par deux ou par trois, le long de quelque sentier montagneux. Quelquefois un poète, d'une race ayant aussi une individualité particulière pour un zoologiste (caractérisée par une certaine insexualité), se promenait avec une Muse, comme, dans la nature, des créatures d'espèces différentes mais amies et qui vont de compagnie. Dans une de ces aquarelles, on voyait un poète épuisé d'une longue course en montagne, qu'un Centaure, qu'il a rencontré, touché de sa fatigue, prend sur son dos et ramène. (R, 2: 422)

The muse is a conventional romantic symbol of the artist's unique inspiration, the constantly deferred subject of the fête painting. The "asexual" poet conventionally symbolizes the artist's indifference to real objects of desire, like those represented in his paintings, and the artist's sole interest in his artistic vision of these objects. And the "poète" in the mountains symbolizes the artist's solitary search for self in nature, which marks the death of society's conventional signs for self (R, 3: 1037–38). The clear conventionality of these romantic symbols of a unique self reveals them to be social modes of expressing a self, which question their symbolic meaning and render them ironical. Irony negates the conventional symbol of the unique poet and reveals it to be the artificial product of society's conventional signs and structures.[41]

The mythological watercolors foreground and develop the ironical implications of their conventional romantic symbols by narrating the inescapable return of the isolated modernist consciousness, which seeks a sublime essence of self, to the purely conventional social and rhetorical signs that make symbolic representation possible. The poet, the muse, and the Centaur are thus painted in the performance of everyday social actions. Elstir's muse, who, theoretically, exists only to inspire the artist, is represented as "une espèce fossile mais qu'il n'eût pas été rare, aux temps mythologiques, de voir passer le soir, par deux ou par trois, le long de quelque sentier montagneux." Similarly, the painter's muse is an everyday woman who likes to take walks and to talk every evening with her female friends. The poet, who, theoretically, lives only for his solitary act of creation, "se promenait avec une Muse, comme, dans la nature, des créatures d'espèces différentes mais amies et qui vont de compagnie." Elstir's asexual, mythological poet, who finds a unique artistic inspiration in his muse, takes a walk with her as would any man who desires and seeks out the company of a woman. Finally the deadly Centaur, the death of signs of self that the poet seeks out in his search for artistic life, becomes an everyday, conventional vehicle of life by which the poet, fatigued by his vain search for his sublime self, returns to, and communicates with, society: "épuisé d'une longue course en montagne,... un Centaure, qu'il a rencontré, touché de sa fatigue, [le] prend sur son dos et [le] ramène."

Elstir thus reawakens the symbols' literal and conventional representational meanings of a woman, a man, and a domestic horse. These reawakened representational meanings ironically undercut the symbolic meanings of muse, poet, and Centaur by treating the latter as purely conventional, social vehicles of communication between social beings. The paintings reinforce this transformation of the mythological symbols into ironical negations of their symbolic meanings by heightening the realism with which the symbols and the surrounding landscapes are portrayed. In some of the paintings the landscape virtually erases the symbols and their figural meanings, as in several of Gustave Moreau's paintings:[42]

Dans plus d'une autre, l'immense paysage (où la scène mythique, les héros fabuleux tiennent une place minuscule et sont comme perdus) est rendu, des sommets à la mer, avec une exactitude qui donne plus que l'heure, jusqu'à la minute qu'il est, grâce au degré précis du déclin du soleil, à la fidélité fugitive des ombres. Par-là l'artiste donne, en l'instantanéisant, une sorte de réalité historique vécue au symbole de la fable, le peint et le relate au passé défini. (R, 2: 422)

Just as the narrator's waking consciousness eventually erases its dreams and memories of multiple bedrooms in order to construct for itself a place in space and time, so Elstir's paintings situate their mythical scene at a specific time of day by means of a realist treatment of the precise angle of the sunlight and of the fleeting quality of the shadows. Stopping time at the specific, chronological instant when the symbols perform their social, rather than poetic, actions – a stopping of time made possibly by the narrator's past definite tense – the watercolors seem to situate the mythical within a visible, representable socio-historical reality.

Rather than dramatize the flight of the space of the present within time, the ironical aspect of the Instant spatializes the temporality of the present by creating what the narrator calls the "mensonge" of realist art (R, 3: 881). The watercolors ironically negate the romantic symbols of a unique self by creating the illusion that the subject, the poet or the "I," actually denotes a real person who existed and a real social and natural world that produced this person. But this ironical reading of the self as a product of the social is in turn undercut by the clearly mythological nature of the social scene. This foregrounding of the fictional nature of the social ironically undercuts the realism with which the painting ironically undercuts the individuality of the poet. The narrator develops this irony of irony in an earlier manuscript version of the same passage:

Je me disais: ce coucher de soleil, cet océan que je pourrai à nouveau, quand je le voudrai, contempler de l'Hôtel ou de la falaise, ces flots identiques, c'est un décor analogue, surtout l'été quand la lumière l'orientalise, à celui où Hercule tua l'Hydre de Lerne, où les Bacchantes déchirèrent Orphée... [C]'est seulement par ce que j'introduisais d'étranger en elle qu'elle était d'aujourd'hui, c'est seulement parce que je la mettais à l'heure de ma vision quotidienne que je trouvais un accent familier à la triste rumeur qu'entendit Thésée. (*R*, 1: 1162)

The painting's realism deceives viewers into projecting their present social reality into a mythological past, creating the illusion that the mythological past can be experienced historically, even as the mythological nature of the scene ironically negates this deceit. It is just such an ironical realism that motivates the narrator when he repeats his past conviction that he had fully awakened and was fully conscious of his pitch dark bedroom: "Certes, j'étais bien éveillé maintenant, mon corps avait viré une dernière fois et le bon ange de la certitude avait tout arrêté autour de moi, m'avait couché sous mes couvertures, dans ma chambre..." (*R*, 1: 8). The narrator creates this realism knowing that he was not in the bedroom that he thought he was in.

The ironical aspect of the Instant of first-person narration is thus constituted by an irony of irony that questions not only the personal but also the social determination of art. It uses conventional, realistic social and natural signs to ironically negate symbols of a unique self, yet it also uses the mythological symbols to ironically negate the illusion of realism, to show that it is a social artifice. This is the same ironical aspect of the present that the narrator dramatizes on the Guermantes Way, in Marcel's encounter with Mme de Guermantes in the Combray church. The young Marcel's mind ironically transforms the Duchess from an everyday woman with a big nose and red face into the ideal, medieval Duchess about whom he has read and dreamed, a legendary symbol (*R*, 1: 174–78). But the narrator's ugly description of Mme de Guermantes's body ironically undercuts Marcel's childish, symbolic reading of her. However, the ugliness of this description is so exaggerated that it ironically undercuts the physical description, revealing it to be an artificial means by which the narrator mocks his past illusions.

The target of the narrator's irony is not just the romantic notion of a unique artistic self; it is also the notion of a "real," socially defined self. This social irony of irony is at the heart of "l'esprit des Guermantes." The

Guermantes' wit is a sarcastic means of doing verbal battle with their cousins, the Courvoisiers, who proclaim their aristocratic superiority through rigid conformity to ritual social gestures and words. The champion of the Guermantes' wit is Mme de Guermantes. "Oriane" loves to puncture the aristocratic pretentiousness of her fellow nobles by reminding them of details of the real world that they do not want to admit, as in her quip to the Grand Duc of Russia: " 'Hé bien! Monseigneur, il paraît que vous voulez faire assassiner Tolstoï?'" (*R*, 2: 447). In response to elitist, aristocratic rituals – such as saying hello with "un certain salut, fort laid et peu aimable en lui-même, mais dont on savait que c'était la manière distinguée de dire bonjour" – she offers the "gentil bonjour de la main" of a middle-class woman (*R*, 2: 448). Mme de Guermantes's wit mocks the symbolic meanings of aristocratic names, which signify an identity that is defined by a fixed social hierarchy and history. She responds with gestures that proclaim her common nature, as a member of the dominant bourgeois society of the latter half of the nineteenth century. And she reinforces this bourgeois realism with words that broadcast her intellectual egalitarianism. Significantly, her husband uses the same pretension of everyday realism and egalitarianism, if without wit, to negate Marcel's theoretical pretensions of the superiority of Elstir's expressive art: "Du reste, il n'y a pas lieu de se mettre autant martel en tête pour creuser la peinture de M. Elstir que s'il s'agissait de la *Source* d'Ingres ou des *Enfants d'Edouard* de Paul Delaroche. Ce qu'on apprécie là-dedans, c'est que c'est finement observé, amusant, parisien, et puis on passe" (*R*, 2: 501). Realism thus becomes a means of ironically negating the errors of artistic elitism and aristocratic (rather than monopolistic and imperialist) elitism. It would be interesting to explore the extent to which Jameson's bourgeois monopoly capitalism is itself a repetition, rather than a distinct transformation, of aristocratic social elitism.

But the realism and egalitarianism with which Mme de Guermantes's irony mocks the symbolic pretensions of aristocratic names, including her own, is itself subject to irony, for her egalitarian wit is a means of establishing the superiority of the Guermantes over their cousins, the Courvoisiers, as well as her superiority, through her wit, over all the other Guermantes (*R*, 450–51). Hence her mocking of Swann's refusal to present to her his déclassé wife and his daughter, a meeting which he knows she would not in actuality permit. Her "bonhomie" and bourgeois egalitarianism are only a means of creating her wit. Swann does not take them literally.

The ironical affirmation and negation of individual uniqueness or social egalitarianism in the *Recherche*, whether in Elstir's realist, mythological paintings or in the social reality of the Duchess's dinner, negates any theory, not only of what art is and does, but of what society is and does. The ironical realism of the watercolors may appear to assert the priority of the social over the individual, the paintings' irony of irony negates the possibility of establishing such priorities. The self can no more be identified as the product of a flight from social history than as a product of socio-historical determination.

The structures of both the individual and the social are determined in part by the same rhetorical nature of language: its irony of irony, which puts into question any individual or social definition of the subject. In another passage where the narrator describes another Elstir watercolor, *Miss Sacripant*, he argues that realist illusion functions to question the claim that language can achieve an abstract truth, such as the truth of the subject. Realist deception and self-deception "contente en nous un matérialisme inné, combattu par la raison et sert de contrepoids aux abstractions de l'esthétique... comme si, ce charme, le peintre n'avait eu qu'à le découvrir, qu'à l'observer, matériellement réalisé déjà dans la nature et à le reproduire" (*R*, 1: 847–48). The narrator's descriptions of the mythological paintings' realist scenes are ironical counterweights to the paintings' abstract characterizations of the present subject of narration, either as a unique or a purely conventional, socially determined subject.[43]

But irony, like allegory, eventually marks its own failure to constitute the text or society. Just as the narrator's allegory of forgetting fails to say what it is doing, remembering or forgetting a self, and opens up to the possibility of a non-allegorical, ironical reading, so irony, as will be discussed in Chapter 4, eventually denies its power to negate that which it asserts, and opens up to the possibility of allegory and the struggle between remembering and forgetting. Irony and allegory are two deceptive aspects of the Instant of Proust's first-person narration between which the "I," like the waterlily in the Vivonne, always alternates. This alternation marks the failure of these rhetorical modes, and thus of language, to account for the real contingencies of textual and social events.

Not surprisingly, Marcel's meditation on Elstir's ironical, mythological watercolors culminates with his remembering his own and the guests' forgetting, and Marcel's remembering of his forgetting marks his return to allegory: "J'eus peur qu'on m'eût oublié" (*R*, 2: 419). The subsequent passage, on the Guermantes, recounts Marcel's attempt to become a part of, to be remembered by, the most elite aristocratic society. The story of the dinner, however, only seems to culminate in the narrator's discussion of the irony of irony that structures the Guermantes' wit. Mme de Guermantes's endless repetition of increasingly tired witticisms eventually functions only to put off the inevitable departure of her guests. It defers her fear of being forgotten, of dying in her guests' eyes, which their departure will inevitably evoke in her (*R*, 2: 545–46). Life's laughs and recognitions are always over too soon. They are fleeting. Irony may try to control allegory and history, it cannot help but be swept away into history's forgetting.

CHAPTER 3

Lying, irony, and power: Proust's deceptive allegories

I have argued that the story of Marcel's search to remember unique past selves and to write an autobiography is riddled with forgetting. It turns out to be an allegory of the narrator's deconstruction of the distinction between remembering and forgetting, which makes possible an autobiographical search for the past, and an allegorical deferral of this search. Allegory repeatedly puts itself into question and opens up the possibility that the narrator's allegory is an illusion created by a fundamentally ironical narrator. The story of Marcel's search for self thus produces not only two representations of the present instant of the first-person narrator's discourse – the allegorical aspect of the present as the temporal flight of the personal present into forgetting and the ironical aspect of the present as that which produces and negates signs of the personal and of time – it dramatizes a redefinition of allegory as a product of irony. Only indirectly do the passages we have studied suggest the reverse transformation. It is time to explore the story of Marcel's search to become an ironical, rather than an allegorical, writer.

The ironical reading of first-person narration in the *Recherche* is rooted in the narrator's dramatization of, and commentary on, lying in love, art, and society. Irony, like lying, invents a representation of reality. But it includes indirect signs that disclose this misrepresentation. The roles of lying and irony, like those of forgetting, create an essential bridge between Proust's narrator and Beckett's narrators in his later trilogy. Part of the fascination of Beckett's early *Proust* is the extent to which large parts of the essay, particularly the discussion of Marcel's obsession with Albertine's possible lying about her lesbian affairs, present another side of the *Recherche* from the one presented by the essay's passages on involuntary memory. At times Beckett writes as if the romantic and symbolist aspects of Proust's novel are reconciled in his theory of involuntary memory.[1] At other times, he dismisses involuntary memory as a regression from symbolism to romanticism.[2] Beckett's essay on the *Recherche*, like the *Recherche* itself, is thus divided between the two aspects of the Instant that we studied in the previous Chapter. It foregrounds a remembering narrator who seeks to recapture past and present selves that are fleeing into forgetting. But it also discusses an ironical narrator who deceitfully invents past and present selves.

The structure and history of the writing of the *Recherche* give support to the argument that the *Recherche* is in part structured by a linear movement, from a focus on memory and forgetting to a focus on lying and irony. The first three volumes of the novel emphasize the narrator's remembering and, to some extent, forgetting, although they increasingly discuss the theme of lying. The fourth, fifth, and sixth volumes – *Sodome et Gomorrhe*, *La Prisonnière*, and *Albertine disparue* – emphasize lying and forgetting. Proust put a much greater emphasis on lying in the passages and volumes that he wrote after the beginning of the war in 1914, particularly in the passages on Albertine in the second half of the second volume, *A l'ombre des jeunes filles en fleur II*, and in the fifth and sixth volumes, *La Prisonnière* and *Albertine disparue*.[3]

The transition from memory to lying was still taking place in the final corrections of the last typescript of *Albertine disparue*, which Proust made just before he died. His increasing emphasis on lying towards the end of his life was apparent in the final typescript of the volume which was published by Grasset in 1987.[4] The earlier uncorrected and handwritten manuscript of *Albertine disparue* – published in the Pléiade edition as *La Fugitive* – focused on Marcel's attempt and failure to show that his dead lover, Albertine, had lied to him about her lesbianism. It included about 200 pages, to which Beckett devoted substantial attention, on Marcel's gradual forgetting of her, or rather on his forgetting of his obsession with her homosexual desire, as he slowly accepted his uncertainty about whether she lied:[5] "Mais pourquoi croire que c'était plutôt elle qu'Andrée qui mentait? La vérité et la vie sont bien ardues, et il me restait d'elles, sans qu'en somme je les connusse, une impression où la tristesse était peut-être encore dominée par la fatigue" (*R*, 3: 623). But, in Proust's final corrections of the typescript, he crossed out the pages on Marcel's forgetting and had his protagonist abruptly conclude, immediately after Albertine's death, that he had received a letter providing "proof" that "elle [lui] avait menti." Proust then skipped directly to the passage on Venice, where Marcel discovers that his forgetting of Albertine has come to completion.[6]

If, as the editors of the new Grasset edition suggest, these corrections are a key to the novel's "plan secret," then Proust's final corrections lead to two possible readings. The editors read the corrections as distinguishing love, which is now shown to be a lie, from autobiographical art, which is sincere.

The writer's lies, unlike the lover's, would indirectly express the essence of the author's self.[7] But the corrections can also be read as identifying art with love's lies. The writing and reading of the *Recherche* would then take the form of the ironical aspect of the instant dramatized by Elstir's watercolors: the ironical affirmation and negation of signs of the past.[8] This ironical reading of the *Recherche* relies upon the possibility of reading Albertine as a metaphor for the subject of art, the first-person narrator.[9] In order to interpret the significance of the ironical reading of the *Recherche*, including that of the new manuscript's revelations that Albertine lied, we must read them within the context of what the rest of the novel has to say about lying, repetition, music, and narrative. This chapter will discuss the development of the narrator's theory of ironical narration. Chapter 4, the last chapter on Proust, will discuss the narrator's definitive rejection of the possibility of identifying the text with the ironical aspect of the Instant.

The narrator's commentary on Albertine is, Beckett says, "the Proustian *discours de la méthode.*"[10] The narrator develops the consequences of Albertine's lying for his first-person discourse in passages in *La Prisonnière* on Wagner's and Vinteuil's music. In the narrator's reading of Vinteuil's chef d'œuvre, his septet, he replaces the rhetoric of remembering and forgetting that dominates the first half of the *Recherche* with a vocabulary of difference and repetition. Vinteuil tries to differentiate his art from the works of past artists and from his own past art, in order to express indirectly the hidden similarity of his unique musical "accent" that characterizes all of his works. This process of deliberate differentiation implicitly takes place within the signs of Elstir's "fête" painting, although the narrator does not use the word "differentiation." The painter tries to differentiate his unique manner of seeing from the conventional signs of objects and subjects that he repeats. The process of differentiation ends in a discovery of how the painter artificially produces signs of difference. In the latter half of the *Recherche*, the narrator focuses on the role of producing artificial differences in the creation of art and the expression of self:

[C]'était justement quand [Vinteuil] cherchait puissamment à être nouveau, qu'on reconnaissait, sous les différences apparentes, les similitudes profondes ... qu'il y avait au sein d'une œuvre; quand Vinteuil reprenait à diverses reprises une même phrase, la diversifiait, s'amusait à changer son rythme, à la faire reparaître sous sa forme première, ces ressemblances-là, voulues, œuvre de l'intelligence, forcément superficielles, n'arrivaient jamais à être aussi frappantes que ces ressemblances dissimulées, involontaires, qui éclataient sous des couleurs différentes ... (*R*, 3: 256)

All great artists, according to Proust, carry out the process of differentiation that takes place in Vinteuil's septet.[11] The act of differentiation is as conventional as the signs that it differentiates from each other. It is also artificial, since it produces "différences apparentes," differences that Marcel knows to be deceptive and thus reads ironically. According to the narrator's theory, the production of deceptive differences engenders the repetition of a hidden, ineffable difference:

ces ressemblances dissimulées, involontaires, qui éclataient sous des couleurs différentes, entre les deux chefs-d'œuvre distincts; car alors Vinteuil, cherchant puissamment à être nouveau, s'interrogeait lui-même, de toute la puissance de son effort créateur atteignait sa propre essence à ces profondeurs où, quelque question qu'on lui pose, c'est du même accent, le sien propre, qu'elle répond. (R, 3: 256)

On the surface, differentiation fragments Vinteuil's composition into a collection of ironically deceptive differences. But the ironical repetition of deceptive differences creates the repetition of a real but ineffable difference that "ressou[d] en une armature indivisible" these "fragments épars" (R, 3: 255). Artistic differentiation takes the form of a romantic irony of irony. It repeats bourgeois society's construction of artificial differences, but in an ironical mode, which fully knows that these differences misrepresent the artist. However, it also ironically undercuts this cynical irony by creating a hidden repetition of the unique difference that defines the artist's unique self.[12]

Proust's construction of art as a resemblance that can only be expressed through difference has deep roots in German romantic thought, as can be seen in the title of Goethe's famous poem "Dauer im Wechsel."[13] For Schelling, deceptive difference hides the reality of unity: "[L]a diversité des formes... fait illusion."[14] For Goethe, deceptive change hides "den gehalt in deinem Busen/ und die Form in deinem Geist" ("the meaning in your heart, and the form in your mind").[15] Similarly, in Marcel's narrative theory, differentiation is deceptive and hides an unnamable, repeated resemblance. But he now defines this indirect resemblance as a unique difference between a work and previous works, as well as between an œuvre and previous œuvres. He thus discloses the irony of irony that implicitly structures the romantic notion of resemblance through difference. Romantic permanence is a conclusion drawn from a process of differentiating the work from its own differentiations. It is a negation of negation that romantics and Marcel's reading of the septet assume to be the equivalent of an affirmation, an affirmation of a resemblance, a unique difference repeated throughout the authors' works.

Whereas *Combray* links the narrator's search for past selves and his allegory of forgetting to his mother and maternal grandmother, the ideal protectors and readers of his selves, *La Prisonnière* associates the search to become an ironical artist with his father, the family agent of social irony and power. Marcel develops his theory of an autobiographical art based on a romantic irony of irony at a moment when he discovers that, despite his apparent resemblances to his mother's side of the family, many of his actions now repeat those of his father and paternal aunt. He has begun to show Albertine the same "froideur glaciale" and to treat her with the same "vélléités arbitraires" that his father, as an authority figure, showed to his family (*R*, 3: 109–10). This cold, ironical superiority, he discovers, is part of a strategy of control that his father inherited from Tante Léonie, then passed on to him. Tante Léonie loved to create false threats to the family's sense of security in order to reinforce the sense of her power over them (*R*, 3: 352). Marcel's father repeats Léonie's neurotic patterns in an ironical mode. He periodically threatens the family's sense of security by making them think that the world is different than they believe it to be, fully knowing that it is not: "[M]on père... ne nous signifiait jamais une décision que de la façon qui pouvait nous causer le maximum d'une agitation en disproportion, à ce degré, avec cette décision elle-même" (*R*, 3: 109–10).[16] The father then periodically reveals his deceit (and irony) by showing that the world has not really changed. For example, when the father sent the frightened Marcel to bed without his habitual goodnight kiss, then told his wife to spend the night in Marcel's bedroom (*R*, 3: 352). In *Combray*, the father's strategy is exemplified by the family walks near Combray, when he would deliberately make everyone feel lost, so that they might better appreciate his power to bring them home safely:

Tout d'un coup mon père nous arrêtait et demandait à ma mère: "Où sommes-nous?" Epuisée par la marche mais fière de lui, elle lui avouait tendrement qu'elle n'en savait absolument rien. Il haussait les épaules et riait. Alors, comme s'il l'avait sortie de la poche de son veston avec sa clef, il nous montrait debout devant nous la petite porte de derrière de notre jardin qui était venue avec le coin de la rue du Saint-Esprit nous attendre au bout de ces chemins inconnus. (*R*, 1: 115)

The father ironically creates in wife and son a fear of being lost, of symbolically dying, then laughingly discloses that he has brought the family home to everyday life. He discloses permanence within change.

The father's ironical revelation that the apparent change he wrought in his family's life during their walk was deceptive is a laughing revelation of this deception, and thus of his irony. One could conclude that the father's irony is a sadistic means of creating fear in his family and then revealing that this fear was only a product of his power to manipulate their emotions. But Marcel wants to read this revelation of deceit as an ironical negation of his father's cold irony, a negation of negation, that affirms the father's fundamental compassion: "Peut-être même que ce que j'appelais sa sévérité, quand il m'envoyait me coucher, méritait moins ce nom que celle de ma mère ou ma grand'mère, car sa nature, plus différente en certains points de la mienne que n'était la leur, n'avait probablement pas deviné jusqu'ici combien j'étais malheureux tous les soirs..." (*R*, 1: 37). It is this ironical negation of the father's ironical negations, and the conclusion that it produces an affirmation, that Marcel reads into Vinteuil's septet. The septet begins "au milieu d'un aigre silence, dans un vide infini." It creates an "atmosphère froide, lavée de pluie, électrique – d'une qualité si différente, à des pressions tout autres, dans un monde si éloigné de celui, virginal et meublé de végétaux, de la Sonate..." (*R*, 3: 250). The seemingly radical difference between the happy world of the sonata and the cruel world of the septet is, however, as deceptive as the father's cruel creation in wife and son of the fear of being lost:

> Je me trouvais en pays inconnu... Or à ce moment, je fus précisément favorisé d'une telle apparition magique. Comme quand, dans un pays qu'on ne croit pas connaître et qu'en effet on a abordé par un côté nouveau, après avoir tourné un chemin, on se trouve tout d'un coup déboucher dans un autre dont les moindres coins vous sont familiers, mais seulement où on n'avait pas l'habitude d'arriver par là, on se dit tout d'un coup: Mais c'est le petit chemin qui mène à la porte du jardin de mes amis; je suis à deux minutes de chez eux; et leur fille en effet est là qui est venue vous dire bonjour au passage; ainsi, tout d'un coup, je me reconnus, au milieu de cette musique nouvelle pour moi, en pleine sonate de Vinteuil; et, plus merveilleuse qu'une adolescente, la petite phrase, enveloppée, harnachée d'argent, toute ruisselante de sonorités brillantes, légères et douces comme des écharpes, vint à moi, reconnaissable sous ces parures nouvelles. (*R*, 3: 249)

Art's deliberate and artificial creation of false differences, its ironical taking of a different path that it knows to be deceptive, may appear to be an expression of the composer's and father's ironical cruelty. This ironical cruelty produces its own romantic, ironical reversal. It differentiates the artist from the apparent differences that he creates. Marcel concludes that this differentiation from differentiation affirms a resemblance between all of Vinteuil's works.

The ideal reader of the septet is thus not Marcel's compassionate mother, who erases signs of immoral differences, such as Sand's obsession with incest, in order to express Sand's "accent" in her tone of voice. Rather, the ideal reader is Mlle Vinteuil's lesbian lover, who compassionately helps Mlle Vinteuil satisfy her sadistic desires, even though she does not feel such desires herself. Mlle Vinteuil desires to distinguish herself from her self-sacrificing dead father by breaking his rules and treating his memory sadistically. This deliberate differentiation and profanation takes the form of a sadistic parody of her father's paternity. She laughingly uses her father's very self-denying words to justify spitting on his portrait. In other words, she satisfies the father's desire for masochistic self-denial by sadistically denying his memory. She even jumps into her lover's lap, as if she were her father, "en ravissant à M. Vinteuil, jusque dans le tombeau, sa paternité" (*R*, 163). The substitution of lesbian lover for father, in an act of parodic and cruel differentiation from the father, makes her feel that she has escaped his obsessive rule of self-sacrifice. She feels that she has become a cruel, ironical person whose very act of remembering her father, by repeating his words and looking at his portrait, is an ironical means of profaning him.

But the sadistic scenario, in which Mlle Vinteuil seems to become a cruel ironist who differentiates herself from and kills off her self-denying father, is deceptive, as Mlle Vinteuil's lover and privileged reader knows. Mlle Vinteuil, who feels the need to say "no" every time her lover proposes spitting on her father's portrait, cannot carry out her sadistic acts without the help of her lover: "Les sadiques de l'espèce de Mlle Vinteuil sont des êtres si purement sentimentaux, si naturellement vertueux que même le plaisir sensuel leur paraît quelque chose de mauvais, le privilège des méchants. Et quand ils se concèdent à eux-mêmes de s'y livrer un moment, c'est dans la peau des méchants qu'ils tâchent d'entrer et de faire entrer leur complice, de façon à avoir eu un moment l'illusion de s'être évadés de leur âme scrupuleuse et tendre, dans le monde inhumain du plaisir" (*R*, 1: 164). The lover knows that Mlle Vinteuil's sadistic parody of her father is itself only a parody of sadism, a "simulation de méchanceté" (*R*, 3: 262). Similarly, M. Vinteuil, "s['il] avait pu assister à cette scène,... n'eût peut-être pas encore perdu sa foi dans le bon coeur de sa fille" (*R*, 1: 163). She can never achieve her sadistic pleasure, precisely because for her, as for her father, "[c]e n'est pas le mal qui lui donnait l'idée du plaisir, qui lui semblait agréable; c'est le plaisir qui lui semblait malin" (*R*, 1: 164). As a result, "[a]u moment où [Mlle Vinteuil] se voulait si différente de son père, ce qu'elle me rappelait, c'était les façons de penser, de dire, du vieux professeur de piano" (*R*, 1: 164).[17] Mlle Vinteuil eventually learns to accept her own sadistic pleasures and to sacrifice them to making a gift to her father's memory. Her lover translates the "hiéroglyphes inconnus" of his greatest work, his septet, which he had left unpublished. The sado-masochistic profanation of the father/composer gives way to an ethical sacrifice of this profanation in the act of giving to her father the first performance of his greatest work, which will inspire Marcel's theory of romantic irony (*R*, 3: 262). For, as we have seen, the reborn septet expresses the very same repetition through feigned sadistic differentiation that Mlle Vinteuil's lover reads in her.

This passage links Mlle Vinteuil's feigned sadism to Marcel's theory of art by foregrounding the strong similarities between the compassionate but prudish Vinteuil and Marcel's mother (*R*, 1: 159–60). The daughter's sadistic desire to profane and differentiate herself from her prudish father reflects Marcel's desire to profane and differentiate himself from his prudish mother. Mlle Vinteuil's parodic profanation of her father and her jumping into her "sadistic" lover's lap alludes to Marcel's "sadistic" deconstruction of the signs of self that his mother wants him to express in writing and his increasing identification with his father's ironical attitude towards signs of self, such as Marcel's and his mother's goodnight kiss. Like Mlle Vinteuil, Marcel denies his mother's very maternity by having Albertine – whom he fantasizes as a liar and lesbian whom his mother would condemn and who could not love him – use his mother's bedroom while she is away and give him a motherly goodnight kiss. Marcel substitutes Albertine's apparent lies and illicit pleasure for his mother's apparent sincerity and condemnation of (illicit) pleasure. At the same time he adopts a severe ironical stance towards Albertine's lies. He treats her with the same cruel irony that his father adopted in the face of Marcel's clamoring for his mother's goodnight kiss. But this cruel irony, which gives Marcel the pleasure of thinking that he knows the truth that Albertine hides, only spurs on his desire to be loved by her, his desire for confirmation of his ironical self.

Based on this ironical reversal of the sadistic desire to differentiate oneself from a rule-giving parent, the first-person narrator of *A la recherche du temps perdu* would be an ironical narrator who sadistically negates signs of his past selves (by symbolically killing off the mother and the self she protects), just as Mlle Vinteuil sadistically negates a sign (her father's portrait) of the virtuous self that she has inherited from her father. All self-representation by the narrator of the *Recherche* would be a lie: "Oui, j'ai été forcé d'amincir la chose et d'être mensonger, mais ce n'est pas un univers, c'est des millions, presque autant qu'il existe de prunelles et d'intelligences humaines, qui s'éveillent tous les matins" (*R*, 3: 191). When the narrator says, "I lied about my past" – whether he says this directly, as he does here, or indirectly through his theories of art – he makes his readers ironical accomplices in his creation of autobiographical deceit. This is what the narrator does at the end of *Combray*, when he reveals that he had deceitfully created and maintained the illusion that he knew where, when, and who he was while spending the night remembering his past. The narrator suggests that autobiographical discourse is a process of seducing readers into believing that he is representing his past, in order to reveal to them that he has duped them, just as Marcel's father revealed to his family that he had deceived them into believing they were lost. Proust's narrator makes his readers ironical accomplices in his autobiographical deceit that he is literally representing what is truly different about his past. He does so in order to reinterpret deceit as the only mode of expressing what is truly new and different:

Le mensonge...sur les gens que nous connaissons...sur ce que nous sommes, sur ce que nous aimons, sur ce que nous éprouvons...ce mensonge-là est une des seules choses au monde qui puisse nous ouvrir des perspectives sur du nouveau, sur de l'inconnu, puisse ouvrir en nous des sens endormis pour la contemplation d'univers que nous n'aurions jamais connus. (*R*, 3: 216)[18]

The sadistic theory of writing and reading expounded in the passages on the septet, Albertine, and Mlle Vinteuil is intuited in Beckett's essay. In his comments on Marcel's involuntary memories of his dead grandmother, Beckett underlines the coincidence in the *Recherche* between a painful awareness of time – constant change, deformation, difference, deceit – and a joyful recuperation of the past outside time. This coincidence results in a "contradiction between presence and irremediable obliteration."[19] Albertine, according to Beckett, represents this deceit and painful temporal change as it exists both outside and inside Marcel. She represents Time as that which destroys selves, yet produces a repetition of signs of what it destroys. For this early Beckett, however, Proust's solution is to transform Time and Albertine's lies into a mode, not only of repeating death, but of overcoming it: "Time is recovered and Death with it, when he leaves the library and joins the guests, perched in precarious decrepitude on the aspiring stilts of the former and preserved from the latter by a miracle of terrified equilibrium."[20] Proust's narrator ends the *Recherche* with the image of himself on tall stilts of time, looking down from old age, through the lens of involuntary memory, onto his deepest past on the distant ground. As long as he stays on the stilts of involuntary memory, time's differentiation and death are incorporated into a miraculous repetition and rebirth. When he falls off the stilts of memory, time and death destroy memory. But Proust's precarious stilts of memory are for Beckett only "aspiring," and his escape from death, a "miracle." The Beckett who wrote *Malone meurt* twenty years later will have great fun with the stilted image of a rebirth of self brought on by the death of self in time and by lying.

Like Beckett, Proust's narrator has difficulties seducing himself into believing that the negation of ironical negation, the reversal of deceitful differences into real differences, actually takes place. He is not at all sure whether deceptive autobiographical differentiation repeats real hidden differences defining the author's self or whether it is just an ironical mode of seducing readers into believing autobiographical illusion, then making them accomplices in this seduction. Consequently, the narrator explores a "postmodernist" counter-theory, according to which the autobiographical writer's deconstruction of, and ironical differentiation from, his deceptive representations of past selves only serve to reveal his power to create autobiographical illusion. Any ironical reversal of the writer's power to deceive, as when his father reversed his decision to send Marcel to bed without his mother's goodnight kiss, is not what Marcel hopes for. This reversal is not a compassionate act of preserving self. Rather, it is a lie that hides the narrator's indifference to others, just as his father may have given Marcel's mother to him only in order to sleep in peace. Similarly, at the end of the Montjouvain passage, the narrator comments about Mlle Vinteuil: "Peut-ête n'eût-elle pas pensé que le mal fût un état si rare, si extraordinaire, si dépaysant, où il était si reposant d'émigrer, si elle avait su discerner en elle, comme en tout le monde, cette indifférence aux souffrances qu'on cause et qui, quelques autres noms qu'on lui donne, est la forme terrible et permanente de la cruauté" (*R*, 1: 165). Beyond the oppositions cruelty/compassion and self-satisfaction/self-denial lie the absolute indifference to others that is hidden within all human beings. Perhaps the irony that underlies autobiographical deceit is itself fundamentally indifferent to whether it satisfies or frustrates the author's and reader's desire for signs of the author's past selves.

Marcel is propelled towards this pessimistic reading of irony by his increasing fear that Albertine's expressions of love for him are only deceitful means of seducing him for his money, as his mother alleges: "Je continuais à vivre sur l'hypothèse qui admettait pour vrai tout ce que me disait Albertine. Mais il se peut qu'en moi pendant ce temps-là, une hypothèse toute contraire et à laquelle je ne voulais pas penser, ne me quitta pas" (*R*, 3: 346). Perhaps Albertine's lies are "quelque chose d'infranchissable" that cut off all access to the mystery of her true desires: "Cet amour entre femmes était quelque chose de trop inconnu, dont rien ne permettait d'imaginer avec certitude, avec justesse, les plaisirs, la qualité" (*R*, 3: 385). Perhaps it is Marcel's own self-deceived imaginings about the mysterious quality of women that have been transforming Albertine's lies and desires for women into indirect expressions of a hidden desire for him. What if art, like love, is a deceitful means of creating the pure illusion of expressing an artist's self? What if the narrator's theories of how voluntary forgetting of, and differentiation from, signs of self bring involuntary remembering and repetition of the essence of self are only ironical means of creating the pure illusion of a Proustian difference from the works of other authors?

The narrator's pessimistic reading of autobiography is based on Marcel's fear that his love for Albertine is a pure product of his jealous desire for what he cannot possess: her recognition of him. He fears that the object of his desire is always a lack, a void. Marcel recognizes that his mind alternates jealously, in time, between an intense desire for Albertine's presence, for her desire for him when she is absent, and an ironic indifference to her when she is present. This jealous alternation between what Beckett calls suffering and boredom suggests that Marcel is seducing himself into believing that it is she, her presence, that he wants.[21] Perhaps he has chosen, and desires, an unfaithful woman who makes him suffer only in order to create the fantasy that he desires her presence. Perhaps he chooses to write about his past, knowing that the signs he must use are always conventional and deceptive, as a means of creating the jealous illusion that he can overcome this linguistic infidelity. Whenever Marcel brings Albertine home, he discovers that the true object of his, and all, desire is absence. Desire, including autobiographical desire, exists only as long as objects of desire are absent. He also discovers his own indifference to whether or not Albertine loves him, and thus to whether or not autobiography's deceptive signs reverse themselves into a sincere expression of self.[22] He takes an ironical attitude towards his jealous desires.

Marcel thus desires to overcome his drive, which repeatedly creates autobiographical fantasy by means of an obsessive and masochistic search to possess unfaithful signs of his self, but repeatedly kills these signs off. One way to overcome this death drive is to accept the consequences of his ironical indifference to his desire when she is present, to accept that there is no self:

Mais tandis qu'elle me parlait, et comme je pensais à Vinteuil, à son tour c'était l'autre hypothèse, l'hypothèse matérialiste, celle du néant, qui se présentait a moi. Je me remettais a douter, je me disais qu'après tout il se pourrait que si les phrases de Vinteuil semblaient l'expression de certains états de l'âme analogues à celui que j'avais éprouvé en goûtant la madeleine trempée dans la tasse de thé, rien ne m'assurait que le vague de tels états fût une marque de leur profondeur, mais seulement de ce que nous n'avons pas encore su les analyser, qu'il n'y aurait donc rien de plus réel en eux que dans d'autres. (R, 3: 381)

The object of Marcel's interpretations of Elstir's paintings and Vinteuil's music would not be a unique, ineffable self that is produced by the repeated creation of artificial differences. The sole object of his interpretive desire

Lying, irony, and power

would be the power to deceive himself into believing that he has a unique self. The desire for difference and temporal change that he associates with Albertine, a desire to constantly please new and different women, would only be a metaphor for his own desire to please new and different women, to constantly recreate himself differently: "Mais ce qui me torturait à imaginer chez Albertine, c'était mon propre désir perpétuel de plaire à de nouvelles femmes, d'ébaucher de nouveaux romans... [O]n peut presque dire qu'il n'est de jalousie que de soi-même" (R, 3: 386).[23] Marcel is thus jealous of his own desire for change and deceit. His solution to this jealousy is to accept that he is like Albertine, a liar, and to take an ironical distance from the deceitful words of love for him that he seeks in new and different women.

According to Marcel's materialist hypothesis, the themes of forgetting and differentiation and the deconstruction of signs of self in the *Recherche* are solely means by which the narrator creates a desire in readers for that which signs erase and deny. They seduce readers into desiring and fantasizing that the novel expresses Proust's past selves. Beckett reaches a similar conclusion in the opening pages of *Proust*, which, unlike some other sections of the essay, highlight the negative role of time in Proust. Beckett characterizes Proustian time as a deep "suffering of being" that opens up a "via dolorosa."[24] In such passages, Beckett seems to hint at Proust's pessimistic narrator of *La Prisonnière*, who reduces the self to the fantasized product of a masochistic repetition of the loss of self. Such passages in *Proust* foreshadow Beckett's trilogy, which repeatedly foregrounds a narrator's ironical attitude towards the notion that he desires anything more than absence. For Proust's pessimistic narrator, there is no escape from time or the pain of loss, only pleasure in achieving a stable ironical distance from his obsessive drive to create and demystify illusions of self and past.

The narrator dramatizes the consequences of his analogy between jealous love and art in an earlier passage, where Marcel applies his materialist hypothesis to Wagner's *Tristan* (R, 3: 381).[25] At first, Marcel tries to reject Nietzsche's materialist reading of *Tristan*, which according to him makes no distinction between the great *Tristan* and the vulgar *Postillon de long jumeau* (R, 3: 159). But, when he tries to fit *Tristan* to his autobiographical theory of indirect expression, he discovers that Nietzsche may have been right after all:

Chez [Wagner], quelle que soit la tristesse du poète, elle est consolée, surpassée – c'est-à-dire malheureusement un peu détruite – par l'allégresse du fabricateur. Mais alors, autant que par l'identité que j'avais remarquée tout à l'heure entre la phrase de Vinteuil et celle de Wagner, j'étais troublé par cette habileté vulcanienne. Serait-ce elle qui donnerait chez les grands artistes l'illusion d'une originalité foncière, irréductible, en apparence reflet d'une réalité plus qu'humaine, en fait produit d'un labeur industrieux?... Je continuais à jouer *Tristan* [au piano]. Séparé de Wagner par la cloison sonore, je l'entendais exulter, m'inviter à partager sa joie, j'entendais redoubler le rire immortellement jeune et les coups de marteau de Siegfried; du reste, plus merveilleusement frappées étaient ces phrases, l'habileté technique de l'ouvrier ne servait qu'à leur faire plus librement quitter la terre, oiseaux pareils non au cygne de Lohengrin mais à cet aéroplane que j'avais vu à Balbec changer son énergie en élévation, planer au-dessus des flots, et se perdre dans le ciel. Peut-être, comme les oiseaux qui montent le plus haut, qui volent le plus vite, ont une aile plus puissante, fallait-il de ces appareils vraiment matériels pour explorer l'infini, de ces cent vingt chevaux marque Mystère, où pourtant, si haut qu'on plane, on est un peu empêché de goûter le silence des espaces par le puissant ronflement du moteur! (*R*, 3: 162)

The "silence des espaces" into which Wagner's airplane soars alludes to Pascal's frightening "silence éternel des espaces infinis." According to Nietzsche's reading of that *pensée*, Pascal's silences represent the "*fearful* possibility" that God, the ultimate mystery, exists.[26] Like Pascal, Marcel has hoped that the silences between art's signs represent the possibility that the creator of the world of art exists. But Marcel now accepts Nietzsche's critique of the subject, whether this subject be the creator of the world or of the work of art. The silences that inhabit Wagner's differences between notes and themes, which might signify their hidden creator, are in fact drowned out by the "puissant ronflement" of Wagner's artificial, musical techniques, his loud musical motor. Wagner's music turns out to be a "cloison sonore." This "cloison" is different from the wall that separated the child's bedroom from his grandmother's at Balbec, the wall that enabled him to recapture her presence (and protection from death) by means of three theatrical knocks before he went to sleep. By contrast, Wagner's "cloison" recalls Marcel's last telephone call to his grandmother from Balbec, when the sounds of her dying voice made her seem already absent. These signs of absence, his grandmother's dying voice, created an enormous desire to see her, but a desire whose satisfaction was impossible, because he knew she would soon be dead.

Wagner's music may create the impression of soaring like an airplane into the silent heavens of the composer's past self, the sounds of his musical expression of a self drown out any evidence of self from the present of the work's interpretation. If Wagner's musical signs are a "cloison étanche," all that remains for the listener is the possibility of appreciating the artist's powerful and ironical production of the "illusion d'une originalité foncière" by means of his "habileté vulcanienne." This would be true of all artists. Marcel first thinks of *Tristan* while playing Vinteuil's Sonata, when he recognizes beyond their differences their similar techniques. He now concludes that all self-expressive art is just a repeated technique of differentiation, an artificial means of creating an illusion of a repetition of the same self within difference: "Si l'art n'est que cela, il n'est pas plus réel que la vie, et je n'avais pas tant de regrets à avoir (*R*, 3: 162)."[27] He no longer need regret abandoning writing for his jealous love of Albertine, since art can no more confirm his self than can Albertine. Were he to write a novel, the subject pronoun, "I," would refer only to the writer's act of producing the illusion of an authorial self. It would refer only to the act of enunciation by which the narrator's rhetoric creates an illusion of self.

Proust's ironical, autobiographical rhetoric is best explained by the narrator's discourse on male homosexuality. In the *Recherche*, the airplane and homosexuality are hybrid symbols of the subject as the power to produce and demystify the illusion that the work expresses a self. Thus in a passage of *Sodome et Gomorrhe II*, where Marcel is horseback riding with his deceitful muse Albertine, he comes across the very landscape that Elstir represented so realistically in two of the watercolors that Marcel saw in the Guermantes salon, "Jeune homme rencontrant un Centaure" and "Poète rencontrant une Muse" (*R*, 2: 1029). Once in the real landscape to which the paintings refer, Marcel and Albertine encounter a contemporary, mechanical equivalent of a centaur: an extremely rare (for the early twentieth century) passing airplane and pilot. This mechanical centaur – a human pilot attached to a mechanical device, not unlike a cyborg – is a metaphor for the two riders who are mounted on their horses, particularly Marcel the future artist, whose horse rears back as if it, like the airplane and Wagner's music, were about to take off into the skies.

The novel explores its two centaurs, Marcel and Albertine on horseback, by alluding to passages on the male homosexual who, according to the *Recherche* (if not contemporary psychology), has a "tempérament féminin" within a male body (*R*, 2: 614).[28] When Marcel discovers Charlus's homosexuality, he discovers the hidden female desires upon which the social sign, his male body, rides: "[C]omme dans le centaure le cheval, cet être avait beau faire corps avec le baron, je ne l'avais jamais aperçu" (*R*, 2: 614).[29] The ability of Proust's homosexual to free himself from the constraints of his visible male body and express his fundamental female self and desire is a possible metaphor for romantic art's ability to transcend the material body of its signs and express the artist's ineffable self. Like the romantic aviator who can transcend the noise of his plane's motor in order to discover the silence of the heavens, the homosexual may be a metaphor for the autobiographer's freedom to transcend the artificial illusions created by his rhetoric and soar into his past: "Et, comme un aviateur qui a jusque là péniblement roulé à terre, 'décollant' brusquement, je m'élevais lentement vers les hauteurs silencieuses du souvenir" (*R*, 3: 858). The problem is how to transcend the purely sexual and mechanical production of desire by the homosexual or lesbian centaur. For Proust, all homosexual desire, like Marcel's desire for Albertine, is condemned to desire what he cannot possess. Proust's homosexual is "une créature extraordinaire, puisque s'il ne fait pas de concessions aux possibilités de la vie, il recherche essentiellement l'amour d'un homme de l'autre race, c'est-à-dire d'un homme aimant les femmes (et qui par conséquent ne pourra pas l'aimer)" (*R*, 2: 631). The homosexual is thus a metaphor for that which autobiographical art must transcend in order to satisfy the author's jealous, seemingly homosexual desire to possess a past self.

But Marcel's experience of his own desires for the lesbian Albertine, like his growing knowledge of Charlus, lead him to doubt whether his autobiographical desire for self is any different from the homosexual's desire for a heterosexual lover. This leads him to interpret the autobiographical subject as a hybrid centaur, which is constituted by a social, male appearance riding on a hidden, homosexual desire. After all, the homosexual Proust gives his narrator the appearance of a heterosexual, although this heterosexuality is implicitly put into question by his attraction to lesbian women. In life, Proust must have been an expert in creating a heterosexual persona. But he also clearly worried that behind his false social identities he would find not the asexual poet of Elstir's watercolors but only his homosexual desires to recapture unreachable past selves.

Autobiography in this model is a failed expression of sexual difference. Proust's homosexual centaur, Charlus, is caught in a gap between contrary sexual desires. It is as if he were not fundamentally female, as Proust's narrator claims, but rather a difference between the male and the female. Charlus alternates between his unsatisfiable female desire to adopt a female position – to possess and be possessed by a real heterosexual male – and an equally unsatisfiable desire to adopt a male position, to see himself as virile. Proust's homosexuals have "hérité le mensonge," the need to lie not only to a homophobic heterosexual society, but also to themselves about what they really desire and who they really are (*R*, 2: 632). They are thus masters, not only of social deceit, but also of self-deception. Charlus repeatedly blinds himself to his female temperament and deceives himself into believing that his sexual identity is male, first by acting and dressing in the extraordinarily virile manner of the heterosexual man that he wants to be, and later by desiring young virile men, who cannot love him and whom he fantasizes to be himself. In the male brothel that he owns, he has himself beaten by young heterosexual men who pretend to be vicious in order that his "rêve" of being them "lui donnât l'illusion de la réalité" (R, 3: 840). But, given that Proust's homosexual can never satisfy his female desire for a heterosexual man, one might argue against Proust that Charlus fails as much to be female as he fails to be male. In other words, Proust's homosexual is really caught between two impossible identifications, as male and as female. He becomes a sign of that which cannot be represented: sexual difference. The homosexual relationship in Proust is impossible, just as Marcel's heterosexual relationship with Albertine is impossible, because, as Slavoj Zizek argues based on Lacan, all sexual relations are impossible in the sense that they cannot be symbolized in terms of clear distinctions between the male and the female.[30]

The homosexual's power to produce illusory sexual identities that resemble his male body is critical to the narrator's autobiographical construction of past and present selves. Charlus's desire to find in his same-sex lovers the past, virile self that he imagined he once had expresses an autobiographical desire to resurrect past selves by writing them with his imagination onto his male lovers' bodies.[31] In this mental, autobiographical writing, the present of his imagination identifies with the imagined virile past self with which he makes love, where the virile object of his desire is a highly realist representation of the past self he wanted to have. The homosexual act thus makes his memory and imagination fly into his past selves. Similarly, when Marcel runs into the real landscape that Elstir represented in his realist watercolors, his memory of the watercolors "replaçait les lieux où je me trouvais tellement en dehors du monde actuel que je n'aurais pas été étonné si, comme le jeune homme de l'âge anté-historique que peint Elstir, j'avais, au cours de ma promenade, croisé un personnage mythologique' (R, 2: 1029). Mythological realist discourse transforms Marcel into a real past "jeune homme," the one he desires to recapture, just as realist discourse in *Combray* transports the narrator back into a childhood self. But this homology between homosexual and autobiographical desire for self implies that the narrator's desire for his past self, like Charlus's homosexual desire, is a desire for an imaginary past created by his present sexual desire. His past virile origin is a retrospective creation of his present homosexual desire.

What separates Proust's autobiographical artist from Charlus (and thus from Proust's own homosexuality) is the writer's ability to take an ironical distance from his homosexual compulsion to recapture a virile past. Proust's artist is aware that the past selves about which he writes are productions of his sexual desire. Like Elstir's watercolors, they use realist discourse to create the illusion that the past selves they construct are real. This awareness of artifice allows him to take an ironical distance from products of his autobiographical desires:

> Je me disais: "Quel malheur que M. de Charlus ne soit pas romancier ou poète! Non pas pour décrire ce qu'il verrait, mais le point où se trouve un Charlus par rapport au désir fait naître autour de lui les scandales, le force à prendre la vie sérieusement, à mettre des émotions dans le plaisir, l'empêche de s'arrêter, de s'immobiliser dans une vue ironique et extérieure des choses, rouvre sans cesse en lui un courant douloureux." (R, 3: 831)

It is precisely this exterior, ironical distance that the writer takes, according to Proust's materialist hypothesis, a distance not only from the illusion of being male, but also from the illusion of being female. The writer can write only when he consistently negates, ironically, his sexual identity and, by extension, all identity. The ironic subject of autobiography is thus a hybrid of male and female, subject and object, present and past, and it is neither. The very process of artificially creating an autobiographical difference is always deceptive and hides the breakdown of differences that make autobiographical desire possible.[32]

Does this mean that the motor of the writer's homosexual desire drowns out the silences of the heavens in which his unique artistic self might exist? The passage on Wagner's purely technical production of the illusion of identity, with its Nietzschian deconstruction of the romantic irony in Vinteuil's septet, would suggest that the "author" is a pure product of rhetorical deception. Nietzsche's ironical artist treats *"illusion as illusion."* He "does not wish to deceive" with his creative lies.[33] The truth of autobiography would be the truth that the subject is a lie and that the text is the ironical producer of this lie.[34] Some Proust critics thus speak of the "mythe de l'intériorité" in Proust and the "uniform subcurrent of irony which gives the novel its unity."[35]

In *Proust*, Beckett notes the need for such an ironical distance from the illusion of self:

> [W]hen the alchemy of Habit has transformed the individual capable of suffering into a stranger for whom the motives of that suffering are an idle tale, when not only the objects of his affection have vanished, but also that affection itself; and he thinks how absurd is our dream of a Paradise with retention of personality, since our life is a succession of Paradises successively denied, that the only true Paradise is the Paradise that has been lost, and that death will cure many of the desire for immortality.[36]

Habit is a key to the conventional processes by which not only society, but also art create the illusion of a self. However, habit is also a key to how the mind achieves relief from suffering by means of an ironical distance from the jealous illusion of having an immortal self in the eyes of others: "[M]on sentiment du mystère avait pu s'appliquer successivement à Gilberte, à la duchesse de Guermantes, à Albertine, à tant d'autres. Sans doute l'inconnu, et presque l'inconnaissable, était devenu le connu, le familier..." (*R*, 3: 988–89).[37] In the passages under discussion, the same destruction of mystery takes place in the narrator's relation to his past selves.

The adoption of an ironical position by Proust's narrator in *La Prisonnière* and *Albertine disparue*, which he indirectly theorizes in his discourse on Albertine, Wagner, and homosexuality, represents the act by which Marcel internalizes his father's irony. Like Elstir's centaur, Marcel's identification with his father brings his prodigal lost son home, away from his incestuous and romantic desires for mother and self, and towards the power of irony to repeat and demystify the illusions that these desires create.[38]

Is this the conclusion of the novel? Some parts of the *Le Temps retrouvé* suggest that it is. The final passages of *Le Temps retrouvé*, which recount a matinée at the Prince of Guermantes's, appear to progress from an affirmation of self outside time to a deconstruction of self in time. When the narrator arrives at the matinée, he has a series of involuntary memories. He then meditates alone in the Prince's library on a future novel that would use involuntary memories to recapture his changing past selves and the unique difference of his manner of seeing. But, when he descends to the guests below, in a repetition of Marcel's return from Elstir's paintings to Mme de Guermantes's dinner, he comes face to face with the world of social convention and habit, and thus with the death of self that habit implies. He sees all the aristocratic and upper-bourgeois socialites whom he has known during his life, but they are now old and dying. One might thus interpret Beckett's words, "[f]rom the victory over Time he passes to the victory of Time, from the negation of Death to its affirmation," as an absolute negation of memory.[39] Other passages near the end of *Le Temps retrouvé* interpret this affirmation of death as a resigned acceptance of the reality of both forgetting – "la maladie avait usé... les forces de ma mémoire" (*R*, 3: 1044) – and the "mensonge de la littérature" (*R*, 3: 855): "[M]ême enfin si je n'entreprenais pas, ce dont ma liaison avec Albertine suffisait pourtant à me montrer que sans cela tout est factice et mensonger, de représenter certaines personnes non pas au dehors mais au dedans de nous... du moins ne manquerais-je pas d'y décrire l'homme comme ayant la longueur non de son corps mais de ses années" (*R*, 3: 1045–46). In this scenario, the novel would recount the narrator's final transition from the illusion of an autobiography based on atemporal involuntary memories to the reality of a novel representing "la forme...qui nous reste habituellement invisible, celle du Temps," where the form of time would be the inevitability of the death of all signs of self (*R*, 3: 1045).

The writer thus seems to renounce the autobiographical search for self-expression and seeks to dramatize time's and jealousy's alternation between forgetting and remembering, differentiation and repetition, from the peaceful distance of a habit of irony. Behind the allegorical aspect of the Instant in the *Recherche* – which creates and demystifies the illusion of a past essence of self within the intervals between its too early and too late signs – would hide the fundamental temporality of irony, which repeats the same simultaneous assertion and negation of the illusion of self. The writing narrator's ironical reading of his novel thus ironizes and spatializes the remembering narrator's allegory of time.[40] It reveals what Ross Chambers calls postmodernism's "sorte de modernisme sans pathos du manque": an amoral indifference to the notion of a subject and to the pain one causes others and oneself.[41] Proust's final decision, in his last draft of *Albertine disparue*, to give Marcel the certainty that Albertine lied would thus appear to mark his decision to reveal that his novel is an ironical lie and that the only pleasure it provides is purely aesthetic.[42]

If the narrator's adoption of a position of irony of irony breaks down any difference between art and life, what is the relation between art and society? Art may be, as we have seen, the product of Proust's ironical critique of his homosexual fantasies. But is this ironical critique a product of sociohistorical determinism, as Richard Terdiman and Fredric Jameson argue?[43] As noted in the last chapter, after Marcel meditates on the ironical aspect of Elstir's watercolors, he joins the Duchesse de Guermantes's dinner guests and discovers the ironical aspect of her social wit. One could argue that the ironical aspect of Elstir's art and of Proust's autobiography is itself an elaboration of the ironical aspect of high society's wit at the turn of the twentieth century. This wit involved Mme de Guermantes's ironical negation of elite subjects (noble or artistic) and her affirmation of an egalitarian, bourgeois ironical subject. This bourgeois irony is itself ironically negated by Marcel's discovery that the bourgeois ironical subject is for Mme de Guermantes only a pose, a pure means of establishing her intellectual superiority to her aristocratic peers. There results an irony of irony that is very similar to the irony of irony with which Flaubert and Baudelaire reacted to the short-lived illusions of bourgeois equality during the Revolution of 1848.

However, this socio-historical reading of society and art as an ironical negation of all subjects clashes with Bourdieu's, Terdiman's, and Jameson's socio-historical readings of art, in the same period, as an expression of modernist social structures. These theoreticians identify Proust's art with his remembering narrator, who seeks a sublime subject between the spaces of his signs, ignoring Proust's allegorical deconstruction and ironical negation of such a subject. Vincent Descombes thus applies to Proust Bourdieu's argument that late nineteenth-century art was a means by which society created fictions of the unique bourgeois individual.[44] According to Descombes: "[C]ette transgression, cet incessant renversement des valeurs, c'était justement ce que le groupe attendait de l'artiste en tant que ce dernier incarne à sa façon le sacré du groupe, à savoir l'autonomie individuelle."[45] Terdiman argues that the creation of the bourgeois fiction of the autonomous individual was produced by art's methodical erasure of the signs of its socio-historical production.[46] This historical erasure was a symptom of a more general nineteenth- and twentieth-century socio-historical memory crisis. The modernist period of history produced this crisis of forgetting, he argues, by questioning "the reliability of the semiotic elements that consciousness offers in its representation of the world" and by causing artists to escape the pain of this unreliability by creating deceptive totalizations. Proust's theory of the artist's ineffable, unique accent or manner of seeing, which unifies the entire work of art, is just such a totalization. Although Proust's narrator, according to Terdiman, expresses anxiety about this totalization, he does not reject it. What Proust blinds himself to is the fact that socio-history "malignantly captures us." Socio-history determines art.[47]

Fredric Jameson identifies the social structures that produce modernism's ineffable artistic self as the creation and isolation of centers of power within late nineteenth-century colonial and monopoly capitalism.[48] The questioning of the modernist illusion of the autonomous artist in the late twentieth century, he argues, was brought about by a breakdown of the modernist distinction between high art, which is caught in the modernist illusion of the ineffable subject, and low or commercial art, which is based on convention. This breakdown of the modernist distinction between art and society, he argues, was caused by twentieth-century multinational capitalism's dispersion, fragmenting, and decentering of monopoly capitalism's elite centers of power.[49] This decentering of economic, social, and political power in

Jameson's postmodern era produced a literature that takes an ironical distance from the illusory autonomy that monopoly capitalism attributed to the monopolist, or that bourgeois society attributed to the modernist artist. Whereas modernism ironically negated the notion of a stable, outer center of truth and power and asserted the existence of a stable, inner or hidden center (the autonomous monopolist or artist), postmodernism ironically undercut this inner center as well and produced what Jameson calls postmodern pastiche, an unstable irony that fragments all signs and treats them as lies.[50]

But, as we have seen and as other commentators have long noted, the ironical postmodern narrator who fully questions the subject already exists in Proust, as in Baudelaire. If nineteenth- and early twentieth-century society were indeed doing what Bourdieu, Descombes, Terdiman, and Jameson claim, then they could not have produced Proust's non-modernist, ironical rhetoric. Of course society was much more complex than the social determinists argue. Proust's society is one in which it is already possible to take a postmodern ironical stance towards the homosexual's fantasies of sexual identity and Mme de Guermantes's witty pretensions of a superior social identity. This is not to deny that the modernist and monopolist social structures that these theorists describe were not real and did not influence Proust's novel. There is strong evidence that they did. But in order to argue that these structures "produced" the text and that the text existed to erase its socio-historical production, one must ignore all the evidence in the *Recherche* that does not fit such theorists' modernist view of society, then use the resulting reading to argue that the text is a symptom of a modern social order that produced it. Indeed, one must misread the text as modernist, then use this misreading as evidence of a purely modernist social order that produced it. Social determinism must use its reductive reading of the text as evidence of the truth of its presuppositions about the nature of society, then artificially reverse the causality. If we wish to call Proust a modernist, then, in Lyotard's terms, the future of the postmodern already inhabits the modernist as its past.[51]

Critics have known for quite some while about the postmodern attributes of Proust's novel. Although the narrator's materialist hypothesis – that the subject is an artificial creation of the motor of rhetoric and desire – does not use the language of commodities, his conclusion in some passages that art is no better than life implies, as Walter Benjamin notes, that the "attitude of the snob is nothing but the consistent, organized, steely view of life from the chemically pure standpoint of the consumer."[52] The descriptions of Elstir's watercolors by the Guermantes and their guests are no more than repetitions of the commodified mode of writing, the "compte rendu de Salons," found in middle-class newspapers of the time.[53] The metaphor of consumption itself plays a substantial role in Proust's commodified come-on, the madeleine.[54] Indeed, in Proust's post-1914 drafts of the novel, he not only fleshed out his discourse on lying and irony through the new character, Albertine, he substantially increased references to money, which became an aspect of art.[55] Thus, the passage on Wagner's artificial and ironical art is followed by a transition to Charlus's lover, the venal violinist Morel, whose performances are purely technical. Ironically, it is the emotionless technician, Morel, who later performs the septet that inspires Marcel's theory of Vinteuil's unique, non-technical accent. Morel's presence, as the performer of the septet, thus produces an undercurrent of irony that culminates in Marcel's materialist hypothesis of art. Just as Morel's performances are commodified, so is Morel himself. He is obsessed with money and willing to sell his sexual services to the highest bidder (*R*, 3: 163). The novel also refers to Frédéric Moreau and the postmodern commodification of art around 1848 that Flaubert dramatized in *L'Education sentimentale*. Proust dramatizes the commodification of society itself by narrating the gradual replacement of Mme de Guermantes with the wealthy bourgeois Mme Verdurin, who becomes through marriage the Princesse de Guermantes and the center of elite Parisian society.

Rather than react to the treatment of the commodification of the self with pain and autobiographical self-delusion, as Terdiman argues, Proust's ironical narrator takes the same neutral and indifferent stance implied by Jameson's postmodern, ironical pastiche.[56] His postmodern pastiche ironically repeats and negates both realist art's representations of the conventional, exterior world of society and modernist art's expressions of the unique inner world of the autonomous artist. It treats realist signs of the object and modernist signs of the subject as commodities with an exchange, rather than a use, value.[57] The *Recherche* itself is full of "postmodern" pastiche, as in Legrandin's unaware pastiche of romantic discourse and the narrator's deliberate pastiche of the Goncourt *Journal* in the *Le Temps retrouvé*, whose realism, like that of the watercolors, makes Marcel want to meet again people whom he knew to be banal in reality.

Marcel's repeated return from artistic meditation to society's conventional, consumerized discourse does not signify a recognition that art is determined by social history, therefore. Rather, it signifies the hybrid nature of language's allegorical and ironical rhetoric. Certainly the novel's highlighting of allegory as a means of constructing a sublime subject was not unrelated to modernist socio-economic patterns in nineteenth-century thought, but allegory itself is rhetorical and transtemporal. Similarly, the novel's highlighting of irony is not unrelated to Proust's homosexual psychology and to postmodern patterns in post-1848 society, but irony itself is rhetorical and transtemporal.

Clearly the socio-historical narrative of a movement from late nineteenth-century modernism to late twentieth-century postmodernism breaks down, since the latter is already present in the former. Once we accept that the postmodern is already present in the so-called modernist art that coincided with turn-of-the-century monopoly capitalism, however, we must ask whether the ironical construction of society and art, so beautifully carried out by Jameson, can account for the *Recherche*. Jameson can construct a postmodern space of the world market, a postmodern era of "ever-greater fragmentation" of signs, and a "waning of our sense of history," only because he constructs this space by means of the ironical aspect of language, which makes possible the postmodern rhetoric with which Jameson obliterates individual, social, and historical differences and spatializes time, in order to construct a postmodern world.[58] The fate of Jameson's postmodern space, along with that of the ironical reading of the *Recherche*, thus rides on the possibility of fully identifying a particular social era, or its art, with the ironical aspect of discourse, which is transtemporal.

Socio-historical discourse on collective subjects is not eliminated from the *Recherche*; but it is denied causal authority by the narrator's materialist discourse and ironic rhetoric. Proust is fully aware of the way in which the novelist, or a theoretician like Jameson, uses the ironical aspect of language to create the illusion of an ironical psychology or social structure that determines the text.

Is Proust then fundamentally an ironist who created a purely ironical autobiography? Has his ironical narrator masochistically created a fictional world which, like his fantasized Albertine, necessarily thwarts all his autobiographical desires? The next chapter, the final chapter on the *Recherche*, will explore the narrator's meditation on how irony always turns against itself, negating the possibility of saying that the text is ironical or postmodern.

CHAPTER 4

Proust's forgetful ironies

In the *Recherche*, the remembering narrator treats forgetting as both an obstacle to, and an artistic means of, remembering a sublime essence of the artist's self. It recounts a search to disclose in painting, music, and the novel a unique manner of constructing the world: a difference that distinguishes an artist, a musician, or an author from all other artists, musicians, and authors. As the passage on Elstir's "fête" painting demonstrates, this search for individual difference takes the form of the deconstruction and forgetting of society's conventional signs of sameness, such as the narrator's voluntary or habitual memories of his past selves. The passage on Vinteuil's septet argues that this deconstruction is a deliberate means of differentiating the work from all of its signs of the artist's difference. The purpose of differentiation is to signify indirectly an unsignifiable difference, a remembering and repetition that exist only within forgetting and difference.

The narrator's deconstruction of signs of difference discloses a temporal difference within language; however, this temporal difference condemns all memory to an uncertain relationship with forgetting and differentiation. This is the temporal difference of allegory, which structures the narrator's present of narration as the interval between his unique past impressions and selves, which are always too early to be remembered, and his present words, which are always too late to remember past impressions and selves. Proust's allegorical narrator, unlike his remembering narrator, simply cannot know whether this temporal difference repeats that which it is always too early and too late to represent. But, as discussed in Chapter 3, allegory tends towards a deferral of its very ability to represent itself, to say that it is allegorical. In other words, Proust's allegory of difference ultimately turns against itself, differentiates itself from itself, and reveals its inability to say whether or not it is allegorical at all. This allegorical self-deconstruction opens up the possibility of an ironical reading of allegory as a simultaneous repetition and negation of the allegorical illusion of temporal difference. In such an ironical reading, there is no remembering or allegorical author who intends the text; only an ironical narrator, who simultaneously affirms and negates the illusion that an individual author – rather than the impersonal rhetorical nature of language's allegorical or ironical structures – determines the text's writing. This is the narrator's "materialist" reading of art and first-person narration, which produces an ironical narrator who is fundamentally indifferent to the temporal differences, personal or social, that he creates.

In this chapter, I will argue that the ironical "I" produces and negates not only the allegorical "I," but its own ironical stance. The resulting irony of irony, however, is itself subject to ironical negation, *ad infinitum*. Irony thus never achieves the impersonality of a purely material, linguistic, or socially constructed subject, nor does it achieve indifference to temporal or historical change; rather, it initiates an endless spiral of negations of time, history, individual change, or social change, which repeatedly try and fail to achieve this indifference. Ultimately, irony turns against its own assertion that it is ironical. It reopens, despite itself, the question of self, difference, and temporal change.

The failure of discourse to become ironical takes place because irony of irony falls into the liar's paradox. Immediately after the passage on the dinner at the Duchesse de Guermantes's, where he concludes that all social conversation lies, Marcel visits the Baron de Charlus. Charlus gives Marcel a lesson in the slipperiness of lies. He accuses Marcel of deceitfully maligning him. But, when Marcel denies the charge, Charlus accuses him of accusing Charlus of lying when he said that Marcel lied about him: "Alors je mens! s'écria-t-il d'un ton terrible, et en faisant un tel bond qu'il se trouva debout à deux pas de moi." In order to calm the Baron's hysterical fear and desire of being accused of lying, Marcel attributes the responsibility for Charlus's false accusation to an unknown third party: "On vous a trompé" (*R*, 3: 560). He lies about Charlus's lie – the latter's deceitful accusation that Marcel lied – in order to help Charlus deceive himself into believing that he is not responsible for that lie. He thus becomes co-dependent with Charlus's need to believe that reality, not his own hysteria, is responsible for his belief that others are maligning him. Accusations of lying, Proust noted in *Jean Santeuil*, are always in danger of falling into self-deception.[1] But what about the ironical narrator who accuses Charlus of lying, particularly when Charlus creates the illusion that he is virile? Similarly, is the ironical narrator lying about the Duchess's and her guests' lies? about Albertine's lies?[2]

The fall into lying of those who accuse others of lying is an indirect commentary on the first-person narrator's self-accusation that he lies: "Oui, j'ai été force d'amincir la chose et d'être mensonger...!" (*R*, 4: 191). This statement descends into the endless mise-en-abîme of the liar's paradox, which destroys any distinction between lying and truth-telling.[3] If the narrator is telling the truth that he is performing the act of lying, then his act of truth-telling already contradicts his statement that he is performing the act of lying. If he is lying in saying that he is lying, then he is not lying. In either case, the narrator's representation of his own speech acts ironically undercuts his statement about what these speech acts are doing. It breaks down any possibility of distinguishing between lying and truth-telling and thus the possibility of saying what speech act he is performing. The "ironist's paradox," by extension, means that Proust's ironical narrator can characterize himself as ironical only in an ironical mode. This irony of irony undercuts his ability to distinguish between irony and non-irony.

How then does this ironical negation of language's ironical aspect produce allegory in the *Recherche*? Proust dramatizes the transition from irony to allegory as Marcel's overcoming of his obsession with Albertine's lies when he gradually forgets her, in the passages Proust eliminated from the final typescript of *Albertine disparue*.[4] Whereas irony short-circuits and decenters the remembering/forgetting polarity in the narrator's discourse, forgetting does the same for lying and irony. The narrator explains the transition from lying to forgetting in crucial passages of *La Prisonnière*. He reveals that he does not know whether his accusations that Albertine is lying are truthful or deceptive: "Si... [la nature suivant laquelle j'agissais] n'a pas altéré les intentions d'Albertine au lieu de les démêler, c'est ce qui m'est difficile de dire" (*R*, 3: 347).[5] The narrator is unsure whether his mind hysterically produces an illusion that she is lying or whether it describes her real lies objectively. He attributes this uncertainty to time's production of forgetting:

Il en est malheureusement des commencements d'un mensonge de notre maîtresse comme des commencements de notre propre amour, ou d'une vocation. Ils se forment, se conglomèrent, ils passent inaperçus de notre propre attention. Quand on veut se rappeler de quelle façon on a commencé d'aimer une femme, on aime déjà; les rêveries d'avant, on ne se disait pas: c'est le prélude d'un amour, faisons attention; et elles avançaient par surprise, à peine remarquées de nous. De même, sauf des cas relativement assez rares, ce n'est guère que pour la commodité du récit que j'ai souvent opposé ici un dire mensonger d'Albertine avec (sur le même sujet) son assertion première. Cette assertion première, souvent, ne lisant pas dans l'avenir et ne devinant pas quelle affirmation contradictoire lui ferait pendant, elle s'était glissée inaperçue, entendue certes de mes oreilles, mais sans que je l'isolasse de la continuité des paroles d'Albertine. Plus tard, devant le mensonge patent, ou pris d'un doute anxieux, j'aurais voulu me rappeler; c'était en vain; ma mémoire n'avait pas été prévenue à temps; elle avait cru inutile de garder copie. (*R*, 3: 153)

In almost all cases where the narrator has claimed to demonstrate that Albertine lied to him, this demonstration, he now admits, was dictated, not by memory, but by the "commodité du récit," by narrative syntax, which requires a beginning (her original words) and an end (the words she falsely substitutes for her original words). When Marcel accuses Albertine of lying, he has to invent the past words that her allegedly deceitful present words contradict. The reason he invents her original words is that he has forgotten them, since at the time she pronounced them he had no idea she would someday contradict them. His jealousy is so invested in her being a liar, he creates a story with a fictional beginning and end. He retrospectively invents her past truth-telling, the beginning of his narrative, in order better to invent the present deceit that now hides this truth. Marcel's story of Albertine's transformation of past truth into present deceit may thus be deceitful and, from the point of view of the narrator, ironical. But he will never know. She may have been lying. She may not have been lying.

According to the narrator, the same forgetting that cut off access to what Albertine's present words were doing puts into question any story he might now retrospectively recount about how he originally became a writer and any story about what his writing is doing in the present. Forgetting erases the real "commencement...d'une vocation": the origin of writing. It renders unreadable any statement by the narrator of how he came to write and any statement of what his present words about his past actions are doing, such as being deceitful or ironical. According to the purely ironical reading of the *Recherche*, the present of narration is constituted by the production and negation of a purely fictional, personal subject. But, once the narrator admits that language's memory of its own actions is inhabited by forgetting, that it "avait cru inutile de garder copie" of its ironical origin, that it does not remember its original manuscript, then he must accept that any statement about the ironical nature of his writing and reading, like his statements about Albertine's lies, forgets whether or not writing and reading are doing what he says they are doing. Language's self-forgetting condemns it to being unable to do what it says or say what it does.

The narrator's ironical negation of his statements that language is deceitful or ironical puts into question not only his statement that Albertine was lying to him, but also his pretense of adopting an ironical distance from his past accusations that she was lying. From the point of view of irony, irony keeps turning against itself, in what Paul de Man calls "the narrowing spiral of a linguistic sign that becomes more and more remote from its meaning."[6] But this spiral of irony is not endless, as de Man seems to argue. It comes to an end when it puts into question, through the ironist's paradox, its ability to say that it is ironical. And if irony is not ironical, then its affirmations and negations are not simultaneous either. Irony takes time, if a very short time, while the mind transforms an affirmation into a negation, or an apparent act of irony into a representation of that act. And time in Proust involves forgetting. Irony's forgetting of whether it is acting ironically transforms the ironical subject into a product of allegory. It defers any memory of what the ironist did. It is always too late or too early to repeat this memory. This deferred memory reintroduces allegory as that which seeks a future memory of a past origin: the first-person narrator's actual act. Deferred memory asserts the reality of time and redefines ironical simultaneity as an error. It redefines irony as that which allegory is always too early or too late to represent.

Language cannot represent itself as ironical, therefore, without questioning its ironical nature and taking the temporal form of allegory. The narrator may say, as he does forty pages later, that he is lying. He may mark his discourse as ironical: "Oui, j'ai été forcé d'amincir la chose et d'être mensonger, mais ce n'est pas un univers, c'est des millions, presque autant qu'il existe de prunelles et d'intelligences humaines, qui s'éveillent tous les matins" (*R*, 3: 191). His representations of his present act of first-person narration as ironical presuppose a memory that is always deferred by forgetting. The statement "I lie" in the present of narration not only asserts the unreadability of any representation of language as an ironical speech act and any narrative of the transformation of truth into deceit; it does so by means of an allegory of language's forgetting and deferral of any representation of what (if anything) it is doing.

The narrator locates the source of language's self-forgetting, not in the emotional "maladie" (*R*, 3: 1044) that he later hypothesizes in *Le Temps retrouvé*, nor in social history, but in the rhetorical nature of the grammatical function of the first-person pronoun "I." Albertine seems to have an impenetrable defense against Marcel's accusations that she is lying. She appears to capitalize upon his forgetting of her past words by using "[un] de ces brusques sautes de syntaxe ressemblant un peu à ce que les grammairiens appellent anacoluthe" (*R*, 3: 153). Anacoluthon is a non-grammatical jump, within a single sentence, from one grammatical structure to another. The anacoluthon by which Albertine seems to elude Marcel's accusations jumps from an "I," which may refer to her own past lesbian activities, to a "she," which refers to someone else: "S'étant laissée aller, en parlant femmes, à dire: 'Je me rappelle que dernièrement je', brusquement, après un 'quart de soupir', 'je' devenait 'elle', c'était une chose qu'elle avait aperçue en promeneuse innocente, et nullement accomplie. Ce n'était pas elle qui était le sujet de l'action" (*R*, 3: 153).[7] Albertine's anacoluthon is a rhetorical figure, a type of metonymy, which Marcel would like to read, but cannot read, as a metaphor. This metonymy prevents him from knowing whether she is deceitfully hiding her lesbian actions or whether she is changing the subject in order to avoid his jealous delusions, which she provokes whenever she speaks about women.

This same metonymy inhabits the subject of first-person narration. The narrator's allegorical deconstruction of the subject over time and his repeated ironical negations of this subject reveal signs of self to be temporally and spatially other than they appear to be. The metonymical replacement of "I" with "he" erases any evidence that the "I" refers, not only to a self that intends the text, but also to an ironical or allegorical structure of language that intends the text. This metonymy puts into question the first-person pronoun's ability to perform its grammatical function: to refer to the present act of narration.[8] As a result, the first-person narrator's attempt to speak indirectly about his own act of narration by speaking in the third person about the actions of other characters, like Albertine, or other artists, like Elstir, Vinteuil, and Bergotte, marks his failure to transform their actions into metaphors for his own actions and thus to say what his narration is doing. It ironically negates the allegorical subject that is produced by language's allegory, and it allegorically defers the ironical subject that is produced by language's irony. The act of enunciation becomes totally other.

The "I"'s reference to language's inability to remember whether it refers to itself is the most radical mode of forgetting in *A la recherche du temps perdu*. This forgetting irreversibly alienates the "I" as subject from its act of narration. The first-person narrator cannot unify his text by representing it as an allegory of temporal difference without marking this difference as an ironical product of language's indifference to time. Nor can he unify his text by representing it as an ironical product of language's deceitful creation of temporal differences without revealing that language erases what it is doing over time. In Beckett's words: "The most ideal tautology presupposes a relation and the affirmation of equality involves only an approximate identification, and by asserting unity denies unity."[9] Since the "I" is always inhabited by an unreadable, metonymical relation to a "she," Proust's final manuscript correction, which gives Marcel the certainty that Albertine lied, cannot be a key to what Proust himself was doing. Writing cannot "garder copie" of the original manuscript of the author's actions. The original manuscript is always lost. The origin is always a retrospective invention.

Proust's alternation between the allegorical and ironical aspects of the present of narration prevents readers from ever knowing what he intended or how his language functions. Like Beckett's *Proust*, criticism can only juxtapose and alternate between the two incompatible "ways" of the two Proustian narrators: the allegorical narrator, who seeks to constitute himself in terms of temporal difference, and the ironical narrator, who seeks to constitute himself as spatial indifference to time, by indirectly negating the signs of temporal difference that language produces. Of course, the *Recherche* repeatedly returns to inviting us to imagine that Proust identified with his remembering narrator. It repeatedly emphasizes his allegorical search for difference and his autobiographical fiction of individual difference. These leitmotifs frequently recreate the impression that "Proust" can be identified with the remembering narrator that he hypothesizes in his discourses on Elstir and Vinteuil. The final correction of the typescript, which makes Albertine a certain liar about her lesbianism, can invite a similar reading, if one interprets her lies as metaphors, not for the ironical narrator's lies, but for love's lies only.

Forgetting, like lying, is thus a key to the interplay between the allegorical and ironical aspects of the present of Proust's first-person narrator. Forgetting renders signs of its ironical aspect irretrievable, just as lying renders signs of its allegorical aspect deceptive. Proust characterizes the novel's unreadability in terms of the novel's forgetting of whether it is allegorical or ironical:

Un des matins qui suivirent celui où Andrée m'avait dit qu'elle était obligée de rester auprès de sa mère, je faisais quelques pas avec Albertine que j'avais aperçue, élevant au bout d'un cordonnet un attribut bizarre qui la faisait ressembler à l'Idolâtrie de Giotto; il s'appelle d'ailleurs un "diabolo" et est tellement tombé en désuétude que devant le portrait d'une jeune fille en tenant un, les commentateurs de l'avenir pourront disserter comme devant telle figure allégorique de l'Arena, sur ce qu'elle a dans la main. (*R*, I: 886)

The problem for the narrator is how to name the game that is found in Proust's narrator's hand: his act of narration. Do we, like Giotto, treat the narrator's first-person narration as the production of idolatrous signs of self that must be negated in the search for the true, unnamable, hidden god, the author Proust? Or do we treat this narration as an ironical game that creates and negates illusions of an author, just as Marcel creates and negates the illusion that Albertine loves or does not love him? The act of narration, like Albertine's toy in Samuel Weber's words, is "assez 'diabolique' pour rendre son oubli obligé."[10]

Because Proust's allegory renders his act of first-person narration unreadable, we must redefine the critical moment at the end of the novel, when Marcel descends from the Prince's library to the guests below, where he comes face to face with time and death. This descent from a theory of atemporal art to the contemplation of the negativity of time signifies the death, not of a personal self, but of any theory of what the first-person narrator is doing, remembering or inventing a self:

En effet, dès que j'entrai dans le grand salon, bien que je tinsse toujours ferme en moi, au point où j'en étais, le projet que je venais de former, un coup de théâtre se produisit qui allait élever contre mon entreprise la plus grave des objections. Une objection que je surmonterais sans doute, mais qui, tandis que je continuais à réfléchir en moi-même aux conditions de l'œuvre d'art, allait, par l'exemple cent fois répété de la considération la plus propre à me faire hésiter, interrompre à tout instant mon raisonnement. (*R*, 3: 920)

Proust's "coup de théâtre," his dramatization of the inevitability of time and death, interrupts and defers any completion of the narrator's theoretical story of how the work of art functions. Theory inevitably produces hesitations about its power to generate truth.[11] As the last pages of the novel reveal, Marcel will not surmount this deferral, as he here predicts. He will never escape theory: "L'organisation de ma mémoire, de mes préoccupations, était liée à mon œuvre, peut-être parce que, tandis que les lettres reçues étaient oubliées l'instant d'après, l'idée de mon œuvre était dans ma tête, toujours la même, en perpétuel devenir" (*R*, 3: 1041).[12] Any metaphorical relationship between the theory and the practice of the first-person novel is deferred by theory itself and revealed to be metonymical.

This gap within language between a theory of allegorical or ironical first-person narration and the act of first-person narration does not mean that all first-person narration must constantly alternate between allegory and irony. Proust has the power to repeatedly deny and defer any recognition of the ironical aspect of his narration. But he does not seem to have the power to indefinitely defer irony. His choice of allegory or irony is in part forced. Similarly, Beckett has the freedom to ironically negate over and over his language's allegorical aspect, but he is forced to repeatedly undercut irony with a return to allegory. As a result, an author's repeated preference for one aspect of first-person narration over the other must not be understood as evidence that this aspect represents the author's act of narration. It is only a means of temporarily deferring the impression that the other aspect also determines the text's writing and reading, or that neither aspect determines the text. Indeed, it is precisely by returning repeatedly to an allegorical reading of his novel that Proust overcomes the debilitating effects of his ironical materialist reading and regains his motivation to write.

Narration cannot deconstruct or ironically negate one aspect of the present of narration without reintroducing the other, if not necessarily in the text's statements about itself, at least in the mind of the reader. But, in negating its being determined by one of its aspects, narration is obliged to create the illusion that it is determined by the other: that it has finally figured out how to say what it is doing. The repeated return of the themes of memory and forgetting at the end of the *Recherche*, after Marcel's rediscovery of time and death in the matinée Guermantes, thus signifies, not a victory of allegory over irony but a breakdown of the irony/allegory distinction and a recognition that the text cannot help but fall into the error of positing this distinction. Similarly, the return of Marcel's ethical concerns at the end of the novel puts into question Beckett's positing of an ironical Proust who is totally indifferent to ethical concerns.[13] It breaks down the allegory/irony opposition that makes possible the distinctions between difference and indifference, morality and amorality, while it also asserts the necessity of choosing one or the other. Thus the sudden return of Marcel's moral guilt for forgetting his mother, grandmother, and past selves at the end of the novel. The narrator talks in *Le Temps retrouvé* of expiating his guilt towards those he has forgotten and he dreams of a writing that will be "pour le destin de ces pauvres mortes, un accomplissement" (*R*, 3: 902). Writing takes on the appearance of being a necessary, allegorical product of a prior obligation:

... Tout se passe dans notre vie comme si nous y entrions avec le faix d'obligations contractées dans une vie antérieure; il n'y a aucune raison dans nos conditions de vie sur cette terre pour que nous nous croyions obligés à faire le bien, à être délicats, même à être polis, ni pour l'artiste athée à ce qu'il se croie obligé de recommencer vingt fois un morceau dont l'admiration qu'il excitera importera peu à son corps mangé par les vers... (*R*, 3: 187–88)

However, the narrator's assertion of the author's prior obligation to please an ideal reader, such as his mother, is qualified by "comme si." Death destroys all presuppositions of such an obligation and renders the attempt to carry out a prior obligation ironical. Indeed, for the writer, guilt is both a motivation to disclose his difference through allegory and the indifferent tool of the ironical writer: "Il sait quelles situations, s'il est romancier, quels paysages, s'il est peintre, lui fournissent la matière, indifférente en soi, mais nécessaire à ses recherches, comme serait un laboratoire ou un atelier. Il sait qu'il a fait ses chefs-d'œuvre avec des effets de lumière atténuée, des

remords modifiant l'idée d'une faute..." (*R*, 1: 851). Proust's narrator is both the moralist and the ironist, mother and father, and neither. Yet he cannot not choose at any moment of his text.

The act of writing becomes possible in the *Recherche* not when the narrator has a sudden recurrence of involuntary memories and constructs a theory of the novel based on them, but when he accepts the gap between all theories of narration and the act of narration, a gap that can be theorized, allegorically, as forgetting or, ironically, as deceit. The present of first-person narration, like a trompe-l'oeil painting, is always forgetting and ironically reinventing itself, always disclosing that it is other than it appears. But, in order to write, Proust's protagonist must also situate himself in the passage from irony, which negates the act of representing the past, to allegory, which vainly seeks to perform this act. It is this passage from ironical negation to failed allegorical affirmation that is the very basis of action in Proust and in Beckett.

Beckett's *Proust* intuits the existence of Proust's divided and deceptive first-person narrator. But Beckett does not yet understand the implications of forgetting for this divided narrator, nor has he discovered the necessity of the passage from irony to allegory for the act of writing. Only in rewriting Proust's first-person discourse in the construction of his own narrators – who seem, but only seem, more drawn to irony and indifference than to allegory and difference – does Beckett discover that writing arises out of the incomplete and repeated passage from the ironical impossibility of historically distinguishing his narrator from Proust's to the allegorical necessity of seeking to establish historical difference.

CHAPTER 5

Molloy's Way: The parody of allegory

> That is what has had a fatal effect on my development, my lack of memory, no doubt about it
>
> (*TN*, 337)

Forgetting and lying, along with the discursive modes that make them possible, allegory and irony, play crucial roles in Samuel Beckett's first-person narration, as they do in Proust's. Beckett was profoundly influenced by the ways in which Proust's writing narrator dramatized his forgetting and lying as rhetorical processes that structure and question perception, memory, thought, and consciousness.[1] Beckett's early trilogy of novels – *Molloy*, *Malone Dies*, and *The Unnamable* – foregrounds its narrators' forgetting and lying in a manner that deconstructs and parodies Proust's remembering narrator and his allegory of temporal differentiation and deconstruction. But the trilogy also parodies Proust's (and Beckett's own) ironical narrators and their search for indifference. The narrators in the trilogy thus reread and rewrite Proust's first-person narrator.

On the surface, the trilogy's rereading of Proust's first-person narrator opens up an historical difference between Proust's remembering narrator, who sincerely seeks to express his individual difference through art, and Beckett's forgetful and deceitful narrators, who ironically mock the claim to express individual difference.[2] It is as if Beckett were following Proust's advice that the best way to differentiate one's writing from a precursor's is through pastiche.[3] But Beckett asserts this historical difference, paradoxically, by means of a rhetorical figure that negates historical difference: irony. Beckett's trilogy, I will argue, repeatedly dramatizes the ironical impossibility and the allegorical necessity of situating its narrator in literary history.

The first half of the first novel in Beckett's trilogy, *Molloy*, is recounted by the writer Molloy. The novel initially establishes Molloy's writing situation

79

as a parody of Proust's and his narrator's writing situations: "I am in my mother's room" (*TN*, 7), the narrator begins. A few sentences later, he adds that he writes in his mother's bedroom. Proust's narrator, we know from *Le Temps retrouvé*, writes in a bedroom at his mother's house.[4] Proust himself wrote in a bed, initially located in an apartment that was associated with his mother through a maternal uncle. Neither Proust's narrator nor Proust, however, write in their mother's bedroom, as does Molloy, let alone sleep in her bed. Molloy exaggerates the incestuous overtones of Proust's and his narrator's writing situations. This exaggeration reduces the mother to a privileged sex object and mocks the idolatrous way in which Proust's narrator represents his sacred ideal reader.[5] Rather than idealize a motherly reader, as did Proust, Molloy claims indifference to his mother in sentences that foreshadow Camus's *L'Etranger*. He also claims indifference to his reader, his boss Youdi. A man picks up his pages and returns them after Youdi has corrected them: "When he comes for the fresh pages he brings back the previous week's. They are marked with signs I don't understand. Anyway I don't read them... Was [my mother] already dead when I came? Or did she only die later? I mean enough to bury. I don't know. Perhaps they haven't buried her yet. In any case I have her room. I sleep in her bed" (*TN*, 7).

Molloy's parody of Proustian narration focuses its irony on Proust's remembering narrator, who idolizes his mother and the self she confirms. Molloy alludes here, as elsewhere in the trilogy, to Proust's dramatization of his narrator's waking to consciousness at the beginning of the *Recherche*. As discussed in the Introduction, Proust's narrator wakes up periodically in the middle of the night and remembers where, when, and who he is. He then spends the rest of the night in bed remembering his past, from his childhood in Combray to the present. Like Proust's waking narrator, Molloy narrator – as opposed to Molloy protagonist, the past self about which he speaks – is in his bedroom and is about to recount from memory the story of how he became the writer and first-person narrator whose words we are reading. Unlike Proust's narrator, however, Molloy obsessively turns away from recounting his story and towards critiquing his act of narration. He repeatedly questions his ability to remember his past, emphasizing his forgetting and ignorance: "The truth is I don't know much. For example my mother's death... [My true love's] name? I've forgotten it again..." (*TN*, 7–8). Molloy cannot even remember the words he needs in order to write about his past: "I've forgotten how to spell too, and half the words" (*TN*, 7–8). But he does not really desire to remember his past; it is a habit: "If you think of the forms and light of other days it is without regret. But you seldom think of them, with what would you think of them? I don't know" (*TN*, 8).

Molloy's irony is not a simple *contrario*, an ironical figure that negates his remembering by asserting his forgetting. Molloy's irony also turns against his forgetting, thus negating the very basis for allegory, the remembering/forgetting distinction: "Perhaps I'm inventing a little, perhaps embellishing ... But perhaps I'm remembering things" (*TN*, 8–9). Molloy thus asserts from the beginning his fundamental ignorance about what his mind is doing: remembering or forgetting. Proust's waking narrator may initially forget where, when, and who he is, he eventually constructs a consciousness of his present world and self and convinces himself that his consciousness of present and past is objective. Only at the end of the first section of *Combray* does the narrator reveal his deceit by telling us that his consciousness of remembering was in fact in error, thus revealing the fundamental confusion between remembering and forgetting in Proust. Molloy, by contrast, rarely lets us forget his ignorance. He clearly situates his narration in the difference between remembering and forgetting, lying and truth.

It is as if Molloy narrator, unlike Proust's narrator, never wakes up entirely, never becomes conscious of whether he is remembering or forgetting, telling the truth or lying. He is terminally confused about what his mind is doing. So too is his reader.[6] Molloy cannot construct with certainty a remembered past self, and thus distinguish between his past as protagonist and his present as narrator.[7] His use of the past tense and of temporal adverbs and adjectives does indeed posit a distinction between past and present, protagonist and narrator; but his obsessive reminders of his extensive forgetting undercut these grammatical distinctions, rendering them ironical, so that we cannot determine when he is remembering and when he is inventing his past.[8] What Molloy's narration ironically negates, therefore, is its very pretension to characterize his own speech acts according to the remembering/forgetting distinctions. Consequently, his narrative takes the form of a search to deconstruct the very bases of allegory in order to redefine it as a product of irony.

But, from the very first pages, forgetting and ignorance in *Molloy* are much more than a means of breaking down the forgetting/remembering distinction. They progressively disable the reader's ability to say even that the narrator is performing the rhetorical acts of irony and parody.[9] Molloy recounts this rhetorical disablement of the narrator's power to do what he intends as the gradual crippling of Molloy protagonist's body, which foreshadows the progressive crippling of the bodies of the trilogy's subsequent narrators, as it advances from its first to its last novel. All of the trilogy's narrators find their minds and bodies in "a world collapsing endlessly," which "murmur[s] that all wilts and yields," "down towards an end it seems can never come" in the "indestructible chaos of timeless things" (*TN*, 40).[10] This story of progressive disablement redefines Molloy's ironical rhetoric within an allegory of rhetorical entropy, which defers any conclusion about what his words are doing. It recounts both the ironization of allegory and the allegorization of irony that the present chapter will trace.

From the first pages of the novel, Molloy situates his discourse in what critics have called a "brink" or "breach" between contraries. I will simply call this the gap between language's allegorical and ironical aspects. Molloy marks his narrative as a vain attempt to say what his words are doing. Hence his failed efforts to characterize his beginning as ironical:

> There's this man who comes every week and takes away the pages... It was he who told me I'd begun all wrong, that I should have begun differently. He must be right. I began at the beginning, like an old ballocks, can you imagine that? Here's my beginning. Because they're keeping it apparently. I took a lot of trouble with it. Here it is. It gave me a lot of trouble. It was the beginning, do you understand? Whereas now it's nearly the end. Is what I do now any better? I don't know. That's beside the point. Here's my beginning. It must mean something, or they wouldn't keep it. Here it is. (*TN*, 7–8)

Molloy, on the one hand, expresses his indifference to what his narrative is doing, to whether or not it is recounting a change between past and present. Since narrative presupposes change, he is expressing his indifference to whether or not he is performing the act of narration: "That's besides the point." This pose of indifference to whether he is recounting anything at all renders his use of the words "beginning" and "end" ironical. On the other hand, Molloy expresses anxiety about whether or not he can recount "his" story. He repeatedly says, "Here it is" when referring to "his" beginning. He asserts that it "must mean something," and he expresses concern that the reader will not understand the difference between his past and present: "It was the beginning, do you understand? Whereas now it's nearly the end." Molloy narrator thus gives evidence of trying to reintroduce the category of narrative, to which he has expressed indifference. He takes the position of a subject of allegory.

In the space of a few sentences, Molloy narrator represents his discourse as an act of irony and an act of allegory. He dramatizes his discourse as a rapid alternation between, or a coincidence of, an indifferent subject of irony outside time and an anxious subject seeking a temporal difference in time. To speak of Molloy's relation to Proust's narrator is thus to speak, in part, of Beckett's compression of the interplay between irony and allegory. Beckett plays out this interplay in the space of a few sentences, or even a single sentence. For example, Molloy says "now" in the first sentences of his first paragraph and "here" in the last sentence, because it is the temporal and spatial present of the "I" that he appears to be trying to capture. But he also qualifies his bedroom as "there" and uses a past tense, because he is spatially and temporally alienated from this present. Since irony and allegory are the incompatible ways in which language tries and fails to capture the present of narration, Molloy situates his discourse in the gap between them. He prevents his readers from entertaining for long the reassuring illusion, which they frequently enjoy in Proust, that they know what his words are doing.

Let us consider first Molloy's allegory of the negation of allegory and his disclosure of his parodic irony. This can be done by focusing on the central figure of the mother and on her surrogates, with whom Marcel and Molloy fall in love. Beckett's irony takes as its object Marcel's allegorical walks on the Méséglise Way, which initially dramatize the latter's search for mother and self-memory in the displaced form of nature and little girls. Molloy protagonist begins his predominantly walking voyage towards his mother's house at a moment corresponding to the end of Marcel's. This is the moment when Marcel discovers that he no longer believes that anything is hidden behind the natural objects whose essence he covets: "[J]e cessais de croire partagés par d'autres êtres, de croire vrais en dehors de moi, les désirs que je formais pendant ces promenades et qui ne se réalisaient pas. Ils ne m'apparaissaient plus que comme les créations purement subjectives, impuissantes, illusoires, de mon tempérament" (*R*, 1: 158–59). Molloy has apparently not only ceased to believe in his mother's surrogates; he seems to have ceased to believe in her. Molloy's mother has nothing in common with Marcel's ideal motherly reader whose kiss, like the host, nurtures the resurrection of her son's unique self. Molloy expects to find neither love nor recognition from his mother. He starts walking towards her house only in order to "brin[g] as soon as possible some light to bear on... my relations with my mother" (*TN*, 86). Molloy protagonist wants only to define himself in relation to his mother.

Molloy's relation to his mother thus parodies and profanes Proust's fiction of a mother who nurtures her son's unique self. Molloy wants his mother/son relationship to be purely impersonal. It is based on the universality of his Oedipal desire for her, not on a desire for her recognition of him. However, impersonality turns out to be only a desire for impersonality. When a maternal social worker in a police station offers him tea and cakes, just as Marcel's mother offered him tea and madeleines, Molloy, unlike Marcel, refuses to partake or to remember. Indeed, he throws them down, as if they were poison. His mother's (or her substitute's) offer of nurturing poisons him by provoking his sexual desire, which he wants to have no basis in the motherly object of his desire: "And there are days, like this evening, when my memory confuses [the women I have loved] and I am tempted to think of them as one and the same old hag, flattened and crazed by life." (*TN*, 59). By replacing Marcel's ideal nurturing mother with a flattened and crazed old hag, and by replacing Marcel's chaste desire with Molloy's sexual desire, Beckett parodies Marcel's fantasy of an ideal nurturing mother and of the nurturing "filles en fleurs" that he substitutes for her.[11] He redefines this desire for life as a desire for death. The goal of Beckett's parody of Proust is thus the death of any desire for difference: "Need of my mother! No, there were no words for the want of need in which I was perishing" (*TN*, 34).[12]

The narrator's ironical description of his mother and her substitutes is not just an act of profaning her and of parodying Proust's nurturing mother. It is also an erasure and perishing of the very notion of self. Molloy, like Marcel, seeks to kill off his self by killing off his mother and adopting an ironical, fatherly position. But this symbolic suicide takes the form of identification with mother: "I have taken [my mother's] place. I must resemble her more and more" (*TN*, 7).[13] For Proust's narrator, becoming (like) mother means giving birth to a self through writing, just as the mother gave life to him: "[Mon oeuvre] était pour moi comme un fils dont la mère mourante doit encore s'imposer la fatigue de s'occuper sans cesse…" (*R*, 3: 1042). But Molloy's mother, and the writing Molloy who adopts her position on the pot, gives birth only to waste matter. She "brought me into the world, through the hole in her arse if my memory is correct" (*TN*, 16). Molloy the writer takes his mother's place on her chamber pot and gives birth to himself, through writing, just as she gave life to him, but in the form of dead matter: "[M]y mother['s] charity kept me dying" (*TN*, 22).[14] For Molloy, there is no birth, only a purgatory in which the repeated act of giving birth to self becomes indistinguishable from an act of killing off the self. He thus hopes to "finish dying," to achieve the indifference of an ironical attitude towards the drive towards self-representation in first-person discourse (*TN*, 7). In this way, Beckett redefines Proust's allegory of a search for self as an allegory of Molloy's search to kill off a self and treat all representations of self ironically.

Sexual desire for mother is both a desire to distinguish the male self from the mother's female self and a desire to erase this sexual difference and become mother. It is a desire to be both male and female, or neither. Molloy's utterly confused sexual "relation" to his mother parodies the distinct sexual differences that Proust's narrator tries in vain to maintain by characterizing even his male homosexuals as fundamentally female and his lesbians as really male. In contrast, Molloy reminds his reader of his impotence to clearly distinguish sexual identities. Thus his comments on the mother-surrogate Lousse: "Perhaps she too was a man... Perhaps after all she put me in her rectum" (*TN*, 57). The satisfaction of physical sexual desire, for Molloy, does not establish sexual difference. Rather, sexual relations are a mutual masturbation in which both partners play both sexual roles: "Shall I describe [my mother's] room? No. I shall have occasion to do so later perhaps. When I seek refuge there, bet to the world, all shame drunk, my prick in my rectum, who knows" (*TN*, 19).[15] Homosexual desire ironically breaks down sexual difference, making it impossible to represent. Difference thus produces a desire for what it lacks: absolute indifference to desire.[16]

Desire also erases temporal difference in the form of the genealogical cause and effect relationship between mother and son: "We were so old, she and I, she had had me so young, that we were like a couple of old cronies, sexless, unrelated, with the same memories, the same rancours, the same expectations" (*TN*, 17). This seemingly atemporal, sexless non-relation between mother and son is the model for the non-relation between narrator and protagonist. Desire ironically erases the temporal relation between the narrator's present and past selves, transforming them into mere repetitions of the same empty signs. Desire becomes an ironical creation of the indifference of habit.

The ironical aspect of Molloy's expressions of desire creates an apparent historical difference between the latter's discourse and the discourse of Proust's narrator. However, Beckett's ironical attitude to desire can parody Proust's autobiographical desire for self only by repeating the latter's ironical, writing narrator. Beckett makes this literary historical repetition clear by having Molloy repeat the Montjouvain episode, which concludes the passages on the Méséglise Way in *Combray*. Molloy says: "I called her Mag because for me, without my knowing why, the letter g abolished the syllable Ma, and as it were spat on it, better than any other letter would have done" (*TN*, 17).[17] Molloy's rewriting of his mother's name so that it spits on its signification of maternity recalls not only the spitting of Mlle Vinteuil's lover on the portrait of her father, but also the passage's indirect allusion to Marcel's desire to profane his mother and his self.[18] But Molloy throws his incestuous and angry desire to profane and to forget his own mother and self in his reader's face (in the face of the reader's conventional expectations). In contrast, Proust's narrator's final statement in the Montjouvain passage about the desire for, and the cruelty of, indifference to the pain that it causes only implicitly spits on his mother's name by generalizing Mlle Vinteuil's psychology. This statement nonetheless foreshadows Molloy's search for indifference to his mother by treating her name sadistically.

The Montjouvain passage, which is the culmination of the passages on Marcel's search for self on the Méséglise Way, also prefigures Molloy's discourse by redefining this search, in ironical and parodic terms, as a violent, mocking erasure, rather than an imprinting, of self. Mlle Vinteuil invites her lover to spit on her father's portrait, and thus on his name and memory, by saying: "Oh! ce portrait de mon père qui nous regarde, je ne sais pas qui a pu le mettre là, j'ai pourtant dit vingt fois que ce n'était pas sa place" (*R*, 1: 162). In doing so she repeats her father's self-deprecating obsession with putting a copy of one of his compositions on the piano before his guests arrive, then denying himself the satisfaction of playing the composition after they arrive by saying "Mais je ne sais qui a mis cela sur le piano, ce n'est pas sa place" and putting the composition away (*R*, 1: 113). Mlle Vinteuil's repetition of her father's gesture of self-erasure and self-denial replaces his composition, which he takes as a sign of self, with his portrait, then retrospectively redefines her father's self-denying habits as a masochistic mode of profaning signs of self. Her parody transforms Vinteuil's allegorical search to remember his self in his music (through difference and deferral) into the cruel and ungrateful gesture of a sadistic daughter who ironically repeats signs of his (and indirectly her) self, in order to give herself the pleasure of laughing at the illusions of self and memory that they create.

But Mlle Vinteuil's sadistic parody of her father's masochistic ritual is only a parody of sadism. It can never make her feel that she is completely different from her prudish and loving father, that she, unlike him, is cruel and seeks only her pleasure: "Au moment où [Mlle Vinteuil] se voulait si différente de son père, ce qu'elle me rappelait, c'était les façons de penser, de dire, du vieux professeur de piano" (*R*, 1: 164). Her sadistic parody of her father's self-denial only gives her an "illusion de s'être évadées de [son] âme scrupuleuse et tendre, dans le monde inhumain du plaisir" (*R*, 1: 164). The lover's act of spitting on the father's portrait is thus an unselfaware parody of parody. It questions any identification of Mlle Vinteuil with the desire to be cruel or to seek only her pleasure in the repetition and negation of signs of self. Parody of parody breaks down the memory/forgetting, pain/pleasure distinctions, suggesting indifference to such distinctions. This is why Proust proposes, as the only possible remedy to Mlle Vinteuil's sadism, that she accept her drive to profane her father as just an example of humanity's indifference to whether its actions cause pain or pleasure to others or to itself: "Peut-être n'eût-elle pensé que le mal fût un état si rare, si extraordinaire, si dépaysant, où il était si reposant d'émigrer, si elle avait su discerner en elle, comme en tout le monde, cette indifférence aux souffrances qu'on cause et qui, quelques autres noms qu'on lui donne, est la forme terrible et permanente de la cruauté" (R, 1: 165).[19]

Mlle Vinteuil's (her lover's) parodic spitting on the photo of her father, which is an indirect spitting on the father within her, translates Proust's hidden parody of his own memories of self, of his remembering narrator, from the point of view of his ironical, materialist narrator: "La profanation d'un de mes souvenirs par des lecteurs inconnus, je l'avais consommée avant eux" (R, 3: 902). Similarly, Mlle Vinteuil's unaware parody of her deliberate parody of her father's memory is Proust's parody of the pretension to power of his materialist, ironic, and parodic narrator. Parody of parody in Proust thus seems to bring to culmination the walks on Marcel's Méséglise Way with an irony of irony that negates desire and posits an ironical indifference to one's own manifestations of desire.[20] Thus Beckett's reading of the *Recherche* as an "ablation" of desire.[21]

Molloy parodies the love for mother that nurtures Proust's remembering narrator by repeating Proust's parody of his remembering narrator. By rewriting his mother's name so that it spits on itself, as "Mag," Molloy repeats Mlle Vinteuil's spitting on her father's portrait and Proust's spitting on his loving, remembering mother and reader. Beckett's parodic irony thus negates the proper name's reference to the son's mother, who is different from him and who nurtures her son's different self. It redefines this name as an artificial construction of a mother/son relationship that is motivated only by his desire for such a relationship: "My name is Molloy, I cried, all of a sudden, now I remember... [Mother's] name must be Molloy too" (TN, 23). But this very parody of the family name is, as in Proust, a parody of parody since, as we have seen, Molloy, like Proust, repeatedly asserts his (desired) indifference to any desire to be cruel to mother and self by asserting his indifference to whether or not he remembers them.

Molloy's repetition of Proust's parody of parody foregrounds the complex literary historical relation between Beckett's narrator, as the supposed literary son, and Proust's narrator, as the hypothetical literary father. The very attempt by the literary son to differentiate himself parodically from his literary father only repeats the latter's self-parody and parody of this self-parody. Beckett's parody of Proust's remembering narrator and his parody of that parody thus only appear to distinguish Beckett from Proust. Molloy's discourse on mother and self is a literary historical repetition of its precursor's discourse that negates any historical difference between the two. To spit on Proust's name, as a popular reference to a unique remembering self, is thus to spit on Beckett's own name, as signifying an ironical differentiation from Proust's non-ironical remembering narrator. Beckett's parody of Proust thus redefines the names "Proust" and "Beckett" as signs that ironically spit on both their signification of a self and their ironical negation of a self, which reveals only a desire for ironical indifference to the self/non-self distinction. Beckett's parody of Proust thus turns out to be a parody of his own desire to distinguish his writing in literary history from Proust's.

Molloy's repetition of Proustian self-parody specifically targets Proust's remembering narrator's redefinition of self-consciousness in terms of artistic impressions:

[N]ous n'identifierions pas les objets si nous ne faisions pas intervenir le raisonnement. Que de fois en voiture ne découvrons-nous pas une longue rue claire qui commence à quelques mètres de nous, alors que nous n'avons devant nous qu'un pan de mur violemment éclairé qui nous a donné le mirage de la profondeur! Dès lors n'est-il pas logique, non par artifice de symbolisme mais par retour sincère à la racine même de l'impression, de représenter une chose par cette autre que dans l'éclair d'une illusion première nous avons prise pour elle? Les surfaces et les volumes sont en réalité indépendants des noms d'objets que notre mémoire leur impose quand nous les avons reconnus. Elstir tâchait d'arracher à ce qu'il venait de sentir ce qu'il savait; son effort avait souvent été de dissoudre cet agrégat de raisonnements que nous appelons vision. (*R*, 2: 419)

According to Proust's remembering narrator, the impressionist artist presupposes that consciousness of world and self is structured artificially and linguistically according to a logic of names. His impressionist artist brings out this linguistic structure of conscious representation by deliberately demystifying and erasing the conventional names with which his consciousness retrospectively reconstructs world and self, and by differentiating his impressions from these names. But this demystification also functions as an unreadable sign of the artist's ineffable "manner of seeing" or "accent," which exists only in the space between consciousness's conventional names and defines his unique artistic self.[22]

Beckett dramatizes Proustian impressions as early as *Watt*, where they are purely a mode of deconstruction, not of expression.[23] In *Molloy* this deconstruction becomes a parody of Proustian impressions, of involuntary memories of impressions, and of consciousness as it is represented at the beginning of the *Recherche*. Beckett's parody of Proustian consciousness occurs in a passage that recounts Molloy's stay in the house of Lousse, a lover and mother-substitute.[24]

Molloy narrator parodies Proustian impressions in order to redefine consciousness in solely linguistic terms. He parodies his own ability, and indirectly Proust's narrator's ability, to wake up and become fully conscious: in other words, to remember where, when, and who he is. Early on in his narration, Molloy narrator, like Proust's narrator, casts doubt upon all conscious perception – "And what do I mean by seeing and seeing again?" (*TN*, 15)[25] – as well as on the rational means by which his mind constructs objects of perception – "I raised my head and saw a policeman... Elliptically speaking, for it was only later, by way of induction, or deduction, I forget which, that I knew what it was" (*TN*, 20). Only retrospectively can Molloy's mind impose a conventional name on what he has seen and rationally determine, by deductive or inductive reasoning, what it is, name it. This is of course the same belated certainty that Proust's waking narrator arrives at when he finally decides that he has achieved a consciousness of which bedroom he is in and of what self is in it.

During his stay at Lousse's house, however, Molloy loses his capacity to arrive, by deductive or inductive reasoning, at the certainty that a specific name, like "policeman," corresponds to a specific thing. He becomes "virtually bereft... of consciousness," finding himself imprisoned within the Proustian impressions that precede consciousness (*TN*, 54). Molloy's impressions, like Proust's, are highly subversive means of deconstructing the subject/object distinction that makes consciousness possible. He thus finds it "hard to name what was mirrored [in my one seeing eye], often quite distinctly... [M]y attempts at taste and smell were scarcely more fortunate" (*TN*, 50). Not only is he incapable of naming things, he cannot name names, for the sounds of names become "pure sounds, free of meaning" which he cannot identify. Names float around in Molloy's mind, in the same way that a kaleidoscope of bedrooms swirl around in the gradually waking mind of Proust's narrator, without his being able to attach them to things. Molloy's inability to logically name things puts into question any necessary relation between names and things and thus the possibility of identifying objects of consciousness. For Molloy, as for Watt before him, "there could be no things but nameless things, no names but thingless names" (*TN*, 31).[26]

Molloy's impressions also question any necessary relation between names and the subject of consciousness. In order to name the subject, the subject must become its own object. It must become a consciousness of consciousness. But for Molloy "even my sense of identity was wrapped in a namelessness often hard to penetrate, as we have just seen I think. And so on for all the other things which made merry with my senses" (*TN*, 31). Whereas the pre-conscious impressions of bedrooms experienced by Proust's narrator are eventually erased by his mind when it constructs a consciousness of the bedroom in which he is sleeping, Molloy spends months being defined by the kaleidoscope of his pre-conscious impressions.[27]

Rather than produce a purely ironical stance towards consciousness, this pre-conscious breakdown of the subject/object distinction coincides with an alternation between the allegorical and ironical rhetoric that we found in Proust's passages on Elstir's paintings of the two aspects of the Instant. As daylight fades from Molloy's window and darkness fills his bedroom, "the night... lit the chandelier, which I had left turned on" (*TN*, 38).[28] This sentence combines the allegorical rhetoric of Elstir's "fête" painting and the ironical rhetoric of his watercolors, a combination that can be found in a single Elstir painting, *Port de Carquethuit* (*R*, 1: 836–38).[29] Like the "fête" painting, the first half of Molloy's sentence – "the night lit the chandelier" – erases the literal meanings of "night," which can light nothing, and "chandelier," which must be lit by a switch or matches. This erasure of the literal differentiates Molloy's clause from its words' conventional meanings by giving them figurative meanings. The sentence personifies the night as an agent who illuminates a chandelier, and it transforms the chandelier into a bizarre lamp that is illuminated by darkness. The result of this turning of tropes from literal to figurative meanings is a Proustian impression that, according to Proust's remembering narrator, deconstructs the conscious link between names and things and expresses Molloy's different manner of seeing the world in the past: his difference as a past subject. But, like Elstir's watercolors, the second half of the sentence – "which I had left turned on" – returns to the literal meaning of the lamp as if it referred to real things. It seems to redefine this impression and the unique subject it produces as rhetorical deceptions and to render them ironical. The lamp was in fact already on, but the narrator only became aware of this when it became dark, which produced the illusion that the night lit the chandelier. But, as in Proust's mythological watercolors, although this turning of signs back from figurative to literal meanings questions the subject, it cannot be taken as a return to literal representations of objects. For Molloy has already deconstructed any link between names, like "dark" and "chandelier," and things. His reading of his impression thus ironically asserts and negates both its literal representations of objects and its figurative representations of a subject. But of course, in doing so, it simply repeats Proust's meditation on the turning of tropes in Elstir's paintings.

Molloy thus appears to alternate between, on the one hand, an allegory that deconstructs a literal reading of signs of objects and constructs a figurative reading of the subject, and, on the other hand, an ironical negation of this figurative reading of the subject and an ironical reconstruction of the literal readings of objects.

But Beckett, like Proust's writing narrator in *La Prisonnière*, repeats Marcel's meditation on Elstir's two aspects of the Instant in order to comically parody not only Proust's remembering narrator's theory of artistic impressionist expression but also his theory of the writing of autobiographical involuntary memories. According to Proust's remembering narrator, involuntary memories transform him into a different person, a past self. He can see the world at a specific moment of the past through his past self's eyes. A similar effect is produced by the contemplation of another artist's impressionistic art, which enables Marcel to see the world through Elstir's eyes, to temporarily be Elstir. Molloy too has the experience of becoming a past, other self: "Yes it sometimes happens and will sometimes happen again that I forget who I am and strut before my eyes, like a stranger. Then I see the sky different from what it is and the earth too takes on false colours... I vanish happy in that alien light, which must have once been mine..." (*TN*, 42). But Molloy is not at all sure that this past manner of seeing was his. Indeed, he mocks that very notion. His "fauteuil magique" comically transports not only his mind into the past, but also his crippled body: "Je cherchai mes vêtements. Je trouvai un commutateur et le tournai. Sans résultat. Quelle histoire! Tout cela me laissait passablement indifférent. Je trouvai mes béquilles, contre un fauteuil. On trouvera étrange que j'aie pu faire les mouvements que j'ai indiqués, sans leurs secours. Je trouve cela étrange. On ne se rappelle pas tout de suite qui on est, au réveil."[30] Molloy's last sentence in this quotation alludes to a statement of Proust's remembering narrator at the beginning of the *Recherche*: "et quand je m'éveillais au milieu de la nuit, comme j'ignorais où je me trouvais, je ne savais même pas au premier instant qui j'étais" (*R*, 1: 5).[31] Like Proust's waking narrator, Molloy remembers a past self. He is reborn in the mind of a past, noncrippled self. But Molloy is also reborn into his past body, the body of a non-cripple. He miraculously walks again. This confusion of a sign of the past, a memory, with the physical past itself, is absurd. Involuntary memory, for Molloy, is an illusion: "And if I had not lost my sense of smell the smell of lavender would always make me think of Lousse, in accordance with the well-known mechanism of association" (*TN*, 48).[32]

But Molloy can never achieve the indifference towards which his irony and parody of Proust's remembering narrator tend, as can be seen by quoting the entire passage on his becoming a past stranger:

Yes it sometimes happens and will sometimes happen again that I forget who I am and strut before my eyes, like a stranger. Then I see the sky different from what it is and the earth too takes on false colours. It looks like rest, it is not, I vanish happy in that alien light, which must have once been mine, I am willing to believe it, then the anguish of return, I won't say where, I can't, to absence perhaps, you must return, that's all I know, it's misery to stay, misery to go. (*TN*, 42)

The joyous Proustian act of sincerely becoming a past conscious subject turns out to be a deceptive suspension of Molloy's present disbelief. It is immediately followed by a return to his present, anguished, ironical consciousness, which denies the reality of the past he remembers. But the present ironical voice that negates his remembered past consciousness is itself, ironically, an illusion, which hides the absence of a subject. This absence of voice ironically undercuts his present ironical voice. To become a past, remembered self or the present ironical creator of the fiction of a past self, are, both, willing suspensions of disbelief. Molloy's misery is thus to be caught in a state of becoming, but never being, self-conscious. He can never be a past or present conscious subject, because of language's irony of irony. "He" is caught between his ironical negation of the existence of the Proustian allegorical subject of the search to become a past self and his ironical negation of that negation.

Molloy's attempt to parody Proust's remembering narrator from the stance of an ironical subject ultimately puts into question the very subject/object, present/past, narrator/protagonist distinctions that make consciousness and autobiography possible, but it can do so only by repeating and developing critiques of these polarities that already exist in the *Recherche*. For in the first pages of novel, Proust's narrator redefines the notion of a fixed object of consciousness as a possible confusion of object and subject: "Peut-être l'immobilité des choses autour de nous leur est-elle imposée par notre certitude que ce sont elles et non pas d'autres, par l'immobilité de notre pensée en face d'elles" (*R*, 1: 6). We can never be certain whether we are representing an immobile real object or the projection of an immobile subject's mind: "Le témoignage des sens est... une opération de l'esprit où la conviction crée l'évidence" (*R*, 3: 190).[33] The subject of consciousness may only be the "produit d'un labeur industrieux" (*R*, 3: 162).

Beckett's parody of Proust's remembering narrator thus foregrounds the latter's backgrounded critique of consciousness. Beckett particularly emphasizes his narrator's, like Proust's narrator's, forgetting. Even when Proust's waking narrator forgets where, when, and who he is, he still has "le sentiment de l'existence comme il peut frémir au fond d'un animal" (*R*, 1: 5), the sense of being an existing subject. The narrator can feel that he is, even if he cannot say when, where, or who he is. Molloy not only forgets where, when, and who he is, he forgets to be: "Oui, il m'arrivait d'oublier non seulement qui j'étais, mais que j'étais, d'oublier d'être."[34] Molloy's forgetting comically redefines being – to which the "I" theoretically refers – as something that one must remember to do, as a retrospective product of human action. Being is a construct of the verb "to be" and the descriptive syntax that retrospectively attributes being to the pronoun "I." The being of the subject is not a fixed and closed entity, like the closed jars of Marcel's selves on the Méséglise and Guermantes Ways. Rather, as Proust's narrator later discovers, the jar of self always communicates with its other for Molloy: "Then I was no longer that sealed jar to which I owed my being so well preserved, but a wall gave way and I filled with roots and tame stems..." (*TN*, 49).[35]

By reducing the subject to a purely linguistic subject, Molloy's irony renders narrative reversible. It discredits signs of narrative and obliterates historical difference. In Molloy's bedroom in Lousse's house, the moon, which is cut into three parts by the two bars in the bedroom window, was "moving from left to right, or the room was moving from right to left, or both together perhaps, or both were moving from left to right, but the room not so fast as the moon, or from right to left, but the moon not so fast as the room. But can one speak of right and left in such circumstances" (*TN*, 39). In this relativistic description, which is reminiscent of Beckett's descriptions of Knott's house in *Watt*, the spatial coordinates with which the narrator narrates movement – right and left – are reversible. Movement can be narrated either as the moon's movement from left to right or as the room's movement from right to left, or as both moving right at different speeds or both moving left at different speeds. The reversibility of the spatial coordinates with which we represent time erases the distinctions between mobile and immobile, time and space. It leaves only the spatial juxtaposition, within the text of erroneous temporal representations, of the subject's coming or ceasing to be. It also creates in the reader's mind a spatial and ironical juxtaposition of these representations and of the knowledge of their error. Molloy's irony of narrative prevents him from saying what, if anything, the moon, the room, or the words with which he represents them are doing.

Molloy's irony cripples language's ability to describe the relation between a conscious subject and object, one object being the act of narrating change.[36] Or, rather, irony for Beckett is language's mode of crippling its own claim to describe and narrate, to represent space or time.[37] Molloy's ironical negation of all subjects is "spoken" by language's impersonal rhetorical structures, which make possible the production of subjects of description or of narration. Language itself becomes the subject of discourse. But the crumbling of the physical body, which increasingly affects the successive narrators in Beckett's trilogy, dramatizes a crumbling of the body of language in Beckett, which is brought about by forgetting: "L'Amnésie dont souffre Molloy vise... à placer le sujet en face de ces structures verbales qui l'avaient constitué depuis toujours et qui sont en train de s'effondrer."[38] Moran initially walks well, then loses the use of a leg. Molloy starts out hobbling and ends up crawling. Malone never leaves his bed. The narrator of *The Unnamable*, who cannot situate himself in space or time, fails even to be physically born.[39] This crumbling and disappearance of the physical body of the narrators represents the crumbling of language's own body, of its distinctions between subject and object, past and present, space and time, description and narration.

Molloy's allegory of his past search to define his relation to his mother thus recounts the crumbling of the linguistic relationships that would enable him to construct this relationship. It does so, however, by recounting, over time, the allegorical deconstruction of the narrator's constructions of time and being and of language's redefining these constructions in terms of the spatial difference that separates them from their simultaneous ironical negations. After leaving his Proustian half-awake state in Lousse's house, Molloy goes to the seashore, where he spends his time sucking, over and over, sixteen stones in a row by always having four in each of his four pockets, as if he could do what he fails to do: avoid sucking the same one twice (*TN*, 70). This mechanical and meaningless repetition replaces the signs of difference – which his impressions constructed and deconstructed in Lousse's house – with an ironical revelation of the materiality of language as a relation between words that are as indistinguishable as pebbles on a beach. The seemingly magical reversibility of Molloy's Proustian impressions thus gives way to the compulsive semantic reversibility of contrary signs, which treats language's production of differences ironically, as hiding a purely formal interplay between material signs. Molloy associates this material play of signs with the sterility of anal sex, which resembles the sex he may have had, unknowingly, with Lousse: "I apologize for having to revert to this lewd orifice, 'tis my muse will have it so... [I]s it not rather the true portal of our being and the celebrated mouth no more than the kitchen-door. Nothing goes in, or so little, that is not rejected on the spot, or very nearly"

(*TN*, 80). Writing and reading become a purely ironical ritual of trying to suck difference from the fundamentally indistinguishable stones of language, an ironical insemination of meaning that is sterile.

The goal of Molloy's compulsive repetition is to live in the ironical space of a present that is absolutely indifferent to meaning, consciousness, and being: "[D]eep down it was all the same to me whether I sucked a different stone each time or always the same stone, until the end of time" (*TN*, 74). But once again Beckett's narrator fails, this time to find refuge in the verbal space of irony. Molloy leaves the seashore and goes to a forest where he meets and murders a homosexual whom he "could have loved" (*TN*, 83). He constructs the illusion of loving someone who loves his ironical, anal, indifferent self. But the murder of the homosexual destroys this self-identification with the irony of irony that negates the object and the subject. This murder throws him back into the breach between language's ironical negation of any subject that its rhetoric creates and allegory's desire to become and defer a linear narrative.

Molloy thus tries to resume his allegorical search, over time, for his mother and for an explanation of his relation to her, even though he knows that any such explanation is impossible. He tries to leave the forest by going, in what he believes to be a straight line, towards his mother's house. In other words, he attempts to construct his present as the beginning of a linear narrative of time, a movement towards a distinct future end. But he only succeeds in going in a circle. Then, he deliberately tries to go in a circle, as does irony, and ends up going in a straight line towards his mother's house (*TN*, 85). Only irony can open up the possibility of allegory at this point of his journey.

Molloy is thus confounded in his attempts to do what he says he is doing. Whenever he seeks to be ironical, a voice of language tells him to be allegorical, and vice versa. It is this subversive voice of language that first commanded him to carry out his "duty" to seek his mother and to elucidate his relation to her, but then produced his ironical negation of this search: "Ne me rappelait-il sans cesse au devoir que pour mieux m'en montrer l'absurdité? C'est possible. Heureusement qu'en somme il ne faisait qu'appuyer, pour ridiculiser par la suite si l'on veut, une disposition permanente et qui n'avait pas besoin d'apostrophe pour se savoir velléitaire."[40] But he would appear finally to say what language is doing. The impersonal voice of language seems to narrate both Proust's self-parody and Beckett's repetition of this self-parody in the deceptive form of a parody of Proust. Language's voice would produce Molloy's repeated return from apparent irony to apparent Proustian allegory.

However, Molloy's voice of language ultimately puts itself into question:

> And when I say I said, etc., all I mean is that I knew confusedly things were so, without knowing exactly what it was all about. And every time I say, I said this, or I said that, or speak of a voice saying, far away inside me, Molloy, and then a fine phrase more or less clear and simple, or find myself compelled to attribute to others intelligible words, or hear my own voice uttering to others more or less articulate sounds, I am merely complying with the convention that demands you either lie or hold your peace. For what really happened was quite different... In reality I said nothing at all, but I heard a murmur, something gone wrong with the silence, and I pricked up my ears, like an animal I imagine, which gives a start and pretends to be dead. And then sometimes there arose within me, confusedly, a kind of consciousness, which I express by saying, I said, etc., or... I quote from memory. Or which I express, without sinking to the level of oratio recta, but by means of other figures quite as deceitful, as for example, It seemed to me that, etc., or, I had the impression that, etc., for it seemed to me nothing at all, and I had no impression of any kind, but simply somewhere something changed, so that I too had to change, or the world too had to change, in order for nothing to be changed."[41] (*TN*, 88)

According to Molloy narrator, whenever he claims to repeat his past statements or to represent his past thoughts, he must do so by means of conventional, intelligible, but deceitful rhetorical figures, such as allegory and irony. However, these figures mask the reality that he in fact said and thought nothing. First-person narrative is thus a means by which language consistently questions whether its words can represent what takes place in the world, the mind, or in language's wanderings from one rhetorical figure to another: "I no longer know what I am doing, nor why, those are things I understand less and less..." (*TN*, 45).[42] Language cannot say what it is doing. It can only foreground the absence of any sound or thought that might signify what it is doing. Language simply adopts poses of the life and poses of the death of the non-linguistic subject: "I pricked up my ears, like an animal I imagine, which gives a start and pretends to be dead."

Consequently, language cannot represent what causes it to switch between allegorical and ironical discourses, as Molloy's successful act of leaving the forest seemed to suggest. As in Proust, allegory only opens up the possibility of irony, it does not cause it, and irony of irony only opens up the possibility of allegory, it does not cause it. Molloy thus attributes all change to a totally incomprehensible, contingent event: a silent, ineffable something that has gone wrong with the silence, a "murmur" in the silence, a change that causes him to change, which he vainly represents as allegory, but which immediately appears to ironically hide no change at all.

Without words or thoughts to say why he sometimes tells the allegory of his return to mother and self or why he ironically negates that return, Molloy is without a single voice that can be said to be his or language's. Molloy narrator's repeated allegory of the construction and deconstruction of self-consciousness, as well as his repeated fall from allegory into an ironical questioning of the polarities that make self-consciousness possible, thus culminates in a statement of first-person narration's error and its blind, inexplicable repetition of, and wandering between, allegory and irony.

Molloy dramatizes his first-person discourse as the interval between a forgetful ironical voice – whose successive self-negations tend towards ironical simultaneity and indifference, but forget whether they are actually being ironical – and a deceptive allegorical voice – whose successive differentiation, forgetting, and deferral in time reveal their misrepresentation of what they are doing. The necessity of irony reappears only after it becomes clear that allegory hides the impossibility of saying whether there exists a memory, self, and past to seek. The necessity of allegory reappears when it becomes evident that irony forgets the impossibility of eliminating memory, meaning, and time.

For Molloy, the voices of irony and allegory are "two fools," "one asking nothing better than to stay where he is and the other imagining that life might be slightly less horrible a little further on" (*TN*, 48).[43] Molloy's discourse appears to be both ironical and allegorical, but the foolishness of both voices suggests that it may be neither: "My life, my life, now I speak of it as of something over, now as of a joke which still goes on, and it is neither, for at the same time it is over and it goes on, and is there any tense for that" (*TN*, 36).[44]

The end of Molloy's first-person narration freezes the narrator's first-person discourse in a revelation of the narrator's allegory behind the protagonist's irony, a passage from irony to allegory that makes writing possible. After recounting his past fall into a ditch, the narrator states in his last sentence: "Molloy could stay where he happened to be," as if his search for his mother had lost all meaning for him (*TN*, 91). Molloy narrator seems to say that, in the past, he had achieved in the ditch an indifferent ironical stance towards his desire to find mother and self. But whose conviction is this? His past conviction? His present conviction? Both? Whereas the ironical protagonist may have thought that he could stay where he was – in apparent indifference to his search for mother and self – Molloy narrator opens up an explicable temporal gap between the protagonist's past and his present of writing. He also refers to the protagonist in the third, rather than the first, person, as if they were not the same people: "Molloy could stay where he happened to be" (*TN*, 91). The narrator thus recalls that, according to the scene of narration, he did not stay in the ditch. He arrived at his mother's house and began to write. This reminder ironically undercuts the protagonist's ironical stance and announces an unrepresentable passage to the allegory of his coming to write.

    The final unrepresentable passage from irony to allegory in *Molloy* puts into question the appearance that Beckett is simply repeating Proust's parody of parody in the Montjouvain passage. It reopens the unanswerable question of whether Beckett, like Proust, must situate his act of writing in the passage from irony's spiral of negations, which renders historical difference impossible, to allegory's necessary search and deferral of the expression of historical difference.

CHAPTER 6

Moran's Way: The forgetful spiral of irony

Molloy's seemingly allegorical narrator, who initially pretends to seek out mother and self, tries to take refuge from allegory in transhistorical irony of irony, and parody of parody, which he already found in Proust. However, this very attempt to be fully ironical produces a repetition of allegory. Molloy narrator thus traces a failed attempt to transform the allegory of his past search for, and deconstruction of, self into a pure present of irony. In the second half of *Molloy*, Moran narrator, who imagines himself to be purely ironical, recounts the failed process of transforming his past and present ironical selves into an allegorical narration like the one that Molloy initially appears to adopt.

Moran narrator has no interest in Proust's remembering narrator. Rather, like Proust's writing narrator, he tries to adopt a purely ironical stance towards allegory. Like Proust and his writing narrator, Moran is an insomniac who writes during the night: "It is midnight. The rain is beating on the windows... I can't sleep. My lamp... will last till morning... My report will be long... I remember the day I received the order to see about Molloy..." (*TN*, 92). Moran narrator's reference to his present writing of a report on his past investigation of Molloy creates the impression that he, unlike Molloy, can voluntarily remember the past. But he soon demystifies this impression of memory by underlining his ignorance: "What I assert, deny, question, in the present, I still can. But mostly I shall use the various tenses of the past. For mostly I do not know, it is perhaps no longer so, it is too soon to know, I simply do not know, perhaps shall never know" (*TN*, 105). Moran narrator cannot really know, any more than Molloy narrator can, whether his words represent or misrepresent the past he narrates, although he nonetheless writes in an assertive manner that hides rather than reveals his lack of control. He can only assert that his present assertions about his past are acts of lying, not because they misrepresent his past (which he cannot know), but because they mask his present ignorance about the past with seemingly accurate representations.

Moran narrator's awareness of his ignorance and deceptiveness in speaking about his past repeats the position of the ironical writing narrator that Proust's narrator discloses at the end of *Combray*. Unlike Proust's remembering narrator – who believes at the beginning of *Combray* that he has succeeded in remembering where, when, and who he is, and who discovers at the end of *Combray* his error – Proust's ironical writing narrator knows from the beginning that "his" awakened consciousness of world and self is a mental construction and misrepresentation. He thus retrospectively represents himself as deliberately creating the false impression, over almost 200 pages, that he was accurately representing his present and past. At the end of *Combray*, he discovers nothing. He only reveals his act of deception, his sleight of hand. This revelation of his lie about the past invites a rereading of *Combray* as the writing narrator's ironical assertion and indirect negation of his apparent certainty that he is remembering the past the way it really was and as his revelation of his creative power.

Moran narrator, by contrast, warns us, from the beginning of his report of his past investigation of Molloy, that his narrative misleads us whenever he acts as if he is certain about representing his past accurately.[1] He reveals that he is using past tenses deceitfully and displaces the readers' attention away from the past he is ironically constructing and towards the present of constructing this past, about which he writes in present tenses. The only speech acts that he can successfully perform, he asserts, are the speech acts of assertion, denial, and questioning. He can objectively represent only his present of writing, his ironical creation of a past that may or may not relate to a real past.[2] He can thus assert in the present that his act of narrating his past is ironical: it asserts that the past was such and such; it denies the truth (not the act) of this assertion, and it raises the question of what really happened. Moran's emphasis on his ability to identify and perform at least three speech acts in and about the ironical present of his writing makes him appear to be an earlier version of Molloy, who has not yet achieved Molloy's belief that he is totally "dispossessed" of any certainty about what he is doing. But Moran is not necessarily an earlier version of Molloy. He deals with an aspect of language that Molloy does not explore: speech acts.

Moran's story about his past and about the relationship between his past actions and his present of writing – his assertion that the protagonist represented in his report became the present narrator who is writing this report – must thus be taken with a large grain of salt. His report seems to narrate the story of how Moran protagonist, who reported himself to be an ironical and powerful performer of perlocutionary speech acts of manipulation, became the present narrator, who can do no more than assert, deny, and question. But, by the narrator's own admission, this gap between the "past" character, who thought he could act on others and remember his acts, and the present narrator, who believes he can only assert, deny, and question in the present tense, is unbridgeable. Moran protagonist saw himself as a deceitful performer of perlocutionary speech acts who used words not only to manipulate others, but also to represent these past speech acts to his employer in his report. He based the felicity of his speech actions on their effects – the manipulation of others and the communication of past events – whereas Moran narrator bases the felicity of his speech acts on their verbal performance only.

A deceitful and paranoid manipulator, Moran protagonist resembles the Marcel who lies to Albertine in order to imprison her in his parents' apartment, and who lies to himself by transforming her in his mind into a deceitful manipulator of him. Unlike Marcel, however, Moran protagonist does not believe that his speech acts of lying may constitute acts of artistic differentiation. In his mind, his words are pragmatic instruments of work only, of persuading others to give him the information he wants, in the same way that words function as persuasion for Marcel's diplomat father or for the brilliant ambassador Norpois.

But work for Moran protagonist is a middle-class "job," a habit and technique, whose actions alone define the self: "[T]o see yourself doing the same thing endlessly over and over again fills you with satisfaction" (*TN*, 133). But Moran believes that he is someone who does his everyday work better than everyone else, which he paradoxically appreciates most when he is not working and is watching others work badly: "Seeing something done which I could have done better myself, if I had wished, and which I did do better whenever I put my mind to it, I had the impression of discharging a function to which no form of activity could have exalted me. But this was a joy in which, during the week, I could seldom indulge" (*TN*, 93). Moran's work is to "see about" people like Molloy who, according to Moran, take on value only as objects of his work, as confirmations of the superiority of his work: "I am paid to seek. I arrive, [the prey] comes away. His life has been nothing but a waiting for this, to see himself preferred, to fancy himself damned, blessed, to fancy himself everyman, above all others" (*TN*, 110–11). When Moran finds his prey, like the Old Testament God, he "pass[es] judgement" on him. He "deliver[s]" him from "the outer turmoil's veil," from the world's chaotic veil that hides the real social order (we could also read these words as signifying the veil that hides reality's chaos). Moran's work and judgments, he imagines, transform the disorder produced by those who think themselves "a being apart" within society as a whole into the order of society's habits and conventions. This social act gives these deluded individuals their proper place within society's order. They become members of what he calls "man." Moran thus believes himself to be a uniquely perspicacious and powerful defender of the social order against its deluded, individualist, and not-fully human sources of chaos.

Moran protagonist's superiority resides in his ability as an "agent" to say whatever he needs to say, whether it be true or false, in order to discover and judge the chaotic individualist he has been ordered to find. Like the narrator's ironical non-perlocutionary statements about his past, the protagonist's perlocutionary speech acts in carrying out an investigation are representational lies. They lie about the fact that the representation does not matter. But, in the protagonist's case, speech acts mask a performative act of manipulation, the use of a purely apparent constative speech act to deceive and guide "that docile herd." Moran protagonist thus places himself, like Proust's writing narrator, in the tradition of Nietzsche, if from a much less radical point of view (*TN*, 129). Even his body is a representational lie, whose skills he wishes to pass on to his son: "I wanted [my son] to walk like his father, with little rapid steps, his head up, his breathing even and economical, his arms swinging, looking neither to left nor right, apparently oblivious to everything and in reality missing nothing" (*TN*, 128). Similarly, Moran's house is just a "contrivance" (*TN*, 114). The protagonist's words, appearance, behavior, and place work only to the extent that they hide their true function, which is to deceive others in order to seek out and judge chaos and reproduce social order.

Moran protagonist believes that he not only can perform, he can represent his past perlocutionary acts of manipulation. When he reflects upon his actions during his moments of repose, reports them to his boss Youdi, or teaches them to his son, he treats his words as acts of representation rather than acts of manipulation. Like those who reduce language to speech acts, he paradoxically imagines that his words can represent his speech acts, even though these are indifferent to representation. He may teach his son to lie to others, he also teaches him not to lie to him, just as Moran must not lie to his boss: "It was imperative my son should not imagine he was capable of lying to me with impunity" (*TN*, 95).[3] If, by telling the truth about his lies, Moran is trying to manipulate his son into becoming like him, he definitely does not want his son to manipulate and lie to him, at least not yet.

By reporting truthfully to his boss his deceitful speech acts and by giving lessons in deceitful manipulation to his apprentice son, Moran protagonist treats both readers of his words as ironical accomplices in his lies and in the manipulations they perform. Indeed, he acts as if he and his readers were all members of a secret Masonic-like society of middle-class male secret agents who "knew [their] business" and carried it out conscientiously, with great self-satisfaction: "We thought of ourselves as members of a vast organization" (*TN*, 94, 107). Moran's fantasy of a society of elite investigators, who eliminate dangerous and mysterious sources of disorder like Molloy, constructs a model of history in which the secret knowledge of deceptive speech action is handed down from father to son. Moran receives the instructions describing his future actions from Youdi, a father figure. He then passes on similar instructions to his son, also named Moran, who passes them on to his teddy bear, named Moran. This paternal, historical process has its origin in a distant and sacred past, which the narrator treats ironically: "For what I was doing I was doing neither for Molloy, who mattered nothing to me, nor for myself, of whom I despaired, but on behalf of a cause which, while having need of us to be accomplished, was in its essence anonymous, and would subsist, haunting the minds of men, when its miserable artisans should be no more. It will not be said, I think, that I did not take my work to heart" (*TN*, 114–15).

Moran protagonist's megalomaniacal self has less in common with Proust's manipulative characters than with Balzac's powerful few, like Vautrin, who create fictional selves in order to protect the social order in France, but who represent themselves truthfully to their symbolic sons. Vautrin tries to teach Rastignac, his chosen son, to carry on his powerful practice of lies and aliases. He will have succeeded, he believes, on the day when Rastignac will deceive and manipulate him, when he will replace him as a son does a father.[4] Similarly, Moran imagines with pride that his son, who is still "a little on the young side,... a little on the soft side, for the great deeds of vengeance," will one day be capable of slitting his father's throat (*TN*, 131). But, from the point of view of Moran narrator, the protagonist's middle-class pretensions puncture his illusions of being a Balzacian Vautrin. Moran protagonist thus harkens back to Balzac's short story, "L'Illustre Gaudissart," in which a pretentious, Parisian traveling salesman, who believes that he can sell anything to anyone by saying whatever he needs to say, is himself duped into buying non-existent wine by a "naive" provincial.

But the powerful actor that Moran protagonist imagines himself to be, unlike Gaudissart, already "despairs" of himself, since his self-representations as a powerful ironist are themselves becoming ironical. He becomes less and less sure that his descriptions of his future speech acts describe the act he or his son will need to perform in order to find and judge Molloy: "Thus to my son I gave precise instructions. But were they the right ones?" (*TN*, 103). This doubt about whether he is describing the right speech act reflects the narrator's ironical negation of his ironical manipulation, which deflates the protagonist's self-image as a powerful Balzacian Vautrin who manipulates the Nietzschian "herd." The narrator's irony of irony presents the protagonist as an over-selfsatisfied, pretentious and paranoid middle-class father, but the latter is already seeing evidence of his error and weakness.

Moran's increasing doubts about his power to manipulate others are already present when he receives his instructions from Youdi to leave home and go out into the "world in which all are plunged" in order to find and judge Molloy. He is not at all sure that Youdi's messenger did not forget his boss's actual instructions. He may even have imagined Gaber's arrival with the instructions (*TN*, 110). He may have received the wrong instructions or only imagined that he received instructions, just as he may be giving his son the wrong instructions. As a result, he begins to question whether he can actually carry out the instructions that his mind gives to his speech and physical acts. He does not seem to be able to do what he tells himself he is doing or should do.

This ironical gap between the protagonist's words and actions gets worse when he leaves his house and finds himself, like Molloy, abandoned to "the spray of phenomena," where his "eyes search in vain for two things alike." The contingency of phenomena puts into question the very possibility of his perceiving two of his acts as the same. It undercuts any learned rule or instructions that might define action within the social order, or give Moran a place within this order according to his speech acts. Moran tries to resist this dispersion of his consciousness of his actions: "It is at the mercy of these sensations, which happily I know to be illusory, that I have to live and work." But his self-assured acting self is "drown[ed] in the spray of phenomena." The contingency of perception forces Moran to look outside his conventional acts, which are supposedly indifferent to meaning, for a self that is other than the acting self that society tells him he ought to be. Only in this spray do "I find myself a meaning" (*TN*, 111).

By giving himself over to phenomenal differences and to a search for a self within difference, Moran redefines his self-representation as an ironical and powerful actor within an allegory of a search to say what he is doing and do what he is saying. This allegory deconstructs and defers any possibility of his performing the actions he wants to perform, of being the person society wants him to be, indeed of knowing what society wants him to be. Rather than calculating rationally what he needs to take on his trip in order to find Molloy, Moran retreats to his bed in the dark, where his imagination, rather than his reason, holds sway. He constructs a world of "finality without end," where "no investigation would be possible."[5] In this world, where endings fail to end and where words and deeds flee each other, difference becomes impossible: "Molloy could not be, nor Moran either for that matter." And yet "Moran could bend over Molloy." "[T]he falsity of the terms [the names 'Moran' and 'Molloy'] does not necessarily imply that of the relation, so far as I know" (*TN*, 111). But the very search to trap and eliminate the chaotic object of his desire, Molloy, the search to be a powerful person who always satisfies his desires, breaks down this order of desire. It creates a new relation between Moran and Molloy, in which they share, as in Hegel, the similar inability to do what they say they want to do or to say what they are doing. Rather than chaos being a veil of the social order, the social order is a veil of chaos.

Moran's narrative of his search to find and judge his seeming contrary, Molloy, only seems to identify him with Molloy. The act of dominating his contrary appears to transform him into that contrary. Moran says of the Molloy he imagines: "Now, a prisoner, he hurled himself at I know not what narrow confines, and now, hunted, he sought refuge near the centre" (*TN*, 113). Moran's Molloy alternates between a violent flight from a socially defined center into a world of diverse, uncontrollable perceptions, and a return towards this center. The life of Moran's Molloy is thus organized by the linear and circular movements that we found in Molloy's discourse on himself and that figured the interplay between allegory and irony. But Moran's Molloy, unlike Molloy's Molloy, is obsessed with control. He alternates between the poles defined by Moran's desire: to regain control over his life and reestablish the social order and a socially defined self, his "center"; and to lose control, to flee his center to the periphery of his scattered perceptions and desires. Immediately after imagining his Molloy, therefore, Moray seems to become the Molloy he has created: "Then I was nothing but uproar, bulk, rage, suffocation, effort unceasing, frenzied and vain. Just the opposite of myself in fact. It was a change. And when I saw him disappear, his whole body a vociferation, I was almost sorry" (*TN*, 113); "Was I secretly glad that this had happened to me, perhaps even to the point of not wanting to get well?" (*TN*, 145). In his Molloy, Moran discovers a projection of his own alternation between an attempt to construct and an attempt to destroy a powerful, socially defined self whose words coincide with his deeds.

Moran can recreate an illusion of self-control only by repressing his desire to be like his imaginary Molloy. He must "rein back his thoughts within the limits of the calculable, so great is his horror of fancy." He must "patiently" turn his life away from imaginary representations of the outer world and "towards the outer world" of calculated action "as towards the lesser evil" (*TN*, 114). But his success is only short term.

The protagonist's attempts at ironical deception and manipulation of others thus project onto them not only his own attempts at self-deception and self-manipulation, but a split between manipulator and manipulated. They announce his efforts to abandon ironical speech acts in favor of a Molloy-like allegory of wandering:

It was then the unheard of sight was to be seen of Moran making ready to go without knowing where he was going, having consulted neither map nor timetable, considered neither itinerary nor halts, heedless of the weather outlook, with only the vaguest notion of the outfit he would need, the time the expedition was likely to take, the money he would require and even the very nature of the work to be done and consequently the means to be employed. And yet there I was whistling away... (*TN*, 124)

As stated earlier, the protagonist's search to abandon irony is announced by the narrator's ironical negation of his past ironical manipulation of others. Immediately after the narrator recounts the protagonist's belief that he knew what he was doing and thus who he was, the narrator renders this belief ironical by disclosing the protagonist's inability to coincide with his self-representation: "How little one is at one with oneself, good God. I who prided myself on being a sensible man, cold as crystal and as free from spurious depth" (*TN*, 113). Whereas the protagonist asserted his unified, coldly calculating nature as a subject of the speech act of ironical manipulation, the narrator ironically negates the protagonist's certainty of what he was doing. He asserts the split nature of any subject of speech acts. The very act of representing oneself as a powerful ironical manipulator is the ironical product of self-manipulation.

The narrator's irony of irony discloses the protagonist's failure to describe his speech acts unambiguously. Theoretically, the protagonist's actions are dictated by his boss Youdi's instructions and the social order they represent. The felicity of Moran's speech acts depends upon the success of Youdi's instructions as descriptions of Moran's speech acts. Moran initially "believe[d] he understood everything about them" (*TN*, 106). But, according to Youdi's messenger, Youdi "doesn't know what he says,... Nor what he does" (*TN*, 94–95). Youdi has no idea what his instructions say to Moran, let alone what they make Moran do. The supposed source and description of Moran's rationally calculated acts and speech acts – his boss Youdi's instructions and the social order – are as split as Molloy's actions. The protagonist intuits this loss of a social ground for his words and actions when he asks about Gaber's instructions: "But were they the right ones?" (*TN*, 103). All descriptions of speech actions are always already structured by an ironical negation of their power to say what these speech acts are doing. The "familiar" "labyrinth" of Moran's mind thus becomes the unfamiliar labyrinth of Molloy's "[u]nfathomable mind" (*TN*, 106). But this unfathomable gap between what words say and do has inhabited his speech acts from the beginning. Moran protagonist begins to fall into a "great confusion" (*TN*, 98).

This fall into confusion takes the form of a transition from lying to forgetting: "The directions which Gaber must certainly have given me with reference to this had gone clean out of my head" (*TN*, 137). Moran's forgetting repeats Gaber's, the first reader of Youdi's instructions. Like a message that burns up the minute the spy has read it, Gaber forgets the instructions he carries the minute his eyes leave the written words. He cannot even remember the meanings of the words he reads. Gaber's forgetting of Youdi's unfathomable descriptions of Moran's future actions represents language's erasure of any original intention, such as that of a social order, motivating not only what language says, but also what its words do. Moran plays out language's forgetting of what it is doing in giving instructions to his son: "What did I tell you exactly? I said. We racked our brains together" (*TN*, 142). Writer, messenger, and reader are repetitions of the same ironical nature of descriptions of speech actions, which renders these descriptions unreadable and the actions unknowable: "The awful thing in affairs of this kind is that when you have the will you do not have the way, and vice versa" (*TN*, 131).[6] Beckett dramatizes Moran's discovery of language's erasure of its descriptions of what it does in the form of Moran's loss of control over his actions. He increasingly becomes physically disabled and wanders blindly, thus coming to resemble Molloy (*TN*, 138).

The protagonist's descriptions of Molloy's wandering mirror the wandering of his descriptions of his own actions, but also the narrator's descriptions of his three speech acts. The narrator has said that he can at least perform the speech acts of asserting, denying, and questioning. But he fails to distinguish between asserting, denying, and questioning. When he recounts his departure from his house in order to investigate Molloy: "I looked round for the last time, saw that I had neglected certain precautions, rectified this, took up my haversack, I nearly wrote my bagpipes, my boater, my umbrella, I hope I'm not forgetting anything, switched off the light, went out into the passage and locked my door. That at least is clear" (*TN*, 126). The narrator's Freudian slip, which replaces the word "haversack" with the word "bagpipes," and his ambiguous syntax – did he nearly write "my bagpipes, my boater, my umbrella" in the place of "haversack," or just "bagpipes" – make it unclear whether he is asserting that he was preparing to work, ironically denying that he was preparing to work, or posing the question of what he was preparing to do.

The narrator indirectly attributes his impotence to perform the speech acts he initially said he could perform to Freud's "fatal pleasure principle." He interprets the pleasure principle as motivating him to say the first word that comes to his mind, rather than putting off this pleasure in order to seek out the word that will do the work he intends to do (*TN*, 99). As the protagonist gives in to pleasurable thoughts, words, and actions, as he forgets to do his social "duty," he regresses from the certainty that he is conscious of what he is doing to Proustian impressions of his actions. Like Molloy's half-awake impressions in Lousse's house, Moran begins to react to the unfamiliar and increasingly pleasurable spray of phenomena by reversing the way he is supposed to narrate events: "The sky was that horrible colour which heralds dawn. Things steal back into position for the day, take their stand, sham dead" (*TN*, 139). Moran's description of a typical, horrible sunrise alludes to Proust's narrator's revelation, at the end of *Combray*, of how the sunrise put into question his deceived consciousness, throughout the night, of where, when, and who he was. It transforms all consciousness into an habitual representation of the world:

Mais à peine le jour – et non plus le reflet d'une dernière braise sur une tringle de cuivre que j'avais pris pour lui – traçait-il dans l'obscurité, et comme à la craie, sa première raie blanche et rectificative, que la fenêtre avec ses rideaux quittait le cadre de la porte où je l'avais située par erreur, tandis que, pour lui faire place, le bureau que ma mémoire avait maladroitement installé là se sauvait à toute vitesse, poussant devant lui la cheminée et écartant le mur mitoyen du couloir; une courette régnait à l'endroit où, il y a un instant encore, s'étendait le cabinet de toilette, et la demeure que j'avais rebâtie dans les ténèbres était allée rejoindre les demeures entrevues dans le tourbillon du réveil, mise en fuite par ce pâle signe qu'avait tracé au-dessus des rideaux le doigt levé du jour. (*R*, 187)

Moran narrator's pastiche of Proust's narrator retains the latter's representation of returning to an habitual consciousness of the world, but in a lapidary form: "Things steal back into position for the day, take their stand, sham dead." Moran's sentence suggests that his consciousness before the sunrise was true and his perception of reality after the sunrise was false. The acts that we would habitually call a fictional personification of real, inanimate things – they "steal back into position," "take their stand," and "sham dead" – become reality, whereas the habitual perception of these things as inanimate becomes the deceptive taking of a socially prescribed position. As in some of Elstir's paintings, the very distinction between illusion and reality, action and repose, humanness and materiality, breaks down.

Proust's narrator dramatizes a similar stealing back into position of things: "la fenêtre avec ses rideaux quittait le cadre de la porte où je l'avais située par erreur, tandis que, pour lui faire place, le bureau que ma mémoire avait maladroitement installé là se sauvait à toute vitesse." But Proust's narrator marks the house built by memory and imagination as an error. He thus creates the illusion that the house built by his perceptions is real. As he demystifies one mode of objective consciousness, he creates the fiction of another mode of objective consciousness. Proust's "rectifying" sunrise invites readers to fall back into what he calls the "realist lie" of a clear distinction between subject and object. It also puts off reminding readers that his perceptual house is also always in error. By contrast, Moran narrator does not let readers fall back into the error of distinguishing between a distinct subjective subject and a distinct, objectively perceived object. He treats the latter ironically, as a sham, a deception that hides the reality of the former, but he treats this subjective reading ironically as well. Irony of irony, as in Hegel's dialectic of Master and Slave, negates the assertion that all is objective by affirming the role of the subjective in representation. Then it negates the assertion that all is subjective as well.[7]

In telling the story of his past, Moran indirectly recounts an allegory of the discovery that one is always "dispossessed" of one's verbal property. Moran's search for Molloy leads him to adopt the latter's awareness that he does not own his words, that they cannot be reduced to the familiar meanings society attaches to words and that enable him to represent "his" acts and "his" acting self: "[T]he whole of my little property [is] to blame" (*TN*, 123).[8] What is to blame is society's illusion of property, which has led him to believe that he owned his words and deeds, that they were "his." The denial that words have a proper meaning negates the entire paternal, symbolic order that gives the actor and his acts a single meaning that positions them within a fixed social order, a meaning that the father can pass down to his son as his mind passes it down to his actions. Beckett represents this disabling of Moran's belief that he can own his words and actions as his coming to resemble his Molloy-like son. Moran thus reverses the symbolic, historical relation between father and son: "[W]ith me [my son] invariably took the wrong turn, a crossing or a simple corner was all he needed to stray from the right road, it of my election... It was as though he let himself be sucked in out of sight by every opening that offered" (*TN*, 128); "And you, are you capable of leading me?" (*TN*, 130). The son's actions and words remind the protagonist that his assertions of what he is doing, his instructions to himself and to his son, are always misleading. The son thus indirectly teaches not only his father, but also the narrator. The latter learns from his children, his characters, that he cannot perform the speech acts of assertion, denial, and questioning he claims to perform. To that extent he models his actions on his son's, becomes the son of his son, rendering historical causality reversible. As a writer who is overtly constructing his past artificially, the narrator becomes a character in the drama of his own character, he becomes written by his character.

The increased wandering of Moran protagonist's descriptions of his actions foregrounds his desire to kill off the unified and megalomaniacal subject of action and speech action that he has pretended to be. He plays out this murder in a passage recounting his murder of an arrogant stranger who is chasing a Molloy-like character and who physically resembles the Moran protagonist we find at the beginning of the narrative. Like the latter, the stranger confidently acts as if he can consciously control his speech acts and the effects they produce on others. He asks Moran whether he has seen someone who resembles Molloy and expects his question to produce an answer, as if it were an imperative: "It was his turn to laugh. You refuse to answer? he said." He mocks Moran's impotence to speak and act, just as Moran mocked his son: "Have you a tongue in your head? he said." Moran reacts to the stranger's pretensions by ironically negating them and, indirectly, his old identity: "I don't know you, I said. I laughed. I had not intended to be witty" (*TN*, 151). Moran then murders his double, thus acting out physically the narrator's ironical negation of his pretensions of power. This negation of his past identity as speech actor is figured by his body, which he originally interpreted as a powerful sign of his powerful self. His body is now becoming an unreadable sign of self: "Physically speaking it seemed to me I was now becoming rapidly unrecognizable... [T]he face my hands felt was not my face any more, and the hands my face felt were my hands no longer" (*TN*, 170).[9]

Moran protagonist's symbolic murder of his past self by means of ironical negation indirectly kills off the narrator's power to assert that he is performing the act of narrating a linear sequence of actions. The narrator dramatizes his murder of his past narrating self by turning towards Molloy's favorite discourse: description. Rather than recount the sequence of events

Moran's Way

that led up to the murder, Moran defers his narrative by describing the stranger's appearance in realistic detail (much of which I will elide):

> Can you tell me, he said. I shall have to describe him briefly, though such a thing is contrary to my principles. He was on the small side, but thick-set. He wore a thick navy-blue suit (double-breasted)... Do you happen to know, he said. The fringed extremities of a dark muffler... Do you hear Me? he said. But all this was nothing compared to the face which I regret to say vaguely resembled my own, less the refinement of course, same little abortive moustache, same little ferrety eyes, same paraphimosis of the nose, and a thin red mouth that looked as if it was raw from trying to shit its tongue. Hey you! he said. I turned back to the fire. It was doing nicely... To cut a long story short he wanted to know if I had seen an old man with a stick pass by. He described him. Badly. (*TN*, 150–51)

The old Moran, like the stranger, did not describe well, for descriptions were only valid as speech acts of deception and manipulation, inserted within the story of his heroic victory over chaos. By contrast, the new Moran, who knows the impossibility of representing narratable actions, begins to describe well, as can the narrator and Molloy. His detailed descriptions, like Proust's long descriptions, do not constitute a return to the naive notion of unmediated representation.[10] Rather, they serve to create artificially an "effet de réel" whose purpose, as in Proust, is to construct an ironic "contrepoids" to narrative illusion. The narrator's excessively long description of the stranger's appearance is in fact a parody of his own self-descriptions. Its details function to undercut the stranger's and the narrator's illusions that they can describe and narrate their own actions and the actions of others. When Moran narrator finally finishes his description and tries to narrate his murder of the stranger, he thus fails to narrate: "I cannot indicate more clearly how this result [the murder] was obtained, it would have been something worth reading" (*TN*, 151).

Moran narrator's denial of his power to represent himself as a speech acting narrator leads him deliberately to forget Youdi's instructions, which he had mistakenly associated with a narrative commanding his future actions. He replaces Youdi's external instructions with an inexplicable inner, "ambiguous voice" that is "not always easy to follow" (*TN*, 132).[11] This voice tells him to transform his initial report of the glorious paternal cause he thought he was pursuing in Youdi's name into a parody of the paternal pretension to represent one's acts and do what one represents. But the voice commands him as well to continue trying to narrate a different cause:

> [I]f I submit to this paltry scrivening which is not of my province, it is for reasons very different from those that might be supposed. I am still obeying orders, if you like... [T]he voice I listen to needs no Gaber to make it heard. For it is within me

and exhorts me to continue to the end the faithful servant I have always been, of a cause that is not mine, and patiently fulfill in all its bitterness my calamitous part, as it was my will, when I had a will, that others should. And this with hatred in my heart, and scorn, of my master and his designs... It also tells me, this voice I am only just beginning to know, that the memory of this work brought scrupulously to a close will help me to endure the long anguish of vagrancy and freedom. (*TN*, 131–32)

Moran narrator finds himself commanded by an inner master to remain "the faithful servant" of a cause, but a cause that he hates and disowns. He is also commanded to ironically negate any narration of his actions on behalf of this cause: "I was getting to know [the voice telling me things] better now,... I understood it, all wrong perhaps" (*TN*, 176).[12] This confused inner voice thus commands him to continue narrating what he is doing and defining himself as a doer, even as it ironically denies any possibility of such assertions and raises the question of whether he can assert or deny anything at all. The narrator must tell his story to the end, even as he recognizes the impossibility of arriving at this end: "All was about to end, or to begin again, it little mattered which, and it little mattered how, I had only to wait" (*TN*, 161).[13] Moran narrator thus locates his words in a gap between the necessity and the ironically affirmed impossibility of narrative. This gap gives him a little freedom, the narrator suggests.

The protagonist's forgetting of the instructions of his external master, which he believed to be readable, and his adoption of the explicitly unreadable instructions of his internal master, begins the process by which irony gives birth to the allegory of the wandering of his words. The failed narrative of Moran's search for Molloy seems to culminate in Molloy's ironical description of history as an act of "change, in order for nothing to be changed" (*TN*, 88). But it also harkens back to Molloy's allegory of history as a linear deconstruction, a passive wilting "down towards an end it seems can never come" in the "indestructible chaos of timeless things" (*TN*, 40). Moran's discourse thus redefines first-person discourse as both a Proustian deconstruction of self that ends in irony and as the beginning of a Proustian search to become an original, unnamable self: "And what I saw was more like a crumbling, a frenzied collapsing of all that had always protected me from all I was always condemned to be. Or it was like a kind of clawing towards a light and countenance I could not name, that I had once known and long denied" (*TN*, 148).

There results, not a subordination of irony to allegory, but an interplay between the two in the void that now defines Moran's self: "I dragged myself down to the stream. I lay down and looked at my reflection, then I washed my face and hands. I waited for my image to come back, I watched it as it trembled towards an ever increasing likeness. Now and then a drop, falling from my face, shattered it again. I did not see a soul all day" (*TN*, 145). Moran associates the old unreachable "likeness," towards which his self-representations tremble in the stream's changing mirror, with the face of a Molloy-like passerby: "His face was pale and noble. I could have done with it" (*TN*, 146).[14] The passerby acts proud of his humiliating dispossession of self and of his need to beg, as if they constituted a superior identity: "He accompanied this humiliating request [for bread] with a fiery look." But any consciousness of identity that Moran tries to construct out of the stranger's proud humiliation is ironically shattered, like his image in the water, by the unreadability of all signs of self: "I did not see a soul all day" (*TN*, 146).

Moran's own proud tone, even in talking about his humiliation, raises the question of whether he is an earlier Molloy, as some critics have suggested.[15] The Molloy Moran describes above and imagined earlier is more proud and aggressive than the Molloy we found in the first half of *Molloy*. In the first half of *Molloy*, Molloy protagonist tried to negate the allegory of his Proustian search for mother and self and to take refuge, through irony of irony, in indifference and passivity. But the narrative structure implied that the narrator had indeed gone to his mother's house. Activity, or rather trying to act, is always forced on Molloy, as if his will played no role. By contrast, Moran's turn from irony to allegory takes on a seemingly intentional form, as he decides at the end of his story to sell "all there was to sell" and to begin to learn the language of the wild birds and of his inner voice: "I have been a man long enough, I shall not put up with it any more, I shall not try any more" (*TN*, 175). Moran's turn towards allegory appears to be less a passively imposed wandering than an active choice, even though the narrative makes it clear that it is precisely will that Moran is abandoning. The Moran we find at the end of Moran's narrative is thus not identical to the Molloy we find at the beginning of Molloy's narrative. This seemingly stylistic incompatibility marks the impossibility of any narrative that links one to the other in time or that establishes one as more authentic than the other.

Moran's turn towards allegory, like Molloy's, situates him, if differently, in the spatio-temporal void between ironical and allegorical voices. The last words that the narrator writes before leaving his house appear to recount the act by which he began to write the report that is now coming to an end. But they render this beginning, and with it the very act of narration, ironical: "Then I went back into the house and wrote. It is midnight. The rain is beating on the windows. It was not midnight. It was not raining" (*TN*, 176). The narrator's last two sentences, which negate the content of the first sentences of the novel, give the lie to the beginning of his report. The narrator now tells us explicitly what he suggested throughout his narrative: that any assertion he makes is always accompanied by its ironical denial, and that the assertion of this denial is itself subject to denial, *ad infinitum*. This spiral of irony breaks down any distinction between assertion and denial, beginning and end.

But this spiral of irony coincides with the narrative of Moran's departure, his becoming but never being Molloy. For irony of irony, as we have seen, relegates the act of narration to the liar's paradox and produces a turn towards allegory.[16] The liar's paradox – which is produced by the identification of language with the acts of denial or questioning – prevents the reader from saying whether a lie is taking place at all. The assertion "I lie" implies that I am lying about saying that I lie. It states both that I perform the act of lying and that I am not performing the act of lying. Since irony depends upon the power to deliberately misrepresent, to lie, the narrator's failure to say that he is lying means that he cannot say that his words are ironical. As in Proust's passage on his lying about Albertine's lies, language's irony of irony negates its power to say that it is ironical. Irony, which defines the house of Moran's writing, like his beehive, crumbles as his words fall into irony of irony, then become temporally alienated from the spatial present of action and speech action. The present of narration must always put off becoming present: "Translating myself now in imagination to the present moment..." (*TN*, 154). The present of narration in Beckett must necessarily wander towards a present of first-person narration that it ironically knows to be impossible.

How, then, do we read the overall relation of the novel *Molloy*, which combines both Molloy's and Moran's discourses, to Proust's *Recherche*? The key, I believe, is Beckett's allusions to Proust's intertwining, throughout his novel, of allegory on the Méséglise Way and irony on the Guermantes Way. Molloy and Moran, it is well known, perform similar journeys. They leave home, kill off an old self, and end up writing the discourse we are reading.[17] But Molloy's manner of recounting his journey and the rhetoric with which he recounts it, what I will call Molloy's Way, is distinct from Moran's Way of doing so, as are their repetitions of the Méséglise and Guermantes Ways.

Molloy's Way, like Proust's Méséglise Way in *Combray*, takes the initial form of a search for self as a distinct relation to mother. In both, this search becomes an allegory of the deconstruction of signs for mother and self. Proust's allegory deconstructs signs of self in art and love, whereas Molloy's search falls into parody of Proust's and his own allegory by focusing on purely sexual signs of self. But this parodic difference is only apparent. Molloy's fall into irony and parody occurs obsessively, even within single sentences, whereas the Méséglise Way defers the ironical reversal of Marcel's allegory to the final passage, which concerns the sado-masochistic, parodic profanation of an incestuously loved parent, in the Montjouvain episode. Both the Méséglise and Molloy's Ways end in an unsatisfiable desire for ironical indifference: humanity's and Mlle Vinteuil's cruel indifference to the pain they cause and Molloy protagonist's assertion that he can stay in the ditch. Both also suggest, however, the necessity of desire and difference, which Mlle Vinteuil must learn to accept and Molloy cannot escape. They thus both produce a temporal gap between a protagonist who is too young to discover that he cannot achieve ironical indifference to pain and a retrospective narrator for whom it is too late to open up an allegorical difference between past and present, but who cannot help doing so.

Moran's Way, by contrast, resembles Proust's Guermantes Way in *Combray*. Both Moran's Way and the Guermantes Way speak of language as the speech act of producing effects, although the Guermantes Way is about the ironical production of effects in art, high society, and nature, whereas Moran protagonist's Way is about the ironical production of effects on others within a caricatural middle-class society dominated by a Protestant work ethic. Both Ways associate the ironical production of effects with the father as model. The Guermantes Way, like the end of Proust's novel, culminates his story of the ironical production of effects with a return to the impossible search for allegorical difference, mother, and self. Marcel returns home and rediscovers his intense anxiety about going to bed, dying in sleep, and not receiving his mother's goodnight kiss, even though he knows that he can never possess her in his bedroom. Similarly, at the end of the *Recherche*, Marcel, who has reduced all art to ironical artifice based on Nietzsche, suddenly formulates his theory of involuntary memory as a means of recuperating self, even though he knows that he cannot achieve this goal. Moran's Way, as we have seen, tries and fails to posit an ironical model for the employer/employee relationship based on the father/son relationship, but it too culminates in a passage towards allegory and wandering. Whereas the Guermantes Way defers the transition to allegory until the end of the long passage, Moran's narrative increasingly weaves the transition to allegory into his seemingly ironical narrative.

Although Moran's and Molloy's first-person discourses compress, often into single sentences, the formal interplay between the two aspects of Proust's Instant, allegory and irony, they are nonetheless historical repetitions of Proust's interplay between the two aspects of the Instant. But, to the extent that they carry out this interplay differently, including Proust's introduction of an ethical discourse, Molloy and Moran cannot be reduced to mere historical repetitions of Proust's first-person narrators. Beckett's *Molloy* thus situates first-person narration in the gap between Moran's deferred allegorization of the ironical narrator he thinks he wants to be and Molloy's failed ironization of the allegorical narrator he starts out to be when he begins his journey to his mother's house.

Molloy and Moran establish somewhat different historical relationships with the paternal and maternal Proustian narratives that they repeat. Molloy's attempt to constitute himself first as a parody of Proust's remembering narrator, then as a repetition of Proust's ironical and self-parodic narrator, then as a repetition of Proust's allegorical narrator, situates his historical relation to Proust within an historical interplay between irony and allegory. He allegorically distinguishes himself from Proust by his parody, yet denies this historical distinction by marking his repetition of Proust's self-parody, yet finds himself thrown back into the allegory of a search for historical difference. By contrast, Moran narrator seems to deny all historical difference within an unchangeable passing down of the same manipulative techniques from father to son, but falls into a search for a different self, foregrounded by the historical differences between Marcel's timid character and Moran's brash one. Both of Beckett's narrators, of course, mock any notion of high art by locating their interplay between allegory and irony in the worlds of beggars and middle-class workers.

The narrators in *Molloy* simply foreground different sides of the gap between the allegorical assertion and the ironical negation of Beckett's historical difference from Proust.[18] They also appear to engender the narrators in the last two novels of the trilogy: Malone narrator, who tries to succeed in becoming ironical in ways that Moran narrator could not, on the level of the narration; and the "I" of *The Unnamable*, which tries to follow in Molloy's wandering, seemingly allegorical footsteps, but on the level of words alone.

CHAPTER 7

Malone Dies *and the impossibility of not saying I*

> Now the case is reversed, the way well charted and little hope of coming to its end
>
> (*TN*, 182)

The narrator in *Malone Dies*, like Moran narrator, initially convinces himself that he knows what his words are doing: "This time I know where I am going" (*TN*, 180). He also eventually recounts his failure to reduce words to ironical speech acts that function only to manipulate. But rather than concentrate on his past speech acts, as does Moran, Malone narrator concentrates on representing his present acts of constructing fictional stories. He tries to manipulate language in order to reduce it to a pure game. By treating narrative as a game, Malone seeks to escape a Molloy-like or Moran-like search for self, past or present. He tries to erase all reference to a self, such as the pronoun "I."[1]

The imminent death of Malone's dying body is thus a metaphor for the death of self-representation. But he believes that he can bring about the death of mental signs of self before his body dies, so that, when physical death comes, there will be nothing for it to take away from him. He will have nothing to fear or regret before he dies. In order to kill off his symbolic self before he dies, Malone tries to transform his present of narration into the production of purely fictional, third-person stories that have nothing to do with him. They will be pure narrative games.

In order to erase conscious representations of self, Malone narrator must perform the act that his intentions represent: "I shall tell myself stories, if I can" (*TN*, 180).[2] His stories will be preceded by descriptions of his "present situation." These will represent his act of producing these stories: "I ... feel a strange desire come over me, the desire to know what I am doing, and why" (*TN*, 194). He will first describe his present act of writing stories.[3] Then he will tell third-person stories that obliterate any reference to his first-person narration or his dying.

Malone, like Molloy and Moran, repeats aspects of the writing situations of Proust's narrator and of Proust himself. Like Molloy, he alludes to Proust's waking narrator, who cannot yet identify where he is, who he is, and when he is. He writes his descriptions and stories in a bed within a single room. But, unlike Proust's waking narrator, he cannot know the location of his room nor the time, as if he were floating in a decontextualized world where the only space is the room that his present mind represents and the only time the indeterminate future duration between his present act of narration and the future death of his physical power to act. He has no contact with others, not even with the charitable woman who used to feed him. When he looks out of the window and describes a couple in another bedroom, he seems to invent the reality to which these signs refer. Moreover, he has forgotten all that precedes the last two days; all autobiographical signs, except those of the most immediate past, remain uncertain.[4] Malone's only possible certainty seems to be his descriptions of the space and time of his present act of narrating and his desire to erase any temporal anticipation of his physical death.

Not only is Malone unable to wake up to a certain knowledge of his spatial and temporal location, as can Proust, he cannot wake up to sensory or thought representations of his self:

> All my senses are trained full on me, me. Dark and silent and stale, I am no prey for them. I am far from the sounds of blood and breath, immured. I shall not speak of my sufferings. Cowering deep down among them I feel nothing. It is there I die, unbeknown to my stupid flesh. That which is seen, that which cries and writes, my witless remains. Somewhere in this turmoil thought struggles on, it too wide of the mark. It too seeks me, as it always has, where I am not to be found. It too cannot be quiet. On others let it wreak its dying rage, and leave me in peace. (*TN*, 186)

Malone's senses, emotions, words, and thoughts are self-misrepresentations, which "see[k] me... where I am not to be found." His discourse thus radically negates from the beginning all Proustian autobiographical representations of place, other, and self in space, and seeks total indifference, "peace," in an erasure of time. But, whereas he can achieve indifference to the representations of his senses, he cannot escape the pain of thought, which will only cease with his brain's death. He thus attempts to create a narrating situation in which thought "wreak[s] its dying rage" only on "others." He will destroy his thought's painful, vain efforts to represent a self, to say "I," and any thought of the temporal duration between a present in which he is symbolically dead and his body's death.

Malone thus decides to blind himself from now on to the imminent death of his mind and body: "I shall soon be quite dead at last in spite of all...I shall not watch myself die" (*TN*, 179). In order to end self-representation, he will limit his words and thoughts to the narration of stories about others who have nothing to do with him. These stories will conjure away, not physical death as in Scheherazade's stories, but deceptive signs of a self about to die.[5]

In writing his third-person stories, Malone seeks to avoid all references to emotion, because these might make him think of himself. His stories "will be almost lifeless, like the teller...They will not be the same kind of stories as hitherto, that is all. They will be neither beautiful nor ugly, they will be calm, there will be no ugliness or beauty or fever in them any more..." (*TN*, 180). Emotional indifference will constitute, not his forgetting of a real self, but the inability to define himself in cognitive terms as self-knowledge or as self-ignorance: "Words and images run riot in my head, pursuing, flying, clashing, merging, endlessly. But beyond this tumult there is a great calm, and a great indifference, never really to be troubled by anything again" (*TN*, 198). By adopting the position of a symbolically dead, totally indifferent narrator of non-autobiographical, lifeless third-person stories, he will construct a safe haven from the riot of his mind's vain attempts to represent himself as having a self.

In producing "a great indifference" to his dying self, "never really to be troubled by anything again," Malone's stories will cease to appear to be "earnest" expressions of a knowledgeable or ignorant self and will become language games that he mechanically and lifelessly invents. He will treat the words and names in this game ironically, as game pieces that appear to refer to a living and representable self, but that actually refer only to the artificial rules of the narrative game that he lifelessly plays:

I never knew how to play, till now. I longed to, but I knew it was impossible. And yet I often tried...But it was not long before I found myself alone, in the dark. That is why I gave up trying to play and took to myself forever shapelessness and speechlessness, incurious wondering, darkness, long stumbling with outstretched arms, hiding. Such is the earnestness from which, for nearly a century now, I have never been able to depart. (*TN*, 180)

Malone's past, Molloy-like "incurious wondering" and stumbling in darkness, was his "earnest" expression of the vainly repeated search for self-representation. Like Molloy, the younger Malone acted out his incurious wondering about and wandering towards self as a search for knowledge, but his greatest enjoyment came from the search's failure, from his discovery of his ignorance as his only self: "What I sought, when I struggled out of my hole, then aloft through the stinging air towards an inaccessible boon, was the rapture of vertigo, the letting go, the fall, the gulf, the relapse to darkness, to nothingness, to earnestness, to home, to him waiting for me always, who needed me and whom I needed..." (*TN*, 195). It is this sadomasochistic search to represent a self – which brings the rapturous pain of failure, of ignorance – that the ironical Malone now seeks to overcome, not by returning to the social games that he failed to play with other children, but by performing, alone in his mind, the narrative act of playing with language's formal narrative structures: "From now on it will be different. I shall never do anything any more from now on but play" (*TN*, 180).[6] As a purely performative game player, he will finally do what Molloy failed to do. He will say what he is doing and do what he is saying.

Malone wants not only to represent his future ironical attitude towards his narratives, but also to narrate the stages by which he is preparing and will complete his stories: "Present state, three stories, inventory" (*TN*, 182). After earnestly describing his present state as that of an ironical game player and storyteller, he will lifelessly tell stories of the lives of others. Storytelling will enable him to forget, not only the wandering self that seeks knowledge and desires ignorance, but also his narrative position as lifeless, ironical storyteller. He will then achieve "the goal I set myself in my young days and which prevented me from living. And on the threshold of being no more I succeed in being another. Very pretty" (*TN*, 194).[7] If time remains after he finishes his stories, he will inventory his possessions: his pen and exercise-book. These are the material signs of his being a writer of stories from which the writer himself is totally absent: Proust's greatest fear in his passages on Nietzsche and Wagner.

But Malone's very attempt to freely co-opt language's formal narrative structures in a manner that is indifferent to self-representation may put itself into question, transforming his narrative game-playing into a rhetorical mask for his earnest search for a self that is ignorant: "I shall die tepid, without enthusiasm... I still have my little fits of impatience, from time to time, I must be on my guard against them... Yes, I shall be natural at last" (*TN*, 179). In order to succeed in his language game, Malone must continually ward off any repetition of his earnest past desire to represent himself. Repetition of past desire in the present of narration threatens to redefine his seemingly arbitrary and mechanical stories within language's rhetorical production and demystification of self-representations:[8] "I wonder if I am not talking yet again about myself. Shall I be incapable, to the end, of lying on any other subject" (*TN*, 189).[9]

Malone's recognition of the threat that his playful stories will become serious metaphors of self forces him to change his initial rules of narration, to accept a first failure to say what he is doing: "I must simply be on my guard, reflecting on what I have said before I go on and stopping, each time disaster threatens, to look at myself as I am. That is just what I wanted to avoid... After that mud-bath I shall be better able to endure a world unsullied by my presence" (*TN*, 189). He decides that he cannot forget his "need" to represent himself as ignorant. From time to time, therefore, he must remember and describe this ignorant self, not as a truth, but as a means of getting the drive for self-representation out of his system, before returning, at least for a while, to the self-indifference with which he characterizes his ironical language games.

Malone's freedom to ironically produce and negate signs of knowledgeable or ignorant others is thus always under the constant threat of falling back into a seemingly necessary allegorical search for an always fleeting self. Storytelling does not just erase signs of self; it represses these signs in a manner that produces a displaced remembering of them. Malone's purportedly accurate stories of how he will play his ironical game of fictional storytelling repeatedly take on the appearance of lies that hide the truth of his earnest, if vain, search for a fleeting self. Ironical stories about others seem to give way to language's allegory of the "incurious" search for, and deconstruction of, all representations of the subject, including an ironical subject who playfully creates and negates fictional stories.

Allegory emerges from Malone's two (not three as he intended) ironical stories. The first recounts the actions of a fictional character who, according to Malone, has no relation to his self-representations as ignorant. Malone calls this fictional character Sapo, from the Latin, "sapere": to taste of, to taste something, to mentally discern or to be wise.[10] Sapo sought to "[know] what manner of being he was, and how he was going to live... Nothing is less like me than this patient, reasonable child, struggling all alone for years to shed a little light upon himself, avid of the least gleam" (*TN*, 193).[11] Sapo's search for knowledge seems to be the contrary of "the call of... ignorance" with which Malone periodically needs to represent himself (*TN*, 189). Like the young Malone, the earnest Sapo does not enjoy playing games: "He ought to play more games, [his father] would say" (*TN*, 193). Unlike the young Malone, his search for self-knowledge and his actions are not incurious. Rather, he is "avid of resemblances," of metaphor. To create and narrate the search for knowledge by this fictional other, indeed to become him through identification, is to provide the dying Malone with "the air I need, a lively tenuous air, far from the nourishing murk that is killing me"

(*TN*, 193). He will forget self-representation by ironically becoming, in his mind, a person he cannot be.

In order to cease to hear the call for ignorance with which he habitually represents his dying self, Malone thus tries to tell a story of Sapo's search for knowledge. However, his attempt to take an ironical distance from Sapo fails when the contrast between his search for ignorance and Sapo's search for knowledge comes to inhabit Sapo himself, and when Sapo becomes a metaphor for the narrator's own contradictory self: "[F]rom his ignorance of [natural things Sapo] drew a kind of joy, as from all that went to swell the murmur, You are a simpleton" (*TN*, 191). Sapo has not even "learnt the art of thinking" that would enable him to produce knowledge. He does "not know how to look at [nature], the looks he rained upon [all these things] taught him nothing about them" (*TN,* 191). Sapo fails to know because he cannot link names to things in many cases: "He confused the birds with one another, and the trees, and could not tell one crop from another crop" (*TN*, 191). He cannot make conventional links between signs of space and signs of time: "He did not associate the crocus with the spring nor the chrysanthemum with Michaelmas" (*TN*, 193). The result is a "babel raging in his head" that strongly resembles the "[w]ords and images" that "run riot" in Malone's head, which risk destroying his sense of calm, ironical indifference (*TN*, 192–93, 198). As Sapo's search for knowledge becomes indistinguishable from Malone's joyful search for ignorance, Sapo becomes a metaphor for the dual desires that tear Malone apart and destroy his ironical indifference: "I slip into him . . ." (*TN*, 226); "Mais il s'agit bien de moi."[12]

In order to maintain his ironical distance, Malone must treat the very contradiction between his desires for knowledge and ignorance as breaking down the category of self: "Fear to contradict myself! If this continues it is myself I shall lose and the thousand ways that lead there. And I shall resemble the wretches famed in fable, crushed beneath the weight of their wish come true" (*TN*, 193–94). The inability to avoid contradiction leads Malone to revise once again the narrative of his actions during his final days. Not only will he periodically return, during his last days, to his habitual self-representation as ignorant, he will return to it one last time just before his death. He will then indifferently and ironically watch the simultaneous death of both his knowledge-seeking character and his ignorance-seeking, narrating self: "I shall never go back into this carcass except to find out its time. I want to be there a little before the plunge, close for the last time the old hatch on top of me, say goodbye to the holds where I have lived, go down with my refuge" (*TN*, 193); "To show myself now, on the point of vanishing, at the same time as the stranger, and by the same grace, that would be no ordinary last straw. Then live, long enough to feel, behind my closed eyes, other eyes close. What an end" (*TN*, 195).

However, each time Malone is forced to replace a description of his actions with a new one, a previous itinerary with a new itinerary, he raises the question of whether any of his itineraries describe what he is doing. If he cannot identify with self-knowledge or self-ignorance, then how can he know that he is an ironical, indifferent game player? In other words, his ironical negation of self-representation ironically discloses and undercuts his self-representation as ironical. This necessary fall of Malone's irony into irony of irony coincides with passages deferring the ironical indifference that he seeks. It puts off to an unreachable future the discovery of the correct itinerary. This deferral produces allegory: the allegory of his search for a future self-representation as an ironical acting self who is indifferent to self-representation. It also discloses his present ignorance about what he is doing and who he is.

Allegory turns Malone's act of writing into a forgetting of what he has said this act was doing: a pleasurable response to the call of ignorance. It splits the present of Malone's narration between a remembering narrator, who forgets what he said he was doing – "[The stories] will be almost lifeless, like the teller. What was that I said?" (*TN*, 180) – and a forgetting narrator, who forgets whether he is forgetting what he is doing: "I feel the old dark gathering, the solitude preparing, by which I know myself, and the call of that ignorance which might be noble and is mere poltroonery. Already I forget what I have said. That is not how to play." (*TN*, 189) Allegory is always too early to say that the narrator is remembering what he is doing and too late to say that he is forgetting what he is doing. The narrator can only posit, in the form of an unreachable future or a lost past, the existence of a moment when he does what he says he is doing. Malone's descriptions of the rules of the ironical games he claims to be playing thus can never coincide with his actions in a temporal present. Moreover, the very attempt to become an ironical storytelling self who negates any allegorical search for self in time reproduces allegory as the temporal search to become an ironical self. This return to allegory does not constitute the return to a naive belief in self; rather, it marks a discovery that first-person discourse can only disclose a void within the subject between, on the one hand, the allegorical search for, and deconstruction of, an ever-deferred future self or an always lost past self and, on the other hand, the ironical negation of the very notion of a past or future self.

Malone links his failure to tell stories to the structure of the descriptive discourse with which he tries to represent his characters and his actions. A problem lies in the verb "to be," with which language claims to describe, but in fact posits, a fixed relation between noun and thing. Sapo loses the power to believe that the verb "to be" describes a pre-existing relation between names and things. Malone extends this breakdown of the descriptive to language's power to distinguish between different nouns naming allegorical or ironical acts of narration and thus between different nouns defining him by these acts of narration.

Malone finds the source of the breakdown of language's power to describe what it is doing in Sapo's uncanny gulls' eyes, which resemble both Murphy's and Beckett's:

[They] remind me of an old shipwreck, I forget which. I know it is a small thing. But I am easily frightened now. I know those little phrases that seem so innocuous and, once you let them in, pollute the whole of speech. *Nothing is more real than nothing*. They rise up out of the pit and know no rest until they drag you down into its dark. But I am on my guard now. (*TN*, 192)

Malone transforms Democritus' statement – nothing has more reality than anything else – into "nothing is more real than nothing." On the one hand, the statement says that nothingness is more real than something. This reading suggests that Malone's irony and allegory disclose a "real" spatial void at the heart of signs of temporal relations and a "real" temporal void at the heart of signs of spatial relations. On the other hand, Malone's statement can be read as saying that nothing is more real than itself. In other words, nothing is both "more real" and "less real" than itself. This reading breaks down the possibility of characterizing "nothing" in terms of the opposition reality/fiction. It renders unreadable any assertion that there is an atemporal void of indifference at the heart of irony, or a temporal void of deferral at the heart of allegory. Both irony and allegory would only be means of producing the illusion of such a void. Malone's unreadable statement thus situates discourse in the gap between the atemporal and temporal voids produced by ironical and allegorical desire.

Malone's inability to say what he is doing raises questions about the relation between his act of creating a narrating voice by means of writing the pronoun "I" and the voice that intends his writing: "[I]t must be over a week since I said, I shall soon be quite dead at last, etc. Wrong again. That is not what I said, I could swear to it, that is what I wrote" (*TN*, 209). Malone dramatizes a fundamental gap between his writing "I" and the saying "I" that his writing produces: "In vain I grope, I cannot find my exercise-book. But I still have the pencil in my hand. I shall have to wait for day to break. God knows what I am going to do till then" (*TN*, 208). If Malone has lost his exercise-book, then the present tense verb and infinitive, "cannot

[find]," along with the pronoun "I" attached to them, do not represent the present of writing in his exercise-book. They can only represent a past time in which he was looking for his exercise-book and not yet writing. But the deictic "I" and the present tense of the verb also refer to (but do not represent) the present of the act of writing "I," which the narrating, speaking "I" is too early to represent.[13] Malone thus splits his voice between a narrating voice that is not yet writing and a writing voice that is no longer narrating, where the act of narrating is too early to be written and the act of writing is too late to narrate.

Conversely, Malone's narrating voice is an effect of writing, which is too late to represent the writing "I" that produced it. Malone's act of referring to himself in writing produces a new narrating voice, a new self, that is other than his writing voice or self: "I write about myself with the same pencil and in the same exercise-book as about him. It is because it is no longer I, I must have said so long ago, but another whose life is just beginning. It is right that he too should have this little chronicle, his memories, his reason,..." (*TN*, 208). Writing gives birth to a narrating "I" that "is no longer I," that is too late to be the writing "I," which is dead. Malone's attempt to give birth to an ironical writing voice, therefore, constitutes only the birth of someone else, an ironical narrating voice with which the writer, Malone, cannot coincide: "Yes, I shall soon be [dead], etc., that is what I wrote when I realized I did not know what I had said, at the beginning of my say, and subsequently, and that consequently the plan I had formed, to live, and cause to live, at last, to play at last and die alive, was going the way of all my other plans" (*TN*, 209).

The rhetorical figure that describes the intrusion of the voice of a writer into the fiction of a narrator, an intrusion that destroys the representational illusion of a narrator, is parabasis.[14] Malone's discourse, like Molloy's, is riddled with repeated intrusions of a writing voice into the narrator's voice: "What tedium" (*TN*, 189); "This is awful" (*TN*, 191). But, in this passage, the intrusive writing voice represents itself as an irrecoverable non-voice, in relation to which any narrator's voice is always spatially or temporally other. Parabasis may take the form of an allegorical or ironical negation of a narrator's voice, but it also turns allegory or irony against themselves, making them negate the very possibility of an allegorical or ironical voice. Allegory reveals itself to be too early or too late and irony reveals that it says too much or too little to coincide with writing.

Malone narrator, of course, wants to represent his own act of writing as an act of ironical storytelling. His realization that his very adoption of an ironical, narrative voice states its own failure to represent his act of writing leads him to lose faith in irony: "I do not depart from myself now with the same avidity as a week ago for example" (*TN*, 208); "But what matter whether I was born or not, have lived or not, am dead or merely dying. I shall go on doing as I have always done, not knowing what it is I do, nor who I am, nor where I am, nor if I am" (*TN*, 226).

Malone's apparent "regression" from the ironical negation of voices back to allegory does not mark a return of his belief in allegory's vain search for self, however. Rather, it produces an increasing awareness of the unbridgeable gap between the ironical and allegorical voices that writing produces. He begins to see himself in terms of a pronoun "I" that passively hears language's interplay between its voices: "I shall hear myself talking, afar off, from my far mind, talking of the Lamberts, talking of myself, my mind wandering, far from here, among its ruins" (*TN*, 216). Malone calls this awareness of being spoken by language "conation" (*TN*, 217): the consciousness of a drive (to speak and think) that appears volitional, but whose origin is unknown.

And yet Malone does not give up trying to do something, to take control of his dying. Since he cannot avoid referring allegorically to his desire to be ignorant, he decides to tell an allegory of an earnest "incurious wanderer," like his past self, whose irony has destroyed any belief in his fantasies of ignorance or of being ironical. Malone's wanderer identifies with a now empty drive to wander, as if, but only as if, he will some day arrive somewhere and know something about who he is and what he is doing. By projecting the failure of his ironical voice and his obsessive return to an allegorical voice onto a fictional character, Malone hopes finally to distinguish himself from this character. Language, not he, will be the producer of the interplay between irony and allegory. He can then forget his passive identification with language's actions by imagining that he is the character in his final story. He will finally die symbolically before he dies physically.

The protagonist of Malone's second and last story is Macmann. If Macmann is an elderly Sapo, as the narrator deems possible, then Macmann has gotten over Sapo's self-defeating desires to know or be ignorant. Macmann has accepted the impossibility of marking differences between voices by means of names, such as "writer," "narrator," and "character." Living has become the experience of the dying of this illusion of difference:[15] "[P]erhaps he has come to that stage of his instant when to live is to wander the last of the living in the depths of an instant without bounds, where the light never changes and the wrecks look all alike" (*TN*, 233). Like Molloy at the seashore, ignorance about what signs mean or do has transformed them into indistinguishable material stones or wrecks without meaning.

But Malone has no illusion that he can control the order in which he passes from one wrecked voice to another. It is in this gray, Beckettian world of uncontrolled wandering, which is produced by the return from irony to allegory, that Malone tries to lose himself, while imagining that this world has nothing to do with him.

For Macmann, the relation between signs is caught up in the allegory of an entropic process of "harmoniously perishing terms" (*TN*, 229). His big coat, a metaphor for the body of language, for the materiality of the signifier, harmoniously perishes alongside his teeny hat, a metaphor for another signifier that the mind confuses with the signified of his coat as signifier. This simultaneous perishing of the terms within signifying relationships makes signs increasingly indistinguishable from one another. It produces neither knowledge nor ignorance, but greater and greater confusion. Macmann is not indifferent to his growing confusion. His face is marked by past passion, by past action perhaps, and by a loss of suffering that may only be temporary: "[P]assion has marked the face, action too possibly, but it seems to have ceased from suffering, for the time being" (*TN*, 228).

Rather than make Malone forget his writing situation, Macmann's story of harmonious perishing begins to reflect back on it. This reflection occurs in Malone's return, once again, to describing his writing situation as a harmonious perishing of signs of self-representation. The description is also a parody of Proust's remembering narrator's representation of man's personal history as a remembered instant outside time. Malone's parody works off Proust's famous image, at the end of the *Recherche*, of old men perched on "de vivantes échasses, grandissant sans cesse, parfois plus hautes que des cloches, finissant par leur rendre la marche difficile et périlleuse, et d'où tout d'un coup ils tombaient" (*R*, 3: 1048). Proust's remembering narrator interprets the old men's bodies on stilts as metaphors for the temporal duration of their entire lives that is recreated by their memory. By means of memory, old people, including old writers, look towards the far away ground of their remembered past, the feet from which the stilts of remembered time separate them: "Je m'effrayais que les miennes fussent déjà si hautes sous mes pas, il ne me semblait pas que j'aurais encore la force de maintenir longtemps attaché à moi ce passé qui descendait déjà si loin" (*R*, 3: 1048). The writer's task is to transform all his different remembered past selves into a unified, autobiographical novel, before his imminent death.

In contrast to the body of the elderly Marcel, which represents the differences that memory and writing resurrect, Malone's body is caught up in the processes of the decay of all signs of difference and the massive accumulation of homogeneously confused, material signs. Time's decay of differences between terms and its accumulation of matter has made Malone's body so immense that his head cannot see the feet of his past, whose heaviness is pulling his head and his present, and thus all self-understanding, towards its grave: "All strains towards the nearest deeps, and notably my feet, which even in the ordinary way are so much further from me than all the rest, from my head I mean, for that is where I am fled, my feet are leagues away... Is that what is known as having a foot in the grave?" (*TN*, 234). Malone's immense body, the materiality of words, has become a grotesque excrescence, which expresses his deep enjoyment at losing all connection between head (signifieds) and feet (material signifiers). This monstrous sign of enjoyment questions any representation of what his body has done in the past or is doing in the present: "[M]y arse for example, which can hardly be accused of being the end of anything, if my arse suddenly started to shit at the present moment, which God forbid, I firmly believe the lumps would fall out in Australia" (*TN*, 235).

The head's ignorance of what the body is doing transforms writing into an involuntary production of excremental words by some uncontrollable force: a subversive materiality of the body of language that obliterates distinctions between the parts of speech in his sentences: "But my fingers too write in other latitudes and the air that breathes through my pages and turns them without my knowing, when I doze off, so that the subject falls far from the verb and the object lands somewhere in the void, is not the air of this second-last abode, and a mercy it is" (*TN*, 234). The air's destruction of any relationship between parts of speech extends to any difference between what words do in different parts of a sentence and confuses the functions of subject, action, being, and object.

Rather than the continuity that Proust's remembering narrator posits between a past object of first-person writing, a past self, and a present remembering subject, personal time in Beckett is a discontinuity between present self, past self, and the verbs that claim to relate them.[16] The very function of language becomes the harmonious perishing of the syntactic distinctions necessary to represent one's own actions, including one's act of writing about oneself:

[S]uddenly all swam before his eyes, he could no longer distinguish the plants destined for the embellishment of the home or the nutrition of man and beast from the weeds which are said to serve no useful purpose... And even he himself was compelled to admit that the place swept by him looked dirtier at his departure than on his arrival, as if a demon had driven him... [I]t was truly as if he were not master of his movements and did not know what he was doing, while he was doing it, nor what he had done, once he had done it.[17] (*TN*, 244)

In telling Macmann's story, therefore, Malone fragments the link that Proust's remembering narrator establishes between voice and writing.

Given the pleasure that Malone now begins to take in his allegory of the harmonious fall of discourse into confusion and disharmony – a pleasure that belies any pretension of ironical indifference – is he not guilty, he asks, of being a willing accomplice in this destruction? Malone explores the moral implications of his possible complicity in the violent breach that first-person narration opens up into voice and writing. First-person writing, we have seen, constitutes a death of the writer in the birth and accumulation of narrative voices that fail to represent what the writer was doing, being ironical or allegorical. As Malone rejects these failed voices, does he not kill them off as well? Is writing not a mode of murder and suicide?

Malone initially alludes to the violence of his repeated symbolic murders and suicides when he recounts the actions of the abusive and incestuous pig butcher, Lambert, whose wife and daughter are regularly visited by Sapo (*TN*, 216). Near the end of Macmann's story and of the novel, Lambert's murderous nature becomes a part of Malone's rejection of fictional voices that fail to make him forget himself or represent his present act of writing: "Moll. I'm going to kill her" (*TN*, 264). Malone dramatizes this murder/suicide by recounting the asylum-keeper Lemuel's practice of hitting characters over the head in order to kill them and of hitting himself over the head in order to dampen his guilt.

Lemuel's murders indirectly characterize all first-person writing as the repeated murder of narrating voices, including Beckett's murders of narrating voices in his previous novels: "[When I die] it will be all over with the Murphys, Molloys, Morans and Malones, unless it goes on beyond the grave... How many have I killed, hitting them on the head or setting fire to them?" (*TN*, 236). These murders of past narrators also include Beckett's repeated, parodic murder of Proust's remembering narrator, particularly in Molloy's and Malone's discourses. But who is responsible for first-person narration's repeated murders of past voices?

In a passage on Macmann, Malone tries to dramatize and ironically undercut this "earnest" moral question about first-person writing. Man would appear to have no control over sin because it is product of his being born, Malone argues by quoting Calderon's "el delito mayor / Del hombre es haber nacido," as quoted by Schopenhauer.[18] But the very act by which writing gives birth to a narrating self makes this self an ironical accomplice in writing's murder of the author's original voice or intention. The act of being born out of writing makes one share Schopenhauer's "guilt of existence itself."[19] The life of a mortal thus makes reparation for this guilty act. But, as discussed in Chapter 1, this original sin produces an infinite ironical abyss of guilt and reparation that ultimately puts into question the possibility of moral distinctions between sin and atonement.

Finding himself in the rain without shelter, Macmann decides to lie prostrate on the ground with his arms outstretched in order to protect from the rain that part of his body that is against the ground. His Christ-like position suggests that his suffering from the rain is punishment for his sin, and perhaps the sin of writing. However, the very act of atonement repeats the sin:

And without knowing exactly what his sin was he felt full well that living was not a sufficient atonement for it or that this atonement was in itself a sin, calling for more atonement, and so on, as if there could be anything but life, for the living. And no doubt he would have wondered if it was really necessary to be guilty in order to be punished but for the memory, more and more galling, of his having consented to live in his mother, then to leave her. And this again he could not see as his true sin, but as yet another atonement which had miscarried and, far from cleansing him of his sin, plunged him in it deeper than before. (*TN*, 240)

Macmann posits that he is guilty of consenting to his own birth, just as Malone feels that the narrative voices that he adopts are guilty of consenting to the death of previous narrators' voices. A life of mortal suffering (in the rain) must atone for Macmann's sin. But life gives birth to more and more voices, thus repeating the sin, which must in turn be atoned for, *ad infinitum*. Conversely, Macmann's act of consenting to be born was itself atonement for a previous sin, itself atonement for a previous sin, and so on, in an infinite regress towards a forgotten original sin. Atonement would appear to be impossible.

But, just as the infinite repetition of sin in the drive to atone prevents him from performing the act of atonement, so the infinite regression of atonement prevents him from knowing whether he originally sinned. In this way, Macmann's drive to atone puts into question any distinction between sin and atonement. Moral discourse always ironically undercuts its power to make moral distinctions. Irony of irony undercuts itself, and this opens up the possibility of a non-guilty pleasure. His sense of guilt disappears as suddenly as it appeared, and he begins to enjoy the rain that punishes him just as Malone begins to enjoy the harmonious perishing of his power to represent what his writing is doing: "But not knowing how to go about it, in order to think and feel correctly, he would suddenly begin to smile for no reason … and give thanks for the teeming rain and the promise it contained of stars a little later, to light his way and enable him to get his bearings, should he wish to do so" (*TN*, 240). Macmann gets up and begins to wander again.

Macmann's allegorical meditation on original sin culminates in a fall of moral discourse into irony of irony. It is thus an ironical parody of moral discourse, as was marked from the beginning by his exaggerated logical reversals. Macmann acts despite his negation not only of distinctions between good and bad acts or intentions, but of causal relations between the subject and thinking: "And truth to tell the ideas of guilt and punishment were confused together in his mind, as those of cause and effect so often are in the minds of those who continue to think" (*TN*, 240).

By adopting an ironical stance towards moral discourse, a Beckett narrator once again repeats Proust's writing narrator. Although Beckett states in his early essay that the *Recherche* is "completely detached from all moral considerations," Proust does indeed raise moral questions.[20] As discussed in Chapter 1, Proust's narrator associates his sense of guilt with his incestuous memories of mother and self, which he experiences as a repeated killing off of his rule-giving mother. He makes reparation for his guilty memories by limiting himself to voluntary memories, which forget his incestuous childhood (and past selves) in the very act of obsessively trying to remember them. But this reparation creates guilt for killing off his compassionate mother and the self she confirms. He thus makes reparation for this guilty act by writing a novel whose translations of involuntary memories recapture her and his past selves. But in doing so he repeats the guilty and impossible act of remembering, which leads him to posit a novel that represents only time.

Unlike Macmann, Marcel attempts to take an ethical step beyond this compulsive destruction of moral distinctions by trying to sacrifice his obsessive search to find and kill off self to language's formal alternation in time between allegory and irony. This sacrifice coincides with his reconceiving his novel as a gift to those his writing symbolically murdered, by inventing them anew and to the reader, who will read, not Proust, but themselves.

Malone seems to adopt the impersonal point of view of language only in order to take refuge in an ironical distance from the compulsive nature of the interplay between sin and atonement, self-remembering and self-forgetting, in which writing dies. He hopes to kill off in advance the self that takes moral or ontological discourse seriously. But this ironical attitude towards the moral creates an ironical self which, despite its lack of content, occupies the position of performing the ironical act of asserting and negating moral discourse; irony gives birth to allegory. Malone's attempt to achieve ironical indifference to the moral question of giving birth or giving death to the self thus only defers reposing the moral question. The impossibility of a moral self is indissolubly tied, in language, to the necessity of positing a moral self.

Allegory thus begins to invade the irony with which Malone tries to deliver himself from the moral question and the fall of self-forgetting into self-remembering. Macmann, as we have seen, reminds Malone that language prevents him from linking subject and verb in a causal relationship. He cannot say what his words are doing, such as performing the speech act of ironically negating the moral. Malone thus begins to feel more and more like Macmann, from whom he had hoped to take an ironical distance. He feels increasingly out of control of what his words are doing. His words begin to express passion, which raises questions of self or guilt. Malone thematizes this loss of control by introducing a third party, "they," who force him to do what he does. "They" represent a voice of language that obliges him repeatedly to return to his dying, ignorant, earnest self: "I have had a visit. Things were going too well. I had forgotten myself, lost myself, I exaggerate. Things were not going too badly. I was elsewhere. Another was suffering. Then I had the visit. To bring me back to dying. If that amuses them" (*TN*, 268). It is "they" who have produced his illusion that he can freely and ironically create and destroy voices and stories, but it is also they who render his act of writing too early and too late to be ironical, indifferent, or amoral.[21]

Malone must thus rewrite the rules of his narration, his itinerary, one more time. He abandons his belief in his freedom to choose to write ironical stories and accepts as his master the impersonal or neutral processes of language, which produce his alternation between allegorical and ironical rhetoric. In other words, Malone attempts to be what Maurice Blanchot will later call Beckett's voice of language: an impersonal voice that is "indifferent to what it says." Language's voice, according to Blanchot, is indifferent to the ontological and moral dimensions of its ironical production and negation of fictions of others and selves.[22] Language is an impersonal, formal system that is structured both by prosopopeia – which gives fictional life to that which is dead, a narrator's voice – and by the negation of this prosopopeia through parabasis – which interrupts the illusion of a narrator's or writer's voice. By passively adopting the necessary position of language, Malone tries to take refuge in language's ironical negation of the very voices that it produces. He thus redefines the "I" as the product of a third-person "they," which, according to Blanchot, is utterly neutral in relation to all objects and subjects of their narration: "the narrative 'He' who expresses the neuter…abolishes every subject, just as it dissolves all transitive action and objectivity."[23]

Malone dramatizes the impersonal power of language to produce and erase voices in the form of the bureaucracy of an asylum in which Macmann finally finds himself imprisoned. In the asylum, Macmann is deprived of all possessions, just as Malone, in Blanchot's asylum of language, cannot say that he possesses even the pencil and exercise-book with which he writes. The asylum tells Macmann what to say and do, just as language tells Malone what to say and do, as if both character and narrator were incapable of linking voice and words: "They said in substance... Take no account of anything, it is we shall think and act for you, from now forward" (*TN*, 256). The asylum speaks to Macmann through two employees: Moll, who tries to give him a voice of self, and Lemuel, who kills off this voice of self and feels guilt for this murder. The central question is whether Macmann can be totally imprisoned within the asylum of language without violating its rules, without escaping from the asylum.

Moll, who, like Marcel's compassionate mother, is charitable, represents language's allegorical construction and deconstruction of metaphors for self and other. Moll teaches Macmann to write and read love letters. Beckett characterizes this exchange of the signs "I" and "you" in the act of written communication as "the farce of giving and receiving."[24] It is a farce, because Malone knows that Macmann has no possessions, no self to give or receive. Macmann's giving and receiving are ironical. Indeed, Moll's charitable sending of love letters only appears to be an act of charity. It is an uncharitable act of taking away as well. The letters are "lethal glue" for Macmann (*TN*, 262). The signs that she sends him, which express her love for his adorable, personal self, do not do what they are supposed to do: awaken his personal voice of love for her. Rather, her gift makes him feel that she is trying to imprison him within a voice of love that she is imposing on him: that she is trying to murder his symbolic self. Charitable words of love make him desire to kill off the other, who pens them, in order to kill off the loving voice that is using them to kill him. The same reversal happens in Moll, when he is the giver and she the receiver of words of love. Giving and receiving signs of self produce the negation of these signs and of the voice they generate. Good, like atonement, produces sin.

This reversal of the giving of self into the act of taking away of self structures the act of exchanging signs as an allegory in which the giving of signs of love is always too early or too late to produce a desire to give signs of love back. The only moment in which the two lovers appear to share mutual feelings is "the brief ["tepid"] period of plenitude between these two extremes when, between the warming up of the one party and the cooling down of the other, there was established a fleeting equality of temperature" (*TN*, 263). This temporal in-between is a moment in which giving is becoming taking away and taking away is becoming giving.

In order to escape language's self-destructive giving of voice, Malone decides to kill off Moll, thus ironically negating giving as an indirect taking away and negating taking away as an indirect giving, in a spiral of negations of moral discourse. He decides to replace Moll, as the voice of language's asylum, with the "malevolent" but guilt-ridden Lemuel, a killer of others and their personal voices by means of a hammer.[25] In doing so, Malone reinterprets Blanchot's ironical negation of ontological or moral voices by a neutral voice of language as a covert, compulsive act of satisfying a sadistic desire to kill off voices and of producing guilt for his enjoyment of this sadistic act. Blanchot's neutralization of voices produces painful, moral voices of guilt and reparation, which he tries to kill as well by hitting himself, his own voice, over the head with a hammer:

Flayed alive by memory, his mind crawling with cobras, not daring to dream or think and powerless not to, his cries were of two kinds, those having no other cause than moral anguish and those, similar in every respect, by means of which he hoped to forestall same. Physical pain, on the contrary, seemed to help him greatly. (*TN*, 267)

Blanchot's neutral third-person voice of language, which claims to speak "in the memoryless present," is an act of neutralization that gives birth to its opposite: a sado-masochistic voice that exceeds any neutrality by obsessively remembering and repeating the pleasurable symbolic murder of past and present voices.[26] By hitting himself over the head with a hammer, Lemuel, like Blanchot, tries to kill, to neutralize the material brain of language that produces these moral voices. He attempts to feel the pleasure of attaining Blanchot's amoral voice of neutrality and indifference. But Lemuel cannot achieve this neutral voice without killing language itself, which is why he must obsessively repeat his murder/suicide over and over.

The transition from the charitable Moll to the sado-masochistic Lemuel as the keeper of the asylum who "think[s] and act[s]" for Macmann thus exceeds the "neutral" laws of the asylum of language in the very act of carrying them out. It reawakens the unanswerable moral question of the writer's, Malone's, pleasurable complicity in language's murder of his characters' and narrative voices, even as it repeats the act of neutralizing moral questions. Malone thus repeats Molloy's and Moran's murders of their past voices and selves. But Malone's and Beckett's very acts of killing off past voices, of "the Murphys, Molloys, Morans and Malones" and of Proust's Marcel, in order to achieve ironic neutrality towards them, only brings them back to haunt him. This return of the question of difference puts into question whether the repetition of language's neutral structures – in the works of the same author and between the works of different authors – can ever be neutral.

Unlike Blanchot's "he," Beckett's "they" is always condemned to confusion about what it is doing:[27] "The fact is they don't know, neither do I, but they think they know" (*TN*, 268).[28] Language may formally produce voices as if it knew that it was the silent, neutral voice speaking this production; it is always also spoken by its failure to say what is speaking its words. It cannot help but be also spoken by other voices, such as psychological, social, and historical contingencies.

Malone experiences the failure of language's "they" to deny all personal voices as a failure to forget his own death. He hopes that the time lag between the dying of his hand and voice, which allegorically and ironically negates the "I", and the dying of his head, whose thoughts will take an ironical, neutral distance from the voices of writing and speaking, will allow him to witness death's final, impersonal negation of all voices, as if they belonged to someone else. "My head will be the last to die. Haul in your hands. I can't. The render rent. My story ended I'll be living yet. Promising lag. That is the end of me. I shall say I no more" (*TN*, 283). But language's failure to do what it says it is doing prevents him from achieving this final ironical negation of voice. Rather than neutralize past subjects, including the moral subject, in a memoryless present, language's formal self-negations repeat past signs of the subject, making the subject of language always other than language says it is.

Malone's project to kill off his self symbolically before dying physically necessarily fails to demonstrate that he has not been writing about himself, about his own desire to kill himself off and about his shame for this desire: "It's the heart's fault... It too is burning with shame, of itself, of me, of them, shame of everything, except of beating apparently. It's nothing, mere nervousness" (*TN*, 274). Malone tries one last time to erase the voice of shame, shame at being a voice, "It's nothing, mere nervousness." It is as if the heart's shame were a mere product of nervousness, as if it were psychological not moral. But of course, he can no longer believe that he can reduce his thoughts to products of a neutral, neurotic machine. He is caught between multiple interpretations of the word "heart," the heart as a metaphor for the neutral materiality of language – as mechanical, linguistic pump of blood, voices, and selves – and the heart as a metaphor for a human voice that speaks language – for individual emotion and desire. Lemuel's repeated shame marks language's failure to resolve this co-existence of the material and the psychological or the moral (and, by extension, the social).

Lemuel thus foregrounds the full significance of Beckett's description, in the "Three Dialogues," of an art that is "the expression that there is nothing to express, nothing with which to express, nothing from which to express, no power to express, no desire to express, together with the obligation to express."[29] Malone's voice is, at once, language's formal negation of the voices it produces, which renders them impossible, and it is the necessity of producing voices that exceed language's neutrality.[30] But this exceeding of language's neutrality, in contrast to Proust's narrator's turning towards language's neutrality, produces an ethical turn. Lemuel frees the prisoners, including Macmann, from the asylum of language, kills off representatives of the asylum, and takes off with them in a boat. His murder and self-flagellation become an ethical sacrifice that is also a gift of freedom to the voices in language's asylum.

At the end of *Malone Dies*, Beckett dramatizes Malone's dying as a negation of negation, a dying of the death of voice in language: "Lemuel... Lemuel is in charge, he raises his hatchet on which the blood will never dry, but not to hit anyone, he will not hit anyone... any more... with his hammer... or with his pencil or with his stick..." (*TN*, 287–88). Malone repeats negations of negations, negations of endings, over and over, while simultaneously repeating the pronoun "I," which he cannot not reproduce, not give back. Thus the failure of Lemuel's murderous hammer/pencil of negation:

> ... I mean never he will never
> or with his pencil or with his stick or
> or light light I mean
> never there he will never
> never anything
> there
> any more.   (*TN*, 288)

Malone's "never... any more" appears to negate the temporal possibility of voice, thus affirming the death of voice. But his statement that Lemuel "will never never anything there any more" negates this apparent negation of the temporal possibility of voice. The double negation states the failure of the "he" or the "they" to be the voice of the death of the "I": the voice of an impersonal language that speaks itself. Hence the return of the 'I' as a totally unreadable intention that is produced by this negation of negation. This return has already been marked by Malone's enormous body, which cannot see what its hands are doing: "I mean never there, he will never never anything there any more."

Language's "never never" repeatedly anticipates a death that it forever defers. Language can never speak, even silently, the death of its voices, just as the mind can never be conscious of the death of its consciousness. Language's repeated anticipation and deferral of its own death thus obligates Malone to speak allegorically once again, as if he also anticipated the birth of a voice. Not surprisingly, this return of hope takes place on Easter weekend, when Malone's bedroom feels more and more like a womb: "I am being given, if I may venture the expression, birth to into death, such is my impression" (*TN*, 283).[31] What is reborn is language's act of writing "I" as a reference, not only to the formal present of narration, but to contingent desires and forces that exceed language: as a gift of voice.

The rebirth of the act of writing in Beckett repeatedly coincides with the passage from irony to allegory, which posits an impossible future expression of meaning: "I mean never there he will never never anything there any more" (*TN*, 288). This is a transition from a spiral of negating temporal signs of voice, which tends towards the disclosure of a spatial void defining an ironical subject, to a sequence of negations of spatial metaphors of voice, which tends towards the disclosure of a temporal void between the too-lateness and too-earliness of meaning, which defines an allegorical subject:

Yet there is no good pretending, it is hard to leave everything. The horror-worn eyes linger abject on all they have beseeched so long, in a last prayer, the true prayer at last, the one that asks for nothing. And it is then a little breath of fulfillment revives the dead longings and a murmur is born in the silent world, reproaching you affectionately with having despaired too late. (*TN*, 277)

CHAPTER 8

The Unnamable: *The death of the ironical self and the return of history*

I have argued throughout this book that the first-person narrators in Beckett's trilogy, like Proust's narrator in the *Recherche*, dramatize an interplay between irreconcilable modes of constructing the first-person narrator's discourse: allegory and irony. The *Recherche* backgrounds this interplay by foregrounding the story of Marcel's search to disclose remembered, personal selves, which becomes an allegory of deconstructing this search. Beckett's trilogy also seems to background this interplay, but by subordinating the notion of self to the impersonal, rhetorical interplay between the structures of allegory and irony. The trilogy thus appears to mark a literary historical transition from Proust's seemingly allegorical narrator to Beckett's ironical narrators.

I have endeavored to show, however, that the trilogy's irony also undercuts this historical distinction by marking itself as a literary historical repetition of the same formal interplay of language between allegory and irony that is already found in Proust. In Proust, as in Beckett, language alone, not a narrator's personal voice, would ironically and impersonally produce and demystify the alternate illusions that are spoken by an allegorical or ironical voice. But the trilogy also puts into question this transhistorical repetition of language's impersonal non-voice by disclosing how the category of voice exceeds language's formal allegorical and ironical rules. This disclosure foregrounds a transition from language's seemingly impersonal, ironical production of allegorical and ironical voices to an allegory of the search for personal and literary historical difference.

In *The Unnamable*, Beckett abandons the narrators' discourses on self that were found in *Molloy* and the first half of *Malone Dies*. There is no longer any question of dramatizing Molloy's search to distinguish his self from his mother's, of Moran's search to be a fatherly acting self, or of Malone's search to become Blanchot's purely linguistic non-voice without self. The narrator of *The Unnamable* seems to have already become Blanchot's unnamable, silent non-voice of language. In other words, there

The Unnamable: *The death of the ironical self*

seems to be no narrator, only language's production and deconstruction of voices that appear to speak the text. It is now a question of whether language alone can be the sole source of the voices produced by the text.

This transition from self to the production and negation of voices has been taking place throughout the trilogy. Its narrators have repeatedly negated the self as a real object of search and adopted an ironical stance towards the voices with which they produce a self. All dramatize the movement towards an impersonal voice, a "he" or a "they," that tells them what to do. But, in *The Unnamable*, narrative voices seem to be spoken only by this "he" or "they," not by the "I" of the text. The novel seems to adopt the silent position of language, which produces the first-person pronoun and the fiction of a present voice. In Blanchot's words, the text seeks to inhabit "[t]he point where language ceases to speak but is, where nothing begins, nothing is said, but where language is always reborn and always starts afresh."[1]

The novel thus initially rejects the very notion that language is spoken by a human voice: "[T]here are no human creatures here" (*TN*, 291, 296). If the novel were to succeed in eliminating all but Blanchot's non-voice of language as the source of its words, the first-person pronoun would refer only to this unnamable, silent voice of the linguistic present of narration. It would be language's, not a human narrator's, "memoryless" present of narration that would produce the pronoun "I" and that would construct the fiction that this pronoun signifies a prior human, narrating voice. Language would retrospectively invent fictions of prior human voices, which we mistakenly believe intend the writing of the text and are referred to by the pronoun "I," until we realize that the very category of voice is ironical.

The question that the text poses is a paradoxical one. Is the impersonal linguistic present of language's producing and negating of personal voices a single voice, which the text can identify as "its" voice?

This voice that speaks, knowing that it lies, indifferent to what it says, too old perhaps and too abased ever to succeed in saying the words that would be its last, knowing itself useless and its uselessness in vain, not listening to itself but to the silence that it breaks and whence perhaps one day will come stealing the long clear sigh of advent and farewell, is it one? (*TN*, 307)

By asking whether the text has a single, silent, impersonal, and unnamable voice, which ironically produces and negates all of its personal voices, the text opens up the possibility that all texts are spoken by one non-voice, which produces the false personal narrative voices that appear to speak them. *The Unnamable* is thus structured, like the first two novels of the trilogy, as an attempt and failure to show that there is a unified voice. But, this time, the unified voice is language itself.

With its very first words, the *The Unnamable* questions the text's power to name and locate a prior, personal voice that speaks its words: "Where now? Who now? When now?" (*TN*, 291). The text's beginning marks its narration ambiguously: either as an identification of the voice that presently speaks its words (Who am I now?) or as a giving birth to the present voice, as if the "now" were in the future (Who shall I be now?). In both readings, the "now" marks an isolated present that breaks with a previous "now." The text begins by exploring the first reading of the questions: "Where, who, and when am I now?" The interrogative pronouns and the question marks seem to signify ignorance about whether there is continuity between past and present or present and future times, places, and voices. It also seems to constitute a call for knowledge to replace this ignorance.

Like the trilogy's previous two novels, these first words recall the beginning of Proust's *Recherche*, which already gives birth to a narrator. But Proust's human narrator narrates this birth of a remembering voice as a past process of waking and rediscovering where, who, and when he really was. He does so from the retrospective point of view of a seemingly unified narrator, who remembers having awakened from self-ignorance to self-knowledge. Only later does Proust's narrator demystify this illusion of self-knowledge by revealing that, in waking, he had invented the self that he thought he was rediscovering. At the beginning of *The Unnamable*, by contrast, the text seems only to be able to ask retrospectively where, who, and when it has become.

Whereas Proust's narrator can retrospectively answer his waking questions, first by becoming conscious of a specific self, place, and time, then by identifying his apparent discovery of self, place, and time to be an ironical invention, *The Unnamable* cannot even ask where, who, and when it is: "Where now? Who now? When now? Unquestioning" (*TN*, 291). The three interrogative pronouns and question marks formally signify speech acts of questioning, but these formal signs do not do what they say they are doing. Can language mechanically produce sentences in the form of questions, without performing the act of questioning? Moran narrator initially thought that he could perform at least the speech acts of affirming, negating, and questioning, but *The Unnamable* undercuts ironically its power to say what its words are doing. For the text now both affirms and negates the power of its speech acts to perform the act of questioning.

Without being able to say what its words are doing, whether they are asking who speaks the text, the repetition of the pronoun "I" ceases to

The Unnamable: *The death of the ironical self*   141

perform the act of referring to a distinct voice that speaks the text: "I say I. Unbelieving." Without belief that it can perform the act of saying, the first "I" in the sentence, "I say I," can only refer to a totally unidentifiable act of enunciating words, and the second "I" can be no more than a repeated word. The text is paradoxically asserting that it is repeating words in grammatically correct order without being able to assert or do something with these words. The only continuity seems to be the irony marked by the words "unquestioning" and "unbelieving," which negate any signs that the sentence's words are doing something or asserting something. But even this ironical denial ironically negates itself, for it indirectly denies its ability to deny that it is questioning or believing.

The challenge of reading *The Unnamable* is to continue reading knowing that the text states the impossibility of identifying a narrative voice that speaks its words and the impossibility of saying that the text is doing or saying something, knowing that it states the impossibility of reading. Words seem to speak and act, knowing that they cannot speak or act: "It, say it, not knowing what... I seem to speak, it is not I, about me, it is not about me" (*TN*, 291).[2] It is as if the text were caught within the present of its simultaneous, ironical production and negation of speech acts and meaning, which indirectly negates this ironical denial of meaning: "Can it be that one day... I simply stayed in, in where, instead of going out..." (*TN*, 291).[3]

The words of *The Unnamable* as "text" thus appear to posit the existence of a prior voice of language that speaks them ironically and ironically negates their ironical negations. But irony of irony does not just fall into an infinite spiral of irony. It also discloses the gap between irony and allegory. The text thus begins to make distinctions between past, present, and future "nows," as if it could "proceed" in a linear direction, from past question to future knowledge: "What am I to do, what shall I do, what should I do, in my situation, how proceed?" (*TN*, 291). In "my," i.e. "language's," situation, how can it begin to do something? "[H]ow proceed? By aporia pure and simple? Or by affirmations and negations invalidated as uttered, or sooner or later? Generally speaking?" (*TN*, 291). To begin by the rhetorical figure of aporia is to use a "figure in which the speaker professes to be at a loss what course to pursue, where to begin, to end, what to say, etc."[4] In this case, aporia begins by denying that text has yet begun. Aporia is constituted by the ironical negation of allegory. The question of how to begin, which allegorically defers its answer into the future, is ironically undercut by the apparent fact that, by posing the question, the text has already begun. But, as we have seen, in this text's "situation," the act of questioning, which ironically undercuts the content of the question of how to begin, is itself ironically negated by the text's denial that it performs the act of questioning. Moreover, this irony of irony reintroduces the gap between irony and allegory. The apparent alternative to the irony of irony that underlies this aporetic question is the alternation between irony and allegory: "[A]ffirmations and negations invalidated as uttered, or sooner..." is irony. "[A]ffirmations and negations invalidated...later" is allegory. *The Unnamable* thus constitutes the novel as that which can never answer the question of whether its negations are caught in a spiral of irony or caught between ironical and allegorical voices.

The Unnamable states explicitly what was only implied by *Molloy* and *Malone Dies*: that language's interplay between irony and allegory structures Beckett's novels. According to de Man, this is the goal of the novel. The "truly perverse assignment [of the novel is to use] both the narrative duration of the diachronic allegory and the instantaneity of the narrative present; to try for less than a combination of the two is to betray the inherent *gageure* of the genre."[5] For Beckett, however, this is the perverse assignment of all texts.

The text thus explores the second reading of the questions that begin it. The narrator is really asking "Where, who, when (shall I be) now?" The ironical appearance of the text's beginning – "Where now? Who now? When now? Unquestioning" – is deceptive in that the object of this irony is not a given place, person, and time, but the text's present invention of a place, person, and time. It is the attempt to invent a future "there and then," which constitutes the present "here" and "now," that the text first explores as an answer to the impossible question "Where shall I be now?": "It would help me, since to me I must attribute a beginning, if I could relate it to that of my abode...I shall say therefore that our beginnings coincide, that this place was made for me, and I for it, at the same instant" (*TN*, 296).[6] The text posits the existence of an abode, as Proust's waking narrator invents his room, through an ironical Nietzschian little bang.[7] This impossible abode is possible only in a "there and then": "I who am here, who cannot speak, cannot think, and who must speak, and therefore perhaps think a little, cannot in relation only to me who am here, to here where I am, but can a little, sufficiently, I don't know how, unimportant, in relation to me who was elsewhere, who shall be elsewhere, and to those places where I was, where I shall be" (*TN*, 301). The impossible acts of thinking and speaking can only take place in the too-lateness and too-earliness of allegorical time, outside of the timeless present of ironical assertion and negation. The present of the text's narration is both outside

The Unnamable: *The death of the ironical self* 143

and inside time, or it is neither in time nor outside it: "Hell itself, although eternal, dates from the revolt of Lucifer. It is therefore permissible, in the light of this distant analogy, to think of myself as being here forever, but not as having been here forever" (*TN*, 295–96).[8]

The necessity of allegory in creating the "abode" of the text's ironical, self-creating "now" means the death of that ironical voice: "I see myself slipping, though not yet at the last extremity, towards the resorts of fable" (*TN*, 308). The dying of the text's ironical voice as it slips into allegory produces a narrative, a fable with a beginning and end, which the text can never become, since allegory is never more than the tendency towards narrative. This necessity of allegory means that the text can never fully identify with the act by which language, according to Blanchot, takes the form of a silent, impersonal present of language that ironically posits and discredits personal voices. Allegory is a constant reminder that the sequence of "heres and nows" in which language ironically constructs a purely fictional self and place is always too early and too late to give a temporal priority to language over voice. *The Unnamable* is both inside and outside the intentionality of language.

But the text tries to subordinate the necessity of allegory to an ironical negation of this allegory. It dramatizes the struggle between an ironical voice of silence and its allegorical "tempters," voices that want "that I should exist and at the same time be only moderately, or perhaps I should say finitely pained" (*TN*, 322). The non-ironical voices try to tempt the text's ironical voice out of its silence, so that without much pain, if not with pleasure, it will die, by becoming a voice that recounts the impossible search for voice: "They have even killed me off... The hard knocks they invented for me" (*TN*, 322–23).

The outer voices of the text's tempters are of course created by language's transition from irony to allegory, which reintroduces the question of narrative. The text attributes this transition to an identifiable voice who, in the past, succeeded in telling stories to the text about what the text's words were doing: "It was he [the character Mahood] told me stories about me, lived in my stead, issued forth from me, came back to me, entered back into me, heaped stories on my head" (*TN*, 309). The story that the text's tempters heaped on its ironical voice is the allegory of search and failure to be a voice that speaks. *The Unnamable*'s ironical voice must repeat the allegorical "lessons" that "they" impose on it, but it does so in order to get these allegorical voices out of the text's system and return to Blanchot's silent, ironical voice that is only "here," "where nothing begins, nothing is said, but where language is always reborn and always starts afresh."

The text thus turns towards allegory's anticipation of the future repetition of a forgotten past story or fable, which served and will serve as a lesson in how to act: "[B]etween me and the right to silence, the living rest, stretches the same old lesson, the one I once knew by heart and would not say, I don't know why, perhaps for fear of silence, or thinking any old thing would do, and so for preference lies, in order to remain hidden, no importance. But now I shall say my old lesson, if I can remember it" (*TN*, 306). The text invents a narrative voice, Basil, whom it quickly renames Mahood. Mahood tells stories in order to give "ostensible independent testimony in support of [the narrator's] historical existence" outside of the ironical, indifferent "here and now" of language (*TN*, 319). In order to provide evidence of a personal voice that survives the passage from one "now" to the next, these stories must displace the ironical space of the "here and now" into the lost past and deferred future of allegory, which the text states to be impossible: "I say years, though here there are no years. What matter how long? Years is one of Basil's ideas. A short time, a long time, it's all the same" (*TN*, 309). The notion of time would allow Mahood to "usur[p]" the "identity" of the text's ironical "here" that gives birth only in an ironical mode to all personal voices. In order to usurp the subject position of this ironical non-voice, allegory would "drown" it out and create a new one that exists in historical time (*TN*, 311, 309).

Mahood's (and "their") first story tempts the ironical non-voice of the text by constituting it within an allegory of the search to become a voice. This story seeks to redefine the purely spatial nature of the "here" in allegorical terms, within an ever-deferred, allegorical search to become the personal voice called Mahood. Were this allegory to become a linear narrative, it would "console me, help me to go on, allow me to think of myself as somewhere on a road, moving, between a beginning and an end..." (*TN*, 314).[9] But allegory is ironically undercut by its reversible, spatial representation, its presupposed abode:

I've been he [Mahood] an instant... I say an instant, perhaps it was years. Then I withdrew my adhesion... I must have got embroiled in a kind of inverted spiral, I mean one [of] the coils of which, instead of widening more and more, grew narrower and narrower and finally, given the kind of space in which I was supposed to evolve, would come to an end for lack of room. (*TN*, 316)

[B]eyond the equator you would start turning inwards again, out of sheer necessity. (*TN*, 317)

The story Mahood recounts takes place on a globe. One pole of this globe represents home, Mahood's original voice through his family's recognition of it. The other pole represents being away from home, non-voice.[10] As spoken by Mahood, Beckett's text would trace a spiral inwards from the equator towards the pole of family and voice, then a spiral back out to the equator, then a spiral inwards towards the pole of non-voice, then a reverse spiral, but without the illusion of finding his family. The end of one narrative constitutes the beginning of the other: "I should no doubt have had to stop, unless of course I elected to set off again at once in the opposite direction, to unscrew myself as it were, after having screwed myself to a standstill..." (*TN*, 316). This reversible spatial model of the narrative of the search for voice has a linear aspect, for when he returns to the pole where home should exist he finds his family dead and the family house in shambles. As a result, when he repeats the return from the pole of non-voice to the pole of voice, he repeats only a desire for home and voice that knows it cannot be satisfied.

Mahood's narrative redefines allegory as a search to kill off signs of voice. Mahood stamps underfoot his family's remains out of "annoyance at having to flounder" in their muck (*TN*, 323–24). Allegory is the text's "obligation, and the quasi-impossibility of fulfilling it," to disclose a single voice over time (*TN*, 320). But allegory fails to convince the text that it speaks the text, since the latter has defined allegory in spatial terms as a "spiral" of irony. It conceives of the globe as the simultaneous negation of the search for home and voice and the negation of the search for a non-voice: "But enough of this nonsense. I was never anywhere but here, no one ever got me out of here" (*TN*, 324). The apparent "there and then" of Malone's imaginary void becomes the "here and now" of the text's "affirmations and negations invalidated as uttered."

However, the very process by which the spatial abode of the "here and now," which the text constructs for itself, ironically negates allegories of voice produces more slipping back into allegory. The text can account for this slippage only by positing a "they" beyond the text: "[I]t's entirely a matter of voices, no other metaphor is appropriate. They've blown me up with their voices, like a balloon, and even as I collapse it's them I hear"; "[T]hey've inflicted the notion of time on me too" (*TN*, 325). "They" in *The Unnamable* is not at first language, as it was in *Malone Dies*, but society, a voice produced by the conventional nature of words, which makes language's impersonal voice identify itself as a personal, human voice:[11] "And man, the lectures they gave me on men, before they even began trying to assimilate me to him!... How they must hate me... To testify to them, until I die, as if there was any dying with that tomfoolery, that's what they've sworn they'll bring me to... Not to be able to open my mouth without proclaiming them... It's a poor trick that consists in ramming a set of words down your gullet on principle that you can't bring them up without being branded as belonging to their breed..." (*TN*, 324).[12] It is thus not an individual voice or a voice of language that tempts the text to find a voice outside language, as is the case for Malone; it is a social voice that provides the conventional words for language's impersonal interplay between its allegorical and ironical rhetoric.

The ironical text decides that it can free itself from "their," society's, unending influence only by agreeing to tell "their" story about the text. The text repeats their story about itself as it repeated its story about its abode: in order to get all their stories, their lessons, out of its system:

It's of me now I must speak, even if I have to do it with their language, it will be a start, a step towards silence and the end of madness, the madness of having to speak and not being able to, except of things that don't concern me, that don't count, that I don't believe, that they have crammed me full of to prevent me from saying who I am, where I am, and from doing what I have to do... (*TN*, 324)

In order finally to identify itself as language's ironical creator and demystifier of fictional voices in the "here and now" of language, the text must tell society's stories of its being a human voice *as if* it were speaking about itself:

They have explained to me, described to me, what it all is, what it looks like, what it's all for, one after the other, thousands of times, in thousands of connexions, until I must have begun to look as if I understood. (*TN*, 324)

I'll fix their gibberish for them. I never understood a word of it in any case, not a word of the stories it spews, like gobbets in a vomit. My inability to absorb, my genius for forgetting, are more than they reckoned with. Dear incomprehension, it's thanks to you I'll be myself, in the end. Nothing will remain of all the lies they have glutted me with. And I'll be myself at last, as a starveling belches his odourless wind, before the bliss of coma. (*TN*, 325)

To return to the coma of silence is to exist outside voice and outside their stories of time, within a pure present of language that speaks its dead voices: "Beyond them is that other who will not give me quittance until they have abandoned me as inutilizable and restored me to myself" (*TN*, 331).

Mahood's second story constructs a first-person narrator who, unlike Mahood's first narrator, does not have a personal voice or move himself in time. Rather, this narrator is forced by society to act as if he had a socially defined voice that speaks in time. Instead of ironically reversing the illusion of an irreversible itinerary around a globe and negating any content of the globe's poles, Mahood has now lost the capacity to speak, write, and act

The Unnamable: *The death of the ironical self*   147

physically: he has no hands or feet and is mute. He is immobilized on the island of the ironical present "here and now" of narration to which the first-person pronoun, he hopes, refers: "The island, I'm on the island, I've never left the island, God help me" (*TN*, 326). He is blind to signs of time and space outside his island of language: "There will be no more from me about bodies and trajectories, sky and earth, I don't know what it all is..." (*TN*, 324). Nevertheless, society can force time on the now of this blind and immobile narrator: "[A]t the period I refer to now this active life is at an end, I do not move and never shall again, unless it be under the impulsion of a third party" (*TN*, 327).[13] A restaurant owner, Madeleine, has placed the narrator's limbless body in a jar in front of her chop-house, which is located in the slaughterhouse district. To the jar she has attached a menu whose socially conventional items speak for the mute narrator. The words of the menu give social voice and intention, signs of collective humanity, to the pure materiality of the first-person pronoun, which has neither voice, nor intention, nor humanity.

Madeleine's menu of words transforms the "I" into a conventional and commercial, "human" sign that intends a conventional meaning – the consumption of meat. The menu speaks the "I" as a conventional voice of commerce. The "I" also refers indirectly to its own materiality, its immobile body. The jarred narrator thus sees a statue that indirectly refers to his material body: "I can see the statue of the apostle of horse's meat, a bust. His pupil-less eyes of stone are fixed on me" (*TN*, 327). The statue of the apostle of horse's meat looks back at Mahood blindly, baptizing him as commercial meat in a jar. He, like horse's meat, is up for sale to the chop-house owner, who buys his meat in order to turn it into a business sign to be consumed by the passing eyes of consumers. But the pupil-less eyes of the apostle of horse's meat also mark the sign's blindness to what society is making it signify and do.

Not only does the menu impose on the "I" a conventional voice of commerce and a story of seeking to satisfy consumer desire; it, and the surrounding area, also make the pronoun signify the act of its social production and consumption. The statue refers metonymically to its production by referring to the slaughterhouse district. Just as the slaughterhouse produces horsemeat for consumption, so the menu transforms the narrator's limbless body into a sign of the chop-house, a sign that is read, consumed, by its readers, the clients. The menu also refers to the production of the materiality of the sign, the narrator's body. Madeleine grows lettuce by fertilizing her garden with the narrator's offal, then feeds this lettuce to the narrator to maintain his body as social sign. Society thus transforms the blind "I" into a mark of society's act of producing and consuming conventional signs and meanings. Since the narrator remains alive, and since the jar is a sign whose contents are a human body, Mahood recounts an allegory of the social deconstruction of a pure voice of language and the social production of signs of a human voice.

But the sign "I" is not as immobile as society thinks it is, and this mobility of the sign raises questions about society's full appropriation of language. The narrator can make his body intend asocial meanings by moving his eyes and head without the "impulsion of a third party" (*TN*, 327). This movement of the sign produces a figurative meaning, which negates the literal meaning that society imposes on it in order to make it refer only to a social, human voice. The narrator rolls his eyes, dashes his "head angrily against the neck of the jar," and lets his spittle flow in a manner that suggests that he cannot be contained within the jars of society's conventional signs (*TN*, 329). At times, the narrator puts into question the very distinction between human and animal by lowering his head into the jar and acting dead, as if he had ceased to function as a social sign of the human desire for society's discursive food and had become the animal meat to which he is forced to refer. Society's very effort to imprison language within a social discourse seems to produce an ironical turning of language's tropes away from society's signs and towards the materiality of signs.

Whereas Mahood's first story discloses the first-person narrator's ironical negation of his alternation between signifying an individual voice and signifying a non-voice within a fixed space, his second story recounts the first-person pronoun's alternation between society's exploiting the materiality of language's formal rhetoric in order to signify a human voice that speaks language and the text's ironical negation of this reference to the human by referring to the material turning of language's rhetorical tropes. The narrator dramatizes this interplay between society's speaking of language and language's negation of society's' voice when Mahood decides to play dead in order to make the frightened chop-house owner, Madeleine, come running, thus pretending to kill off the social self into which she tries to make him. When she arrives, he frightens her all the more, by suddenly giving birth once again to his social self. He rapidly sticks his head out of the jar, like a jack-in-the-box. This sudden reappearance of the social as a living dead redefines social signs of the human ironically, in terms of language's production and demystification of all voices, including society's notion of a human voice.

Having rendered ironical the birth, in language, of a socially human persona, the narrator falls temporarily into the Proustian romantic story, as if,

The Unnamable: *The death of the ironical self* 149

by distinguishing himself from society's signs, he could disclose an individual self. He imagines that his jack-in-the-box antics will make "Madeleine," like Proust's privileged motherly reader, remember him as someone out of the ordinary after he dies. His popping back up when Madeleine comes running to him recalls the rebirth of Marcel's involuntary memories of his childhood at that point in his life when his mother had ceased to discipline him for his lack of will and given him her incestuous love once again, in the form of a madeleine. Mahood imagines that, after his death, Madeleine will replace his head with a "vegetable-marrow, or a big pineapple with its little tuft, or better still, I don't know why, a swede, in memory of me. Then I shall not vanish quite..." (*TN*, 329). But, as in *Molloy*, the fiction of an individual, like that of a social voice, is ironically negated by language's production of this voice.

Language's subversion of the social signs of individuality or of humanity that society tries to impose on it, however, is no more successful in liberating language from society than society is successful in liberating its voice from language. They exist together in mutual negation. Mahood and Madeleine "made a balls of it between us, I with my signs and she with her reading of them" (*TN*, 330). Madeleine can read only madness in language's resistance to social determination, whereas language's turning of tropes towards and away from the conventional meanings that society imposes on it can only produce doubt about a socially defined human or individual voice: "I merely doubt that I am in [the jar]. It is easier to raise a shrine than bring the deity down to haunt it" (*TN*, 343). The very notion that Mahood can roll his eyes and drool, the general turning of language's tropes away from and towards language, negates the notion that the text can exist only in an immobile "here and now."

Society's response to the madness of language's rhetoric is to forcibly transform the sign into a social lie that hides language's mad questioning of society's voices. By putting a cement collar around the narrator's head and immobilizing it, Madeleine forces him to see "approximately the same set of hallucinations exactly," not unlike the inhabitants of Plato's cave. She ensures that her customers will read in him (and he in himself) the same sign of human production and consumption of conventional signs (*TN*, 332).[14] This overbearing mother figure puts the first-person pronoun in a narrative straitjacket. But, as the contradiction between "approximately" and "exactly" suggests, the text not only doubts the social subject Madeleine constructs; it tries to kill off this subject by transforming it into another fictional social voice that is produced ironically by the materiality of language's signs.

Mahood's two stories both culminate in parabasis: the text's retraction of its identification with the fictional narrative voices that it has produced, a retraction that renders these voices ironical: "The stories of Mahood are ended. He has realized they could not be about me" (*TN*, 345). Mahood's stories are, both, "about" the failed attempt to subordinate allegory to irony. They argue that allegory is always already negated by the space between the text's ironical assertions and negations of any voice, including an allegorical one. But these stories fail to reach their ironical conclusion. Mahood realizes, therefore, that they are not about "me," the text. The text is something other than Mahood's attempts to ironize allegory.

The text's last narrator, the "all impotent, all nescient" Worm, marks the text's last attempt and failure to subordinate allegory's production and deconstruction of voices to language's ironical assertion and negation of the voices it mechanically produces. Worm, as an animal, is a narrating voice that is neither individual nor social. It does not even have the "sentiment de l'existence comme il peut frémir au fond d'un animal," which Proust imagines his narrator has when he first begins to awaken: "[Worm's] senses tell him nothing, nothing about himself, nothing about the rest..." (*TN*, 346). Unlike Mahood's two voices, Worm is from the start nothing for itself, neither signification nor action. It is non-human, but rather mobile, dumb materiality, like the formal turning of language's tropes. For the text's only narrator to be a worm is for it to become everything that humanity despises, as in the Christian bible: "But I am a worm, and no man; a reproach of men, and despised of the people" (Psalms 22:6). More importantly, Beckett's Worm resembles another biblical worm. It is a tool of justice that consumes the wicked: "The Womb shall forget him; the worm shall feed sweetly on him; he shall be no more remembered; and wickedness shall be broken as a tree." (Job 24:20).[15] But unlike the biblical worm, Beckett's Worm consumes and erases from memory, not just the wicked, but the very notion of the human, which is at the heart of Christianity. By redefining the first-person pronoun as signifying only Worm's non-human, non-sentient erasure of the human, the text tries to transform the "I" into a non-signifying, moving materiality that no longer refers either to a voice or to language's formal act of enunciation. If the turning of the text's formal tropes becomes Worm's blind unthinking movement, then this turning ironically undercuts any voices that individually or socially chosen words might attach to it.

As pure materiality, Worm can exist only for others, for the words of others that attribute thought, action, and being to the text: "Feeling nothing, knowing nothing, he exists nevertheless, but not for himself, for others. Others conceive him and say, Worm is, since we conceive him, as if there

The Unnamable: *The death of the ironical self* 151

could be no being but being conceived..." (*TN*, 346). Only in society's words does Worm's materiality become a voice that ironically negates the illusion that it has a voice, as when the text says "I am Worm": "It's a lot to expect of one creature, it's a lot to ask, that he should first behave as if he were not, then as if he were, before being admitted to that peace where he neither is, nor is not, and where the language dies that permits of such expressions" (*TN*, 334–35). In saying "I am Worm," the text acts "as if" the "I" were both a voice that affirms its existence ("I am") and a voice that denies its existence ("I am a worm," which cannot exist for itself). Society's words may give birth to Worm as voice, they do so without his coming alive (he "[c]ome[s] into the world unborn, abiding there unliving"), yet without his being able to die (it is "with no hope of death...") (*TN*, 346). The social context prevents the purely material pronoun "I" and the purely mechanical turning of language's tropes from taking refuge in language's materiality, from not acting as if it is or as if it is not.

The text's failure to achieve the neither/nor of the pure materiality of language prevents it from taking Worm as its narrator. All its attempts to speak as if it were Worm take the form of irony of irony: "Let it go through me at last, the right [voice], the last one, his who has none, by his own confession" (*TN*, 347).[16] The text's injunction that Worm's voice "go through me" is ironical, of course, since Worm is defined as the absence of voice, as a non-voice of language. But this very definition of Worm as a negation of voice, its "confession" that it has no voice, is in turn ironically undercut by our knowledge that Worm, as a worm, cannot say that it has no voice, cannot confess:

[T]he instant [Worm] hears the sound that will never stop. Then it's the end, Worm no longer is. We know it, but we don't say it, we say it's the awakening, the beginning of Worm, for now we must speak, and speak of Worm. It's no longer he, but let us proceed as if it were still he, he at last, who hears, and trembles, and is delivered over, to affliction and the struggle to withstand it, the starting eye, the labouring mind. Yes, let us call that thing Worm, so as to exclaim, the sleight of hand accomplished... I'm Worm, that is to say I am no longer he, since I hear. But I'll forget that in the heat of misery... (*TN*, 349)

The very moment when the text adopts as its voice the materiality of language and makes Worm speak about itself, it falls into irony of irony, which undercuts any voice of language. The text's creation of a voice that cannot be reduced to language's pure materiality is thus more than a product of the formal turning of language's tropes. It marks a negation of language's ability to speak itself, as Heidegger would like, without exceeding itself and becoming something more or less than language. Language's obligation to personify, to express, ironically undercuts its ironical negation of the human voices it creates, its ironical negation of expression.

Irony of irony thus subordinates irony to allegory once again: "The voices and thoughts of the devils who beset me... make me say... that since I couldn't be Mahood, as I might have been, I must be Worm, as I cannot be" (*TN*, 347). The text situates itself in a temporal gap between its past failure to be a self-aware, ironical negation of society's voices and the future impossibility of its being the ironical, pure, unself-aware material movement of language.

Beckett's text thus cannot imprison itself within an endless spiral of ironical negations, as de Man believes. At some point, irony negates its own existence and necessarily produces what it knows to be impossible: the search to give a new voice in time. The ironical "here and now" is always already defined in relation to a fleeting allegorical "there and then."

Whence comes this slippage towards the death of the ironical narrator and the rebirth of an allegorical narrator who cannot complete the narrative of his search to kill off voice, who is always "not yet at the last extremity" (*TN*, 308)? *The Unnamable* discusses the transition from irony of irony to allegory in a passage quoted above from the beginning of *The Unnamable*. The passage borrows key words and the bulk of its argument from Proust. The text states at the beginning of its discourse, "to me I must attribute a beginning" (*TN*, 296). The original French version says: "[J]e dois supposer un commencement à mon séjour ici, ne serait-ce que pour la commodité du récit."[17] The phrase "pour la commodité du récit" is borrowed from the passage of the *Recherche* in which Proust's narrator discloses his failure to recount the genesis of Albertine's lies, and thus to prove that she is lying, without himself lying (*R*, 3: 153). As discussed in Chapter 4, Marcel alleges that it is Albertine's stories that deceitfully project their immoral actions onto someone else. His only evidence that her stories are doing this, however, is his memory of her having told the same story in the past, but in reference to her own actions, rather than her friend's. His memory of her first telling of the story is, however, vague and doubtful. In order to convict her of lying in his own mind, he has had to invent, for "la commodité du récit," a distinct beginning and end. He has had to invent a past Albertine, who openly admitted that the actions she recounted were hers. He has had to lie in order to prove that she is lying.

Proust's passage, I argued, puts into question the very possibility of irony. Albertine's transition from "I" to "she" in her two tellings of the same sexually incriminating story is the prototypical gesture of de Man's ironist, whose words deceitfully substitute a false empirical self for a linguistic self, but ironically undercut this substitution. De Man calls this substitution of "she" for "I," this self-aware transference, the ironist's invention "of a form of himself that is 'mad' but that does not know its own madness" (*TN*, 198). In Proust's case, the present narrator masks his present deceitful voice as a past deceitful voice: the protagonist who does not know that he is mad when he projects his deceitful substitution of Albertine's lies for his own onto her deceitful substitution of a friend's lies for her own. The protagonist ironically and madly negates Albertine's substitution of "she" (her friend) for "I" (herself), while the narrator ironically negates the protagonist's blind substitution of "she" (Albertine) for "I" (Marcel). The protagonist is mad but does not know he is mad, while the narrator appears to have overcome the protagonist's madness and achieved self-awareness as an ironical negation of his protagonist's blind lying about lying.

But the present narrator's irony turns against itself in what appears to be another turn in de Man's endless spiral of irony. By accusing his past voice of falsely substituting "she" for "I," he indirectly accuses his present voice of doing the same when it substitutes the protagonist's past empirical voice for his present linguistic voice.[18] Irony marks its own madness. This ironical revelation of language's present deceit throws the narrator's discourse into the ironist's and liar's paradox.[19] Irony cannot state that it is ironical without undercutting its own statement by indirectly calling this statement ironical as well. But, just as we cannot know whether the person who says he is lying is telling the truth about his lying or whether he is lying about his lying, so we cannot know whether the narrator who says he is ironical is telling the truth about his irony or ironically negating the notion that he is ironical. Irony's possible negation of its own ironical status opens the text up to the search for the truth of whether the text is ironical, to the endless failed narratives of allegory: the replacement of Worm with Mahood and his stories. By referring to this passage in Proust, Beckett paradoxically marks his own deconstruction of irony of irony as a transhistorical repetition of Proust's irony of irony.

Beckett also repeats Proust's foregrounding of forgetting as the source of its allegorical deconstruction of irony: "ma mémoire... avait cru inutile de garder copie" (*R*, 3: 153). The words of *The Unnamable*, its manuscript ("copie"), forget not only who the "I" is, but what it is doing: "The fact would seem to be, if in my situation one may speak of facts, not only that I shall have to speak of things of which I cannot speak, but also, which is even more interesting, but also that I, which is if possible even more interesting, that I shall have to, I forget, no matter" (*TN*, 291). The first-person pronoun may refer to the act of enunciating words, the text's words forget what this act is doing. This forgetting is fatal to the ironist, who must know that every affirmation he makes is always already negated. At the heart of the ironist's paradox, therefore, is language's forgetting of its own speech acts, the allegory of its being too late to say what it is doing.

The present of the narrator's speech act, its "here and now," thus takes the form of a past that the text has forgotten and a future repetition that its forgetting defers.[20] Irony is just an aspect, an appearance that seems to reveal the reality of allegory. But allegory is itself only an appearance that seems to disclose the reality of irony.

The Unnamable thus explains why it cannot answer its opening questions about what its voice is: "Where now? Who now? When now?" The reason it cannot answer is not its isolation in an ironical present, since this present is always already becoming non-present, self-forgetting, and self-deferring. The present of the text cannot say what its voice is because it is caught between two non-voices, the non-voices, the voids, of irony and allegory.

The text's transition from irony to allegory thus puts into question the neither/nor logics of irony and allegory. Irony of irony uses a neither/nor logic to situate the text within a "here and now." It negates the assertion that the text is spoken by the past voice of a protagonist, the present voice of a narrator, or an ironical voice of language. Irony of irony, for Beckett, is a formal structure of language, a non-voice, which constitutes the text spatially in an indifferent middle that is neither outside nor inside language: "I am the thing that divides the world in two, on the one side the outside, on the other the inside, that can be as thin as foil, I'm neither one side nor the other, I'm in the middle, I'm the partition" (*TN*, 383). Beckett's irony negates both the text's assertions that it is a linguistic entity within language – "I'm in words, made of words" (*TN*, 386) – and its assertions that it is an empirical entity outside language – "I'm something quite different, a quite different thing, a wordless thing in an empty place... like a caged beast..." (*TN*, 386).[21] But, to the extent that irony negates its very status as a material product of language alone, then it cannot perform the act of its double negation, its neither/nor. It is as much an affirmation as a negation of the human and linguistic voices that words attribute to the "I."

Similarly, allegory is a non-voice that situates the text in the temporal difference between the "no longer" of past words that had a voice and the "not yet" of words that are only becoming a present voice: "[W]herever I go I find me, leave me, go towards me... I'm all these words, all these strangers, this dust of words, with no ground for their settling, no sky for their dispersing, coming together to say, fleeing one another to say, that I am they, all of them..." (*TN*, 386). The text is all of its words, whether they appear ironical or allegorical.

However, the transition from irony – Blanchot's silent, ironical non-voice of language – to allegory – the temporal displacement of irony into the too-lateness and too-earliness of allegory – repeatedly opens up the possibility of a voice that chooses to act in ways that are paradoxically forced on it by society or individual psychology. Language states the impossibility of reducing the text to a material linguistic event, even as it undercuts any attempt to reduce language to a product of social or psychological events.

The transition from irony to allegory thus opens the text up to the question of historical difference, despite Beckett's repetition of Proust's dramatization of the formal interplay between irony and allegory. This repetition paradoxically foregrounds the differences between the two writers' psychologically or socially influenced choices of words. Authors situate the historical relations between their works and prior or subsequent works in the unresolvable difference between the ahistorical and the historical. Beckett's trilogy may create the false impression that it can subordinate the temporal differences of allegory to the spatial differences of irony, as if all signs of historical difference between itself and Proust's *Recherche* were ironical; it cannot help but foreground Beckett's particular use of irony as that which distinguishes his trilogy from Proust's *Recherche*. Proust's *Recherche* may create the false impression that it can subordinate the spatial difference of irony to the temporal difference of allegory, the vain search for lost time, as if historical differences between itself and its precursors and followers were real; his allegory repeatedly produces an irony that puts any distinct literary historical difference into question. Despite Proust's and Beckett's failures to assert or negate literary historical difference, they both privilege the transition from irony to allegory as that which marks the birth of the act of writing – whether it be linguistic, social, or psychological – out of language, which repeatedly tries and fails to speak itself.

Notes

INTRODUCTION

1 Samuel Beckett, *Proust* (New York: Grove Press, 1970). Some of the more recent Beckett critics who have briefly commented upon the relation between the search for self in Proust and Beckett are Leslie Hill, *Beckett's Fiction: In Different Words* (Cambridge: Cambridge University Press, 1990), pp. 2–6 and Steven Connor, *Samuel Beckett: Repetition, Theory, and Text* (Oxford: Blackwell, 1988), pp. 44–45.
2 Paul de Man, "The Rhetoric of Temporality," in *Interpretations*, ed. Charles Singleton (Baltimore: Johns Hopkins University Press, 1970). As I will discuss later, de Man's analyses of the tropes of allegory and irony best analyze their temporal, if not always their spatial, structure.
3 Samuel Beckett, *Three Novels by Samuel Beckett: Molloy, Malone Dies, and The Unnamable* (New York: Grove Press, 1958), p. 293. All subsequent references to pages of this edition of the trilogy will be made within the text between parentheses and will be preceded by "*TN*"
4 "In everyday, common existence,... [language] functions much more as does the cobbler's or the carpenter's hammer, not as the material itself, but as the tool by means of which the heterogeneous material of experience is more-or-less adequately made to fit. The reflective disjunction not only occurs *by means of* language as a privileged category, but it transfers the self out of the empirical world into a world constituted out of, and in, language – a language that it finds in the world like one entity among others, but that remains unique in being the only entity by means of which it can differentiate itself from the world. Language thus conceived divides the subject into an empirical self, immersed in the world, and a self that becomes like a sign in its attempt at differentiation and self-definition." (de Man, "Rhetoric," 196)

"The ironic language splits the subject into an empirical self that exists in a state of inauthenticity and a self that exists only in the form of a language that asserts the knowledge of this inauthenticity." (de Man, "Rhetoric," 197)

"[The author] asserts... the ironic necessity of not becoming the dupe of his own irony and discovers that there is no way back from his fictional self to his actual self." (de Man, "Rhetoric," 201)
5 "[R]enouncing the nostalgia and the desire to coincide, [allegory] establishes its language in the void of th[e] temporal difference [between present and past self]" (de Man, "Rhetoric," p. 206).

Notes to page 2

6 The two selves spatially juxtaposed by irony are "the empirical and the ironic, [which] are simultaneously present, juxtaposed within the same moment but as two irreconcilable and disjointed beings" (de Man, "Rhetoric," 207).

7 I will differ from de Man in my treatment of the interplay between allegory and irony primarily in that I will replace his argument that both modes disclose the same "temporal void" with the argument that they are different ways of relating temporalization and spatialization within the text. De Man, "Rhetoric," 203. I will also argue that de Man tends to overemphasize the redefinition of allegory by irony, without discussing the redefinition of irony by allegory.

8 For the purposes of my argument, I will use the term "literary historical" to signify a temporal, intertextual relationship between the discourses of texts by different authors. Of course the literary historical may also include biographical, cultural, and social events, which may also influence the writing of the texts. But I will designate these added dimensions as "socio-cultural history." Some might argue that I am really distinguishing two aspects within literary history, others that I am distinguishing two aspects within socio-cultural history.

9 For notable exceptions see Serge Doubrovsky, *Writing and Fantasy in Proust: La place de la madeleine*, trans. Carol Mastrangelo Bové with Paul Bové (Lincoln: University of Nebraska Press, 1986) and Margaret Gray, *Postmodern Proust* (Philadelphia: Pennsylvania University Press, 1992).

10 For a paraphrase of Beckett's reading of Proust, see Bernard Brun, "Sur le *Proust* de Beckett," in *Beckett avant Beckett*, ed. Jean-Michel Rabaté (Paris: P.E.N.S., 1984), pp. 79–91. Also see John Pilling, "Beckett's *Proust*," *Journal of Beckett Studies* 1 (1976): 8–29 for a history of the writing of the essay and an analysis, not only of Beckett's essay, but also of those passages that Beckett highlighted or commented upon in his NRF (Nouvelle revue française) edition of *A la recherche du temps perdu*. Some critics who read Beckett's *Proust*, at least in part, as a reading of the *Recherche* are Pilling, "Beckett's"; Connor, *Samuel*, 44–55, 62; Nicholas Zurbrugg, *Beckett and Proust* (Gerrards Cross: Colin Smythe, 1988), pp. 101–72; Richard Terdiman, *Present Past: Modernity and the Memory Crisis* (Ithaca: Cornell University Press, 1993), pp. 159, 181, 213; John Fletcher, "Beckett et Proust," *Caliban: Annales Publiées par la Faculté des Lettres de Toulouse* 1 (1964): 89–100. Linda Ben-Zvi calls *Proust* "an excellent introduction to Proust," but only discusses Beckett's work, in *Samuel Beckett* (Boston: Twayne, 1986).

Some critics who read Beckett's *Proust*, at least in part, as an indirect reading of Beckett's discourse on writing are: Connor, *Samuel*, 44–52, 62; Pilling, "Beckett's Proust"; Zurbrugg, *Beckett*, 101–72; Steven J. Rosen, *Samuel Beckett and the Pessimistic Tradition* (New Brunswick: Rutgers University Press, 1976); Charlotte Renner, "The Self-Multiplying Narrators," in *Samuel Beckett's Molloy, Malone Dies, The Unnamable*, ed. Harold Bloom (New York: Chelsea House, 1988), pp. 97, 99; David H. Hesla, *The Shape of Chaos: An Interpretation of the Art of Samuel Beckett* (Minneapolis: University of Minnesota Press, 1971); Christopher Ricks, *Beckett's Dying Words* (Oxford: Oxford University Press, 1993); Ben-Zvi, *Samuel Beckett*, 24–27; Edith Kern, "Moran-Molloy: The

Hero as Author," in *Samuel Beckett*, ed. Harold Bloom (New York: Chelsea House, 1985), pp. 9, 11–13, 16; Hill, *Fiction*, 2–6; J. Mitchell Morse, "The Ideal Core of the Onion: Samuel Beckett's Criticism," *French Review* 38 (1964): 23–29.

Brun, "Sur le *Proust*," 91 argues, and I agree, that Beckett's *Proust* should be read neither as an accurate reading of *A la recherche du temps perdu* nor as an adequate foreshadowing of Beckett's future novels, although it clearly contains insights about both. Several critics try to read the essay as partly revelatory of Proust's novel and partly an expression of Beckett's own views. Vivian Mercier, *Beckett-Beckett* (New York: Oxford University Press, 1977), p. 90 argues that the first part of *Proust* is "a patient summary of the plot and method of *A la recherche du temps perdu*," but that in the latter part Beckett "states his own views." Zurbrugg (*Beckett*, 6–22) argues that Beckett develops negative and nihilistic currents that Proust's novel indeed contains. Zurbrugg and Brun, "Sur le *Proust*," 91 assert that Beckett ignores Proust's rejection of the negative aspects of his thought for the positive aspects of memory and, according to Zurbrugg, moral virtue. Connor (*Samuel*, 45–55) similarly argues that Beckett's essay "overstates Proust's pessimism, and undervalues the possibility of rediscovering the selves lost to time that is presented in *A la recherche du temps perdu*."

Two of the most interesting, if short, readings of the essay are Hill's and Connor's. Although Hill reads the essay as if it were an accurate commentary on the *Recherche* and on Beckett's work, he focuses on those moments of the essay that speak about logical reversal, oxymoron, and ambivalence in general. Hill makes no analysis, however, of the narrative functioning of Beckett's ambivalence. Connor reads the essay as an accurate commentary on repetition and time in Proust, but as a simplification of the functioning of these themes in *Molloy*. Both make a helpful transition from the essay to the complexity of temporality in Beckett's trilogy.

11 For the assertion that Beckett and Proust are totally opposed, see William Burroughs, "Beckett and Proust," *The Review of Contemporary Fiction* 7.2 (1987): 28–31.

For the assertion that Beckett and Proust are partially similar (particularly as regards the second half of the *Recherche*), but fundamentally opposed, see Zurbrugg, *Beckett*; Doubrovsky, *Writing*, 80–81; Leo Bersani, "Proust and the Art of Incompletion," in *Aspects of Narrative* (New York: Columbia University Press, 1971), p. 166; Olga Bernal, *Langage et fiction dans les romans de Beckett* (Paris: Gallimard, 1969), pp. 60–63, 137–38; and Richard Begam, *Samuel Beckett and the End of Modernity* (Stanford: Stanford University Press, 1996), p. 31.

For an argument that Proust is a precursor of Beckett's negative universe, see David Ellison, *The Reading of Proust* (Baltimore: Johns Hopkins, 1984), pp. 62, 146; Doubrovsky, *Writing*, 76 (Doubrovsky seems to want his madeleine and to eat it too); Thomas Trezise, *Into the Breach* (Princeton: Princeton University

Press, 1990), pp. 52–53, 65, 121; Gray, *Postmodern Proust*, 46, 54–55, 87, 168; and Richard Terdiman, *The Dialectics of Isolation: Self and Society in the French Novel from the Realists to Proust* (New Haven: Yale University Press, 1976), p. 241.

Most of the studies of the relation between Proust and Beckett, with the exception of Zurbrugg's book, have concentrated only on *Molloy*. Thematic studies of the influence of Proust on Beckett's *Molloy* include James Acheson, "The Art of Failure: Samuel Beckett's *Molloy*," *Southern Humanities Review* 17.1 (1983): 1–18; Margaret Gray, "Beckett Backwards and Forwards: The Rhetoric of Retraction in *Molloy*," *French Forum* (May 1994): 161–74; Gray, *Postmodern Proust*, 46; and Doubrovsky, *Writing*, 71–82. Only Doubrovsky carefully compares differences and similarities in the works of both authors. Also see Hans-Hager Hildebrandt, *Becketts Proust-Bilder: Erinnerung und Identität* (Stuttgart: J. B. Metzlersche Verlags Buchhandlung, 1980), which tends to see Proust everywhere in Beckett, and thus leaves one with the impression that Proust is nowhere.

Only Doubrovsky, *Writing*, 80–81 and, to some extent, Gray, *Postmodern Proust*, 46, 55 comment upon first-person narration in both Proust and Beckett's *Molloy*. Gray briefly discusses the replacement of character, self, and voice with a multiplicity of voices, a "postmodern, fractured Beckettian subject or self," in *Molloy*, in her analysis of a similar "postmodern" phenomenon in Proust.

12 Zurbrugg, *Beckett*, 252–68.
13 Acheson, "Art," 3. Zurbrugg, *Beckett*, 255, sees *Molloy* as emphasizing "the desirability of having nothing to express, nothing to say, and best of all, nothing to know." For Beckett's theoretical statement, see Samuel Beckett, "Three Dialogues," in *Samuel Beckett: A Collection of Critical Essays*, ed. Martin Esslin (Englewood Cliffs: Prentice Hall, 1965), pp. 16–22.
14 Zurbrugg, *Beckett*, 254.
15 The critical discourse on the split subject finds an early linguistic discussion in Serge Doubrovsky's reference to Emile Benveniste's "*deictic* 'I' [which] discovers its linguistic void in discourse." Doubrovsky, *Writing*, 74–76, 81; Emile Benveniste, *Problèmes de linguistique générale* (Paris: Gallimard, 1966), pp. 251–57. cf. José Angel García Landa, *Samuel Beckett y la narración reflexiva* (Zaragoza: Prensas Universitarias, 1992), p. 202, who makes a similar reading of the "I" in *The Unnamable*, and Angela Moorjani, "Beckett's Devious Deictics," in *Rethinking Beckett*, eds. Lance St. John Butler and Robin J. Davis (New York: St. Martins Press, 1990), pp. 21–22.

The deictic "I" is split between an accurate reference to the "anonymous" linguistic present of narration and a deceptive reference to an extra-linguistic personal self or identity. Because reference to a real self is a fiction, the first-person narrator can only refer to the signs with which he constructs and deconstructs, in the present of narration, the fictional selves that he appears to be remembering. Gilles Deleuze, *Proust et les signes* (Paris: Presses Universitaires de France, 1964); Doubrovsky, *Writing*, 80–81. On impersonality, see Trezise, *Breach*, 66–121.

16 See Ellison, *Reading* and Trezise, *Breach*. Ellison writes about Proust only and Trezise about Beckett only, not about their relationship, although both state in passing that the *Recherche* and the trilogy share the same structures of first-person narration.
17 See James Reid, *Narration and Description in the French Realist Novel: The Temporality of Lying and Forgetting* (Cambridge: Cambridge University Press, 1993).
18 The past protagonist and the present narrator are narrative signs that forget the narrated past and defer the present of narrating this past: the moment when the narrator would remember his forgetting. On allegory and forgetting see de Man, "Rhetoric," 205: "[I]n the retrospective perspective of the eternal 'now'" of allegory appears "a grim awareness of the de-mystifying power of death, which makes all the past appear as a flight into the inauthenticity of forgetting." Also see de Man, *Allegories of Reading: Figural Language in Rousseau, Nietzsche, Rilke, and Proust* (New Haven: Yale University Press, 1979), 78: "*A la recherche du temps perdu* narrates the flight of meaning, but this does not prevent its own meaning from being, incessantly, in flight."
19 cf. Søren Kierkegaard, *The Concept of Irony*, trans. Lee M. Capel (Bloomington: Indiana University Press, 1965), pp. 272–73.
20 Irony, according to Reiner Warning, communicates its deceptiveness by means of indirect, irony signals. Reiner Warning, "Reading Irony in Flaubert," *Style* 19 (1985): 304–16.
21 Irony is thus a "rhetorical mode" that "asserts its own deceitful properties." De Man, *Allegories*, 115.
22 An ethics of irony, I believe, would have to explore the ways in which irony, in different contexts, deceives some and enlightens others.
23 De Man, "Rhetoric," 194.
24 Doubrovsky, *Writing*, 73–74.
25 Marcel Proust, *A la recherche du temps perdu*, Bibliothèque de la Pléiade. 3 vols. (Paris: Gallimard, 1954). All subsequent references to pages of this edition of the trilogy will be made within the text between parentheses and will be preceded by "*R*" and the volume number.
26 Paul de Man, "Reading (Proust)," in *Allegories*, 57–78.
27 See for example: "Peut-être l'immobilité des choses autour de nous leur est-elle imposée par notre certitude que ce sont elles et non pas d'autres, par l'immobilité de notre pensée en face d'elles" (*R*, 1: 6). The narrator repeats the words "certes" and "certitude" in the first and last passages of *Combray* as if he were vainly trying to convince himself that he had achieved certainty of where, when, and who he was.
28 See also Trezise's discussion of this structure in the trilogy: "Moran the narrator is no longer Moran the character, and the character not yet the narrator." This inability to coincide in time, according to Trezise, describes the "allegorical nature of the first person." Allegory constitutes time as a difference between and as a repetition of "a pre-originary past" (the non-self-identity of the subject of language) and/in "a posthumous future." This posthumous future is the

unreachable moment beyond death when allegory would become a complete narrative. Trezise, *Breach*, 56.

29 Proust's writing narrator does not sleep in his mother's bed, but Marcel's mother does sleep in his bed during the night she spends with him, recounted at the beginning of *Combray*. In the passage, Marcel sleeps in an iron bed that he uses during the warm weather of the summer.

30 Of course, the writing situation of the trilogy's narrators also echoes that of Proust the author. As we know and as Beckett may have known, Proust wrote in his bed in a cork-lined bedroom, in an attempt to seal himself off from the outside world, the way the narrator of *The Unnamable* tries to seal himself off from reference outside of the pronoun "I." Moreover, Molloy writes only after his mother's death, as did Proust.

31 For Doubrovsky, Beckett's rereading of the *Recherche* in the trilogy not only "recalls," it "*denounces* Proust" by removing "the veil that [Proust] hangs" over the linguistic void to which Proust's first-person pronoun refers. Doubrovsky, *Writing*, 76.

32 cf. Trezise, *Breach*, 143. For Trezise this confusion of colors is produced by a sensory dispossession of Beckett's narrators which "contributes by analogy to the understanding of why, in the essentially verbal universe of the trilogy, an ever greater emphasis is placed on its one and only means of representation, that is, language or signification."

33 Some recent Proust critics also tend to constitute first-person narration in Proust as the repetition of the same, impersonal (what Doubrovsky calls "anonymous") narrator that is spoken by language itself. See de Man, *Allegories*, 57–78. See also Ellison, *Reading*, and Gray, *Postmodern Proust*.

34 This relation between action and the passage from irony to allegory also marks the failure of language to account for what it does and thus distinguishes my reading of the interplay between allegory and irony from Paul de Man's.

35 See Doubrovsky (*Writing*, 70–84), who implicitly treats some Beckett passages as a "burlesque" of Proust and focuses on the relation between the *Recherche* and *Molloy* (particularly Tante Léonie and Molloy). In "Beckett," Gray focuses on how *Molloy*'s two narrators, Molloy and Moran, parody certain Proustian themes, then retract this parody. Burroughs ("Beckett," 28–31) characterizes Beckett and Proust in terms of polar opposites, but he does not substantiate his characterization by reference to the novels.

Gray's study posits that *Molloy* contains literary historical references both backwards to Proust and forwards to the rest of the trilogy. This constitutes an important step towards an adequate reading of the ambiguous, literary historical relationship between the writing of the two novelists.

36 I would hope that this book will provide a first step towards future inquiries into the socio-historical relationship between first-person discourse in Proust and Beckett, although the study only speaks to the socio-historical relationship in relation to Proust. If criticism is to make a persuasive argument that Proust's and Beckett's narrators are products of socio-historical processes, then it must demonstrate how these processes influence the temporal structures that

constitute these texts and their literary historical relationships. In other words, criticism must confront the ways in which textual structures resist appropriation by socio-historical structures, as well as the ways in which socio-historical structures resist the reduction of reading to textual structures.

1 REMEMBERING FORGETTING: *LE DRAME DU COUCHER*

1 Walter Benjamin, "The Image of Proust," in *Marcel Proust's* Remembrance of Things Past, ed. Harold Bloom (New York: Chelsea House, 1987), pp. 37–49.
2 Richard Terdiman, "Deconstructing Memory: On Representing the Past and Theorizing Culture in France Since the Revolution," *Diacritics* (Winter 1985): 14; see also Terdiman, *Present Past*.
3 Friedrich Nietzsche, "On the Uses and Disadvantages of History for Life," in *Untimely Meditations*, trans. R. J. Hollingdale (Cambridge: Cambridge University Press, 1983), pp. 59–123; Michel Foucault, *Les Mots et les choses* (Paris: Gallimard, 1966).
4 Beckett, *Three Novels*, 7.
5 For a discussion of forgetting as the fragmentation of a linear narrative line, see Jerry Aline Flieger, "Proust, Freud, and the Art of Forgetting," *Sub-Stance* 29 (1981): 66–82.
6 For a useful summary of past readings of this scene, see Gray, *Postmodern Proust*, 140, 149. Also of interest is her discussion of the scene, pp. 138–48. cf. Ellison, *Reading*, 46.
7 See *R*, 3: 256 for the narrator's discussion of the author's accent in the work of art.
8 What he seeks to remember is *"le souvenir d'une lecture oubliée."* Eliane Boucquey, "Les Trois Arbres d'Hudimesnil: souvenir retrouvé," in *Bulletin de la Société des Amis de Marcel Proust et des Amis de Combray* 38 (1988): 76.
9 Ross Chambers, *Mélancolie et opposition: les débuts du modernisme* (Paris: José Corti), 1987.
10 Sanford S. Ames, "The Ruse of a Condemned Man: First Writing in *A la recherche*, in *Reading Proust Now* (New York: Peter Lang, 1990), p. 49.
11 Samuel Weber, "Le Madrépore," *Poétique* 13 (1973): 43.
12 See Gray, *Postmodern Proust*, 143.
13 For an excellent discussion of the ethical dimension of involuntary memory see Kevin Newmark, *Beyond Symbolism: Textual History and the Future of Reading* (Ithaca: Cornell University Press, 1991), pp. 132–41.
14 Beckett, *Proust*, 49.
15 Marcel Proust, *Contre Sainte-Beuve*, Bibliothèque de la Pléiade (Paris: Gallimard, 1971), pp. 158–59; also see Melanie Klein, "Mourning and its Relation to Manic-Depressive States," in *The Selected Melanie Klein*, ed. Juliet Mitchell (New York: Free Press), 1987.
16 cf. Beckett, *Proust*, 69, where Beckett states that, in Proust, there "is no question of right and wrong."
17 See the discussion of Macmann's attempt to atone for sin in Chapter 7.

18 See Slavoj Zizek, *Enjoy your Symptom: Jacques Lacan in Hollywood and out*, 2nd edn. (New York: Routledge, 2001), pp. 82–105.
19 cf. Chambers, *Mélancolie*, 229–30; Weber, "Madrépore," 43:
Dès lors, la présence de l'objet – qui est invariablement "maternel" – doit être médiatisée, acquise mais tenue à distance: telle est la tâche de la narration et de ses 'métonymies.' C'est là un discours qui cherche à éluder son propre désir en l'exprimant comme "pure" fiction. Et son prototype est cette "lectrice infidèle," la mère de Marcel, qui lit pour lui dans sa chambre en omettant les passages amoureux: infidèle mais, par les accents de sa voix, "admirable."
20 cf. Ellison, *Reading*, 185.
21 In Weber's words, "[l]e sacrifice que Marcel ne peut faire à un père sans principes," the sacrifice of his mother's presence, "se renverse en sacrifice du fils par le père," the sacrifice of memory, mother, and self, and "le sacrifice de la voix" in writing an autobiographical novel. Weber, "Madrépore," 42–43.

2 IMPRESSIONS, THE INSTANT OF ARTISTIC CONSCIOUSNESS, AND SOCIAL HISTORY

1 Beckett, *Proust*, 17, 25–30, 43–46, 55.
2 See Flieger, "Proust," 73.
3 For the question of emancipation, also see Vincent Descombes, *Proust: philosophie du roman* (Paris: Minuit, 1987), p. 153; David Sidorsky, "Modernism and the Emancipation of Literature from Morality: Teleology and Vocation in Joyce, Ford, and Proust," *New Literary History* 15.1 (1989): 13; and Terdiman, *Present Past*, 201–8. "[Cocteau] recognized Proust's blind, senseless, frenzied quest for happiness." Walter Benjamin, "Image of Proust," p. 39.
4 See Fredric Jameson, *Postmodernism: or the Cultural Logic of Late Capitalism* (Durham: Duke University Press, 1991), p. 412 and Descombes, *Proust*, 47–66 for discussions of inherent contradictions in Proust's modernist theory. See Pierre Bourdieu, *Les Règles de l'art* (Paris: Seuil, 1992), pp. 75–164 and Terdiman, *Present Past*, 182 for the emergence – within French social space of the second half of the nineteenth century – of the myth of autonomy from the social.

The story of the first-person narrator's artistic forgetting has important consequences for the first-person plural, the sign of a collective subject that is implied by the sign of a single subject, the first-person. The implied "we" of cultural discourse often reduces the "I" to an expression of the unique attributes of a particular group's discourse on the world. Marguerite Duras's works would thus be the product of her unconscious femininity, which she shares with other women, Bernard Dadié's of his singularly African nature, and Gide's or Proust's of their distinctive homosexuality. However, Proust's allegory of the first-person narrator's artistic forgetting raises the more general question of whether any discourse, personal or social, can be sufficiently autonomous from the impersonal structures of language and of social history in order to be the unconscious remembrance of an historically different, personal or social, forgotten source. cf. Lee Edelman, "Homographesis," *Yale Journal of Criticism*

3.1 (1989): 189 and Jean-François Lyotard, *The Postmodern Condition: A Report on Knowledge*, foreword Fredric Jameson, trans. Geoff Bennington and Brian Massumi (Minneapolis: Minnesota University Press, 1984), pp. 77–78.

5 There are places where the narrator may appear to state that exact images are remembered. But the thing represented is never more than a metaphor for the gaze and the images it evokes: "[u]ne chose que nous avons regardée autrefois, si nous la revoyons, nous rapporte, avec le regard que nous y avons posé, toutes les images qui le remplissaient alors" (*R*, 3: 885). The narrator concludes the same paragraph by saying that "les choses gardaient l'essence" of the past and that "cette essence est en partie subjective et incommunicable" (*R*, 3: 885).

6 cf. Beckett, *Proust*, 64.

7 Beckett, *Proust*, 23. For Proust's narrator, the external objects that occasion involuntary memories are not, as Beckett supposed, retained in memory: "Involuntary memory... restores, not merely the past object, but the Lazaraus that it charmed or tortured..." Beckett, *Proust*, 17, 20, 56. The young Beckett who wrote *Proust* does not seem to realize that Proust transforms Shelling's "identity" between mind and material world into Schopenhauer's identity between mind and its mental world. cf. Anne Henry, *Proust romancier: le tombeau égyptien* (Paris: Flammarion, 1983), pp. 44–57, 49 and Paul Ricoeur, *Temps et récit*, vol. 2 (Paris: Seuil, 1984), pp. 196–98. What form this identity takes and whether it even exists is a subject of these chapters.

8 Georges Poulet, *Etudes sur le temps humain* (Paris: Plon, 1949), p. 373. For opposing views, see Descombes, *Proust*, 271; Henry, *Proust romancier*, 29. Beckett falls prey to the illusion of a passive Proustian art when he is "reminded of Schopenhauer's definition of the artistic procedure as 'the contemplation of the world independently of the principle of reason'" (Beckett, *Proust*, 66). Just as voluntary memory, because it is habitual, is partially involuntary, so involuntary memory, when it becomes conscious or written, is partially voluntary and rational. Also see Poulet, *Etudes*, 397 and Edouard Morot-Sir's comments on the voluntary/involuntary paradox, "The PARADOX of the LIAR and the WRITING I IN PROUST," *Reading Proust Now* (New York: Peter Lang, 1990), pp. 28–29.

9 See Flieger, "Proust," 74–79.

10 Deleuze, *Proust*.

11 The essence produced by Proust's art of forgetting is not the one suggested by Mallarmé's forgetting: "Je dis: une fleur!, et, hors de l'oubli ou ma voix relègue aucun contour... se lève... l'absente de tous bouquets." Edouard Mallarmé, "Crise de vers," in *Mallarmé*, ed. Anthony Hartley (Baltimore: Penguin, 1965), p. 174. Rather than suggest an ideal object, Proust's art of forgetting suggests an ineffable, unique subject. This subject refers to the artist's atemporal manner of seeing, which characterizes his uniqueness at all moments in his life ("Les parties du mur couvertes de peintures [d'Elstir étaient] toutes homogènes les unes aux autres" [*R*, 2: 419]) and his temporal manner of seeing at each moment of his life ("l'être que nous fumes" [*R*, 1: 643]). cf. Anne Henry, *Marcel Proust: Théories pour une esthétique* (Paris: Klincksieck, 1981), p. 59 for a

discussion of the consequences of Proust's romantic interiorization of Mallarmé's "Idea."

12 Schopenhauer, unlike Proust, identifies art with particular perceptions alone: "'What is life?' Every genuine and successful work of art answers this question in its own way quite calmly and serenely. But all the arts speak only the naive and childlike language of *perception*, not the abstract and serious language of *reflection*; their answer is thus a fleeting image, not a permanent universal knowledge." Arthur Schopenhauer, *The World as Will and Representation*, 2 vols. (New York: Dover, 1958), vol. 2, p. 406. By contrast, the particular multiplicity of Proust's childlike impressions have always already been imprinted in the mind as abstract signs. Of course, in positing that differences between these abstract signs retain the essence of particular impressions, Proust posits the paradox of theorizing a non-general essence or a generalized particularity (cf. Deleuze, *Proust*, 123).

13 Descriptions of past impressions and instants are made possible by everyday, as well as artistic, forgetting. Voluntary memory erases impressions from consciousness. By erasing impressions from consciousness, however, it inscribes them indelibly within the unconscious: "[C]e qui nous rappelle le mieux un être, c'est justement ce que nous avions oublié (parce que c'était insignifiant, et que nous lui avons laissé toute sa force)" (*R*, 1: 643). See Flieger, "Proust," 66–69. As Beckett wryly explains: "Strictly speaking, we can only remember what has been registered by our extreme inattention and stored in that ultimate and inaccessible dungeon of our being to which Habit does not possess the key..." (Beckett, *Proust*, 18). Involuntary memory's forgetting of conventional signs enables it to retrieve what voluntary memory's forgetting has locked away for safekeeping in the unconscious. Beckett's word "dungeon" makes it all too clear that the impressions that involuntary memory retrieves are guilty of crimes. They must be locked away, repressed from consciousness, as all-too-clear signs of the incestuous desire for mother in Proust. Beckett, as his trilogy will make clear, is extremely aware of the incestuous implications of Proust's discourse.

14 See Doubrovsky, *Writing*, 79: "If, in our treatment of the text as logograph, we said that the first offer of the *madeleine-tea* functioned, in the play of symbolic substitutions, as *lait-thé* (milk-tea) – Lethe (the mythological river cited by Proust, *Recherche*, vol. 2, p. 116), we can better grasp *which waters* we must cross in order for this 'exquisite pleasure'... to project outside of time." Also see Plato's dialectic, which methodically erases the world's changing appearances, and Schopenhauer's art of universal will, which acts out an "oubli des contenus particuliers de la conscience": "La seule façon d'échapper à la limitation de la volonté particulière était, jugeait Schopenhauer, de s'élever jusqu'à la contemplation du Vouloir universel, contemplation qui ne s'obtient point par une réduction abstraite, mais par un oubli des contenus particuliers de la conscience..." (Henry, *Marcel Proust*, 49). Also see Schopenhauer, *World*, vol. 2: 140: "From *the form of time and of the single dimension* of the series of representations, on account of which the intellect, in order to take up one thing,

must drop everything else, there follows not only the intellect's distraction, but also its *forgetfulness*." And finally, see Proust in "John Ruskin," Proust, *Contre Sainte-Beuve*, 121.
15 Beckett, *Proust*, 64–67. Beckett characterizes this combination of the voluntary and the involuntary as the difference between the artist and the artisan. The artist "has acquired his text" through the passive "contemplation" of his involuntary memories, whereas the " 'duty and task of a writer ... are those of a translator' " who "explains" them by taking them apart. But Beckett does not seem to be aware that Proust's artist not only takes apart the artist's involuntary memories, he provokes them.
16 Henry, *Proust romancier*, 59.
17 Benjamin, "Image of Proust," 40.
18 Descombes, *Proust*, 278.
19 Descombes, *Proust*, 244.
20 Paul de Man, "Autobiography as De-Facement," in *The Rhetoric of Romanticism* (New York: Columbia University Press, 1984), pp. 67–82.
21 Flieger, "Proust," 74–79.
22 Paul de Man argues that *A la recherche du temps perdu* "claims to be the narrative extension of one single moment of recollection." *Allegories*, 67.
23 For a detailed, if one-sided view of how society's impersonal structures "determine," rather than merely influence, the personal artist as a social fiction, see Bourdieu, *Règles*.
 Contrary to what Richard Terdiman has argued, Proust's narrator demonstrates in many passages that he is aware that his work cannot help but partially reflect history, including the socio-historical conditions of its production, even as he asserts that, metaphorically, the work is outside history. Of course Proust would probably not say that these conditions determine, rather than influence, his text. See Terdiman, *Present Past*, 151–239 and Gray, *Postmodern Proust*, 119.
24 *Proust*, 6. "Peut-être l'immobilité des choses autour de nous leur est-elle imposée par notre certitude que ce sont elles et non pas d'autres, par l'immobilité de notre pensée en face d'elles" (*R*, 2: 6). Once again, Beckett's incorrect belief that Proust's novelist enacts a synthesis of the subject and a real external object leads him to misunderstand that reality for Proust is neither mobile nor immobile. Immobility as well as mobility, space, and time are ways in which the mind structures external reality.
25 See Jack Flam, "The New Painting," *New York Review of Books* 41.19 (1994): 52.
26 Beckett, *Proust*, 64.
27 Flam, "Painting," 48–53.
28 Serge Gaubert notes that Proust
 [passe] entre 1895 et 1900 ... d'une lecture référentielle de certains tableaux – de Chardin ou de Corot entre autres – à une lecture qu'il faudrait appeler "structurelle." Tel tableau l'intéresse moins en lui-même que par comparaison avec tel autre du même peintre; mieux, les deux tableaux retiennent son attention parce qu'il peut à partir d'eux construire mentalement un tableau idéal, constitué des seuls caractères différentiés de la manière du peintre. (Serge Gaubert, "Marcel Proust: Le vieil homme

et la peinture," in *Mélanges offerts à Georges Couton* [Lyon: Presses Universitaires de Lyon, 1981], p. 579)
29 See Bourdieu, *Règles*, 162–64.
30 Flam, "Painting," 50.
31 Anne Henry, "Quand une peinture métaphysique sert de propédeutique à l'écriture: Les Métaphores d'Elstir dans *A la recherche du temps perdu*," in *La Critique artistique: Un genre littéraire* (Paris: Presses Universitaires de France, 1983): 221.
32 See Reid, *Narration*, 7–9.
33 *Allegories*, 16.
34 "[Le point de vue] n'est pas individuel, mais au contraire principe d'individuation." Deleuze, *Proust*, 133.
35 "[T]he narrator becomes an incestuously desiring mother – a mother of the very kind that, as a child, he had most wished to have." Malcolm Bowie, *Freud, Proust and Lacan: Theory as Fiction* (Cambridge: Cambridge University Press, 1987), p. 83.
36 Beckett, *Proust*, 51; see Chapter 5 of this book for a discussion of the relationship of this ambiguity to Beckett's *Molloy*.
37 In the fête painting, allegory's temporalization of the Instant, the flight of the present into the past, already reintroduces the question of social history. The flight of the Instant in the fête painting creates the impression that the working-class woman "allait bientôt s'en retourner." She is leaving the space of the personal artistic gaze and rejoining her family and society, just as the artist will do when he stops observing or painting her and as Marcel will do when he remembers his snobbish desire to become a part of the elite social group at the dinner. The allegorical act of erasing signs of social history in order to project a personal vision thus ultimately states allegory's erasure of any signs of that vision and allegory's reinscription into the society that rejects this vision. The status of this reinscription, however, remains in question.
38 Jameson, *Postmodernism*, 411–12.
39 De Man, *Allegories*, 12–19.
40 cf. Proust, *Contre Sainte-Beuve*, 255, 667.
41 cf. Jameson, *Postmodernism*, 412. Jameson mistakenly associates irony with the modernist, when in fact it is a central means by which the postmodern negates modernist illusion.
42 See Diane R. Leonard, "Literary Evolution and the Principle of Perceptibility: The Case of Ruskin, Proust, and Modernism," in *Proceedings of the Xth Congress of the International Comparative Literature Association*, eds. Anna Balakian and James J. Wilhelm (New York: Garland, 1985), p. 133. Also see the description of Elstir's painting of "Miss Sacripant" (*R*, 1: 848).
43 Elstir's wife serves as a similar reminder that, no matter how artificial and ironical language may be, it sometimes fails to deceive or to ironically assert as true what is in fact false. Despite itself, language may coincide with a referent:
> Plus tard, quand je connus la peinture mythologique d'Elstir..., [j]e compris qu'à un certain type idéal résumé en certaines lignes... qui se retrouvaient sans cesse dans son oeuvre... il avait attribué en fait un caractère presque divin... [Il] le rencontra,

réalisé au dehors, dans ... le corps de celle qui était par la suite devenue madame Elstir. (*R*, 1: 850)

See also the narrator's comments on Ossian's poetry, which reminds him that "[l]e passé n'est pas fugace, il reste sur place" (*R*, 2: 418).

3 LYING, IRONY, AND POWER: PROUST'S DECEPTIVE ALLEGORIES

1. Beckett, *Proust*, 28.
2. For example, Beckett, *Proust*, 60–62.
3. Alison Winton, *Proust's Additions*, 2 vols. (Cambridge: Cambridge University Press, 1977), vol. 1, p. 264.
4. Marcel Proust, *Albertine disparue* (Paris: Grasset, 1987). See also Reginald McGinnis, "L'Inconnaissable Gomorrhe: A propos d'*Albertine disparue*," *Romanic Review* 81.1 (1990): 92–104 and René Girard, *Deceit, Desire, and the Novel*, trans. Yvonne Freccero (Baltimore: Johns Hopkins University Press, 1976).
5. Beckett, *Proust*, 43–44.
6. Proust, *Albertine*, 111–12. This "proof" is a letter that situates her death, not in "la Touraine," as the handwritten manuscript stated, but near "la Vivonne," a river not far from Mlle Vinteuil's house, Montjouvain, where he first glimpsed lesbian love. The proximity between Albertine's place of death and Mlle Vinteuil's den of iniquity, along with her admission that she had known Mlle Vinteuil, demonstrates conclusively, Marcel now decides, that her words of heterosexual desire for him were lies hiding her homosexual desires for women.
7. McGinnis, "Gomorrhe," 103; Proust, *Albertine*, 16; Doubrovsky, "Writing," 95. "Solitude is not solipsism: through a book the Other can be transported into us, can live in us." Doubrovsky, "Writing," 69.
8. Proust, *Albertine*, 16; cf. Beckett, *Proust*, 41.
9. cf. Doubrovsky, *Writing*, 48, 74–75; Ellison, *Reading*, 165–85.
10. Beckett, *Proust*, 25.
11. Musical projection through voluntary differentiation also repeats, as in all avant-garde works, the great classical works, which were created, according to Proust's narrator, by the same process (*R*, 2: 420). See Antoine Compagnon, *Proust Between Two Centuries*, trans. Richard E. Goodkin (New York: Columbia University Press, 1992), pp. 253–56.
12. If the repetition of Vinteuil's "accent" is, as Beckett argues, Schopenhauer's "Idea itself," then the Idea can be revealed only by means of repeated, deceptive differences, where voluntary differences are the equivalent of death and where life is the repetition of the Idea or accent. Beckett, *Proust*, 70–72.
13. Descombes, *Proust*, 255; see Deleuze, *Proust*, 56–57 for this post-romantic aspect of involuntary memory in Proust. cf. Henry, *Marcel Proust*, 124–40 for an informative discussion of Proust's German romantic background, the development of German romanticism in French philosophy at the end of the nineteenth century, and an argument that Proust's involuntary memory does conform to a romantic synthesis of subject and object.

14 Henry, *Marcel Proust*, 276.
15 Johann Wolfgang von Goethe, *Selected Verse* (New York: Penguin, 1964), p. 196; cf. Deleuze, *Proust*, 63; Ellison, *Reading*, 96–101; and Newmark, *Beyond Symbolism*, 111: "Who, or perhaps better, what, would be the 'identity' of that which can only be preserved as something totally different?"
16 Doubrovsky, "Writing," 52.
17 See Julia Kristeva, *Proust: Questions d'identité* (London: Oxford University Press, 1998) and *Le Temps sensible: Proust et l'expérience littéraire* (Paris: Gallimard, 1994) on the fundamental role of sado-masochism in Proust. For example, on Proust's asthma: "A moins que l'asthme ne soit, plus archaïquement, la mémoire d'une impossible individuation, d'une caverne sensorielle précisément, où se lovent, amoureux acharnés, mère et enfant. Le narrateur ne peut s'en sortir que par ce violent arrachement lui aussi sensorial qu'est l'autoflagellation asthmique" (Kristeva, *Temps*, 296).
18 For the relation of this optimistic synthesis of lying and forgetting to individual difference, cf. Deleuze, *Proust*, 23–65. For its relation to the modern institution of writing as an act of social/religious individualization see Descombes, *Proust*, 313–22. For readings of lying as totally incompatible with Proustian artistic essence see McGinnis, "Gomorrhe," 103; Ellison, *Reading*, 175–76. It is important to underline that lying in the *Recherche* functions not only as a negation, but also as a possible affirmation of past and self.
19 Beckett, *Proust*, 66–67.
20 Beckett, *Proust*, 2.
21 "Je n'avais plus aucune impatience de voir Albertine" (*R*, 3: 157); Beckett, *Proust*, 16.
22 Samuel Beckett, "Three Dialogues," p. 17. Beckett associates art with "[t]he expression that there is nothing to express, nothing with which to express, nothing from which to express, no power to express, no desire to express, together with the obligation to express."
23 cf. Leo Bersani, "The Culture of Redemption: Marcel Proust and Melanie Klein," *Critical Inquiry* 12 (1986): 415 and Descombes, *Proust*, 65–66.
24 Beckett, *Proust*, 1–17.
25 Proust's narrator uses "materialist" in at least two different senses. In the early discussion of Elstir's watercolors, it means realist illusion itself: "Que de tels objets puissent exister, beaux en dehors même de l'interprétation du peintre, cela contente en nous un matérialisme inné, combattu par la raison, et sert de contrepoids aux abstractions de l'esthéthique" (*R*, 1: 848). In this later passage, "materialist" means "l'hypothèse...du néant" (*R*, 3: 381), where all autobiographical allusion is deceitful.
26 Friedrich Nietzsche, *The Will to Power*, trans. Walter Kaufmann and R. J. Hollingdale (New York: Vintage, 1968), pp. 138–39.
27 cf. Deleuze, *Proust*, 176.
28 For a subtle Lacanian analysis of homosexuality and sexual difference, see Slavoj Zizek, *The Ticklish Subject: The Absent Center of Political Ontology* (London: Verso, 1999), pp. 269–79. cf. J. E. Rivers, *Proust and the Art of Love: The Aesthetics*

of Sexuality in the Life, Times, and Art of Marcel Proust (New York: Columbia University Press, 1980).
29 See Compagnon, *Proust*, 240, 241. According to the narrator, even those homosexuals who have relationships with lesbians "jouent pour la femme qui aime les femmes le rôle d'une autre femme, et la femme leur offre en même temps à peu près ce qu'ils trouvent chez l'homme" (*R*, 2: 622). There are other suggestions that Marcel might be a woman in a man's body. Homosexuals who love women, he says, prefer lesbians (*R*, 2: 622).
30 Zizek, *Ticklish Subject*, 275–76.
31 See McGinnis, "Gomorrhe," 103.
32 Ellison, *Reading*, 166.
33 Nietzsche, "Uses," 96. cf. Ellison, *Reading*, 175.
34 cf. "[T]he truth of love is the lie, but the lie is ultimately the truth of the truth." Sharon Willis, "'Gilbertine' Apparue." *Romanic Review*, 72.3 (1982): 334. See also Ellison, *Reading*, 28–29.
35 See Ellison, *Reading*, 185; Descombes, *Proust*, 247; Gray, *Postmodern Proust*, 44; McGinnis, "Gomorrhe," and Terdiman, *Present Past*, for readings that subordinate referential lying to the ironical revelation of the truth of lying. Ellison's is by far the most interesting. Although he traces an irreversible allegory that deconstructs autobiographical error and reveals the truth of lying and irony, he also asserts that the text alternates, reversibly, between the two.
> Confessional autobiography is the constantly repeated erroneous moment of subjective delusion whose "unraveling" in allegory produces a uniform subcurrent of irony. The congruence of the fictional "Marcel" with Marcel Proust is the deceptive effect of a purely contingent coincidence. Yet the *Recherche* thrives on such deception, and it is impossible for the reader not to participate in the text's referential illusion. Reading, for Proust, involved two mutually contradictory postulations: the movement of appropriation whereby the self, in its efforts to embrace the meaning of textual events, extends beyond the confines of its subjective prison in its search for referential verification (autobiography); and the cycle of dispossession whereby the self's stability is undermined by the disseminated multiplicity of unreadable signs (fictional allegory). (Ellison, *Reading*, 185)

36 Beckett, *Proust*, 13–14. cf. Richard Goodkin, *Around Proust* (Princeton: Princeton University Press, 1991), p. 23, on Proust's uncle as a figure living only in the present, and Willis, "'Gilbertine,'" 344: "Memory, then, appears as spatialized. Albertine is caught at the moment of appearance and disappearance of truth and deception."
37 cf. McGinnis, "Gomorrhe," 102–3.
38 David Sidorsky, "Modernism and the Emancipation of Literature from Morality: Teleology and Vocation in Joyce, Ford, and Proust," *New Literary History* 15.1 (1989): 149: "Through dedication to his vocation, Proust is giving birth to a work of art that signals the restoration of his paternity. In the novel's teleology, the covenant which was broken at the outset by an act of abdication of paternal authority is regained at the conclusion by the son's discovery of the authority of art." Claudia Brodsky, "Remembering Swann: Memory and Representation in Proust," *MLN* 102.5 (1987): 1033, 1035. cf. Doubrovsky, *Writing*, 96, 108.

Notes to pages 63–66

39 Beckett, *Proust*, 51.
40 cf. Georges Poulet, *Proustian Space*, trans. Elliott Coleman (Baltimore: Johns Hopkins University Press, 1977), pp. 105–6.
41 Chambers, *Mélancolie*, 224.
42 This indifference, which the protagonist periodically feels when he is certain that Albertine is in his power, illuminates both his deconstruction of Wagner and his aesthetic pleasure in listening to Wagner. He has, "à admirer le maître de Bayreuth, aucun des scrupules de ceux à qui, comme à Nietzsche, le devoir dicte de fuir, dans l'art comme dans la vie, la beauté qui les tente" (*R*, 3: 159). When Marcel knows Albertine is returning, he ceases to jealously care about whether her words or Wagner's music lie, and he turns towards the aesthetic pleasure given by Wagner's obsessional alternation between moments that are "lointains, assoupis, presque détachés" and others that are "si pressants et si proches, si internes, si organiques, si viscéraux qu'on dirait la reprise moins d'un motif que d'une névralgie" (*R*, 3: 159). In other words, he takes an aesthetic pleasure in a musical reflection of the formal alternation of his own emotions and desires between indifference to and intense jealousy of Albertine. Such aesthetic pleasure is indifferent to whether music or words lie or are truthful. Marcel thus takes an ironical attitude towards truth and falsity and, by extension, Nietzsche's fall, in dealing with Wagner, into the very truth/falsity opposition that he consistently deconstructs elsewhere.
43 Terdiman, *Present Past*, 160–67; Jameson, *Postmodernism*, 412.
44 Bourdieu, *Règles*.
45 Descombes, *Proust*, 321.
46 Terdiman, *Present Past*, 351.
47 Terdiman, *Present Past*, 208, 225. cf. Bourdieu, *Règles*, 426–30, 434–41 on the concept of the double historicization of art.
48 Jameson, *Postmodernism*, 412. Jameson's few comments on Proust tend to reduce the *Recherche* to his model of modernism. Also see Fredric Jameson, *The Prisonhouse of Language: A Critical Account of Structuralism and Russian Formalism* (Princeton: Princeton University Press, 1972), pp. 54–55.
49 cf. Gray, *Postmodern Proust*, 10, on postmodern fragmentation in Proust.
50 For Jameson, modernism is ironical in the sense of a stable irony that reveals a unified subject, whereas postmodern pastiche is more like unstable irony, which he also calls non-ironical: "[Pastiche] is a neutral practice of such mimicry, without any of parody's ulterior motives, amputated of the satiric impulse, devoid of laughter and of any conviction that, alongside the abnormal tongue you have momentarily borrowed, some healthy linguistic normality still exists. Pastiche is thus blank parody, a statue with blind eyeballs: it is to parody what that other interesting and historically original modern thing, the practice of a kind of blank irony, is to what Wayne Booth calls the 'stable ironies' of the eighteenth century." Jameson, *Postmodernism*, 17. In my reading, pastiche, as in Beckett's pastiche of Proust, is a mode of irony of irony, which both is and is not ironical.

51 Lyotard, *Postmodern Condition*, 79: "A work can become modern only if it is first postmodern. Postmodernism thus understood is not modernism at its end but in the nascent state, and this state is constant."
52 Benjamin, "Image of Proust," 44; Pierre Zima, *L'Ambivalence romanesque* (Frankfurt am Main: Peter Lang, 1988), pp. 365–78.
53 Henry, "Métaphores," 211. On Proust and commodification, also see Gray, *Postmodern Proust*, 152–74.
54 cf. Newmark, *Beyond Symbolism*, 125.
55 Winton, *Proust's Additions*, 50, 359.
56 See Gray, *Postmodern Proust* for a general reading of Proust as postmodern.
57 Terdiman, *Present Past*, 238. See Zima, *Ambivalence*, 121:
   Deux développements socio-économiques complémentaires... séparent la *Comédie humaine* de *A la recherche du temps perdu*: d'abord l'apparition d'une classe d'individus oisifs dont la passivité est incompatible avec l'individualisme libéral qui constitue l'arrière-plan idéologique du roman du XIXe siècle; ensuite l'intensification, vers la fin du XIXe siècle, de la médiation par la valeur d'échange qui envahit tous les secteurs de la vie sociale, recouvrant celle-ci d'ambiguïtés et de fausses apparences: de "masques" dans le sens de Bakhtine.
58 Ellison, *Reading*, 133; Zima, *Ambivalence*, 126; Jameson, *Postmodernism*, 405, 410–18.

4 PROUST'S FORGETFUL IRONIES

1 Georges Bataille, "Molloy's Silence," *Samuel Beckett's* Molloy, Malone Dies, The Unnamable, ed. Harold Bloom (New York: Chelsea House, 1988), p. 56; cf. Gray, *Postmodern Proust*, 98, 202.
2 See also the narrator's assertion that homosexual bodies are lies that mask the homosexual's true gender. This assertion comes into question in the later manuscripts when Marcel discovers a heterosexual affair between the homosexual Morel and the lesbian Léa (*R*, 3: 214–16). Winton, *Proust's Additions*, 291; Gray, *Postmodern Proust*, 100; cf. McGinnis, "Gomorrhe," 101.
3 cf. Morot-Sir, "The PARADOX," 23–46.
4 McGinnis, "L'Inconnaissable Gomorrhe," 101; Gray, *Postmodern Proust*, 97, 101.
5 I am endebted to Paul de Man who first brought this passage to my attention.
6 cf. de Man, "Rhetoric," 203.
7 Paul de Man, "The Concept of Irony," in *Aesthetic Ideology* (Minneapolis: Minnesota University Press, 1996), p. 178.
8 cf. Benveniste, *Problèmes*, 251–57.
9 Beckett, *Proust*, 52.
10 Weber, "Madrépore," 47. In de Man's words, it is "forever impossible to read Reading" (*Allegories*, 77).
11 See Paul de Man, "The Resistance to Theory," in *The Resistance to Theory* (Minneapolis: University of Minnesota Press, 1986), pp. 3–20.

12 cf. Newmark, *Beyond Symbolism*, 136:
    By finally claiming that the role to be played by memory in the writer's future is to be understood by analogy to the seed's maturation – which the text itself has already structured as a radical *disruption* of the process of organic development – the later passage may simply be reminding us that, *until* we have allowed this textual "abortion" to redetermine whatever is meant by "nature," "seed," "maturation," and even the concept of "future" itself, we have not *yet* sufficiently read the earlier version.
    cf. Bersani, "Culture," 418, where he associates the narrator's mother with a "reminder of the power of appearances to defeat what may be imagined to lie 'behind' them ... Marcel's mother seeks to ... point, ultimately, to the *possibility of pursuing not an art of truth divorced from experience, but rather of phenomena liberated from the obsession with truth.*"
13 Beckett, *Proust*, 49: "Here, as always, Proust is completely detached from all moral considerations."

5 MOLLOY'S WAY: THE PARODY OF ALLEGORY

1 By Proust's "writing narrator" I mean the one who speaks as if he is writing what he narrates and what we read.
2 I will be using the word "parody" to signify, not a genre, but a rhetorical mode of irony that involves both the repetition of a preceding text and the ironic negation of and differentiation from that text. cf. Linda Hutcheon, *A Theory of Parody* (New York: Methuen, 1985), p. 37. To the extent that parody, like irony, turns against itself and becomes not only self-parody (of the parodic subject) but also parody of parody, it puts into question the acts of negation and differentiation that define it as parodic. It thus tends towards a fictional, indifferent point of view of language, that of the ironic aspect that we discussed in our chapters on Proust, for which all differences are purely artificial and fictional. Parody both is and is not parodic.
3 cf. Beckett, *Proust*, 7. For Proust's attitude towards pastiche, see *Contre Sainte-Beuve*, 140: "Il n'y a pas de meilleure manière d'arriver à prendre conscience de ce qu'on sent soi-même que d'essayer de recréer en soi ce qu'a senti un maître. Dans cet effort profond c'est notre pensée elle-même que nous mettons, avec la sienne, au jour." In speaking about his own pastiches, Proust writes: "Le tout était surtout pour moi une affaire d'hygiène; il faut se purger du vice naturel d'idolâtrie et d'imitation. Et au lieu de faire sournoisement du Michelet ou du Goncourt en signant (ici les noms de tels ou tels de nos contemporains les plus aimables), d'en faire ouvertement sous forme de pastiches, pour redescendre à ne plus être que Marcel Proust quand j'écris mes romans." *Contre Sainte-Beuve*, 690 n; cf. Connor, *Samuel*, 16 and George Painter, *Marcel Proust: A Biography*, vol. 2 (New York: Vintage, 1978), pp. 99–100. Pastiche in Proust is much closer to parody, in Hutcheon's definition, since it also seeks to differentiate itself from the pastiched text.

4 In "Art," 1–18, James Acheson notes that Beckett's narrator, Molloy, repeats the isolation, illness, and act of writing in bed of Proust's narrator.
5 See the first pages of *La Prisonnière* for one of the narrator's strongest hints of this incestuous relationship with his mother (*R*, 3: 9–10).
6 Trezise's argument in *Into the Breach* is that Beckett's narrators in the trilogy situate themselves in the "breach" between polarities, which confuses the two poles in particular ways.
7 Doubrovsky (*Writing*, 75–76) was one of the first to see the similarities between Proust's writing narrator and Beckett's narrator: "The Proustian Narrator, then, writes *precisely* in a Beckettian position. He composes while decomposing himself." In *Writing* (71–76), Doubrovsky develops a fascinating discussion of the relationship between Proust's narrator and the narrator of the first half of *Molloy*. He does not discuss the burlesque tone of Beckett's narrator that distinguishes him from Proust's narrator.

Molloy narrator's confusion about his relation to his past is so great that he cannot even be certain about his uncertainty, just like Proust's narrator when he would awaken in the dark and not know who, where, or when he was: "[J]'étais bien étonné de trouver autour de moi une obscurité, douce et reposante pour mes yeux, mais peut-être plus encore pour mon esprit, à qui elle apparaissait comme une chose sans cause, incompréhensible, comme une chose vraiment obscure" (*R*, 1: 4). Molloy thus parodies both the certainty of Proust's fully awake remembering narrator and the uncertainty of Proust's writing narrator concerning his relationship to his past. See Trezise, *Breach*, on Molloy's confusion.
8 From time to time, I will use the terms "Molloy narrator" and "Molloy protagonist," rather than simply "narrator" and "protagonist" as I did in discussing the *Recherche*. Whereas Proust emphasizes the impersonality of his narrator by naming him only twice, Beckett names his narrators from the beginning. But he makes this distinction ironically, repeatedly reminding us of the artifice, as well as the inevitability, of distinguishing past from present selves and of naming in general.
9 See Gray, "Beckett," on the assertion and retraction of parody in *Molloy*.
10 cf. Acheson, "Art," 4–5 on Beckett's rejection of Proustian laws of the mind and Zurbrugg, *Beckett*, 240 on *Watt*: "Beckettian characters such as Watt find that the transition from the habitual to the non-habitual, or from 'studium' to 'punctum,' merely demarcates the decline from bad to worse." It is not entirely evident that the transition from habitual to non-habitual moves from bad to worse or from worse to bad for Beckett.
11 Marcel discovers the horror of his desire for his mother only indirectly, in the form of his discovery of Albertine's homosexual desires. See Ellison, *Reading*, 157–68 on the sexual and christic connotations of this discovery.
12 Molloy's desire for mother is as always ambivalent. "Want of need" can be read both as a negation of his desire for his mother and as a desire for this desire. See Gray, "Beckett," 167; Zurbrugg, *Beckett*, 118; Ruby Cohn, *Return to Beckett* (Princeton: Princeton University Press, 1976), p. 84.

Notes to pages 84–87

13 Hence the theme of androgyny shared by Marcel and Molloy. Proust's narrator only hints at Marcel's androgyny by discussing the protagonist's obsession with Albertine's androgyny and by discussing the androgyny of male homosexuals in *Sodome et Gomorrhe I*.

14 cf. Samuel Beckett, *En attendant Godot* (Paris: Minuit, 1952), p. 154: "Vous n'avez pas fini de m'empoisonner avec vos histoires de temps?... Elles accouchent à cheval sur une tombe, le jour brille un instant, puis c'est la nuit à nouveau." Also compare Marcel's encomium to asparagus which, eaten and digested, "jouaient, dans leurs farces poétiques et grossières comme une féerie de Shakespeare, à changer mon pot de chambre en un vase de parfum" (*R*, 1: 121). The homosexual metaphor of eating asparagus produces excrement that is transformed into Baudelairian perfume and artistic impressions.

15 "Décrirai-je la chambre? Non. J'en aurai l'occasion peut-être plus tard. Quand j'y chercherai asile, à bout d'expédients, toute honte bue, la queue dans le rectum, qui sait." Samuel Beckett, *Molloy* (Paris: 10/18, 1963), p. 24.

16 On the breakdown of sexual difference and the failed attempt to erase the debt to mother and give birth to self, see Leslie Hill, *Beckett's Fiction: In Different Words* (Cambridge: Cambridge University Press, 1990), pp. 70, 91–92, 99.

17 Connor, *Samuel*, 18. cf. Moorjani, "Beckett's Devious Deictics," 21 on the psychological relationship between this destruction of the mother and the process of mourning. For a discussion of Beckett's parody of Proust's grandmother's three taps as a sign of ignorance or ignorance of signification, see Gray, "Beckett," 166–67; cf. also Zurbrugg, *Beckett*, 148. Molloy also calls his mother, as Charlus calls aristocratic women, "the Countess Caca" (*TN*, 17).

18 Marcel's profanation of mother repeats his desire for self-effacement. See *R*, 1: 438, where his mother admires in M. de Norpois the fact that "il parlait de lui-même le moins possible."

19 On involuntary memory and pain, cf. Richard Terdiman, *Present Past*, 185–239. Terdiman's social determinist presuppositions produce a reading of Proust that resembles Molloy's to the extent that it greatly exaggerates the role of pain in Proustian memory. But he interprets this individual pain as being caused by an historically determined knowledge of the impossibility of individual autonomy. Whereas Molloy, like Proust, repeatedly puts into question the pleasure/pain distinction, Terdiman simply replaces the pleasure of individual autonomy with the pain of the knowledge of the individual's determination by history.

20 On Proust's awareness of self-parody, see *R*, 2: 153–78. After commenting on the actress Rachel's spiteful nastiness towards another actress and on her lover Saint-Loup's jealous nastiness towards her, and after illustrating Marcel's own jealous nastiness in describing Rachel, whom Saint-Loup seems to prefer to Marcel, Proust's narrator turns to recounting the actions of a male dancer in female clothing. This dancer, who is seemingly oblivious to actors, journalists, and members of high society, dances an autonomous, ideal "rêve extasié" (*R*, 2: 177). When Rachel looks at the dancer, Saint-Loup gets jealous. The dancer then proceeds to parody the feminine self that he has been playing:

"[I]l se mit à refaire le mouvement de ses paumes, en se contrefaisant lui-même avec une finesse de pasticheur et une bonne humeur d'enfant" (*R*, 2: 178). This dancer, I would argue, is Proust's indirect representation of his own self-parody of his idealistic remembering narrator and a precursor of Molloy's self-parodying characters. The male dancer's evocation of a female sylph is itself a mode of self-effacement (of his male identity), but it also becomes a parody of female self-expression, whose repetition in front of the jealous Saint-Loup can only underline the absurdity of the dancer's being a male rival for Rachel's favors. Similarly, the remembering narrator's jealous desire to re-possess fleeting, past selves is a parody of female self-expression. The dancer's pastiches of his own parody of female self-expression remind Saint-Loup that he, and indirectly Proust's remembering narrator, is expressing, by denying it, his desire to construct a fictional feminine self. In *La Prisonnière*, the narrator will more closely link Marcel's jealous desire to possess/be the deceitful Albertine with the lesbian Albertine's deceitful stories of her past "female" actions and with the writing narrator's desire to construct a fictional, female self.

21 "[Memory and Habit] are the flying buttresses of the temple raised to commemorate the wisdom of the architect that is also the wisdom of all the sages, from Brahma to Leopardi, the wisdom that consists not in the satisfaction but in the ablation of desire: 'In noi di cari inganni / non che la speme, il desiderio è spento.'" Beckett, *Proust*, 7.
22 See Chapters 2 and 3.
23 cf. John Fletcher, *The Novels of Samuel Beckett* (New York: Barnes & Noble, 1964), 76–77, 79, 84 and Zurbrugg, *Beckett*, 238, 242–43.
24 cf. Edith Kern, *Existential Thought and Fictional Technique: Kierkegaard, Sartre, Beckett* (New Haven: Yale University Press, 1970), p. 11.
25 "The most successful evocative experiment can only project the echo of a past sensation, because, being an act of intellection, it is conditioned by the prejudices of the intelligence which abstracts from any given sensation, as being illogical and insignificant, a discordant and frivolous intruder, whatever word or gesture, sound or perfume, cannot be fitted into the puzzle of a concept" (Beckett, *Proust*, 53). See Pilling, "Beckett's *Proust*," 18 for a discussion of the passages that Beckett underlined in the *Recherche* relating to the question of perception.
26 On the reproduction/erasure of Watt's inverted discourse, see Connor, *Samuel*, 36–37 and Kern, *Existential Thought*, 177–93. On the split between names and things see Kern, *Existential Thought*, 191.
27 There is a similar subjectivism in *Murphy*, although not associated with the bedroom metaphor and tending uncritically towards solipsism (Mr. Endon), rather than its own ironical reversal as in *Watt* and *Molloy*. cf. Connor, *Samuel*, 20, 25.
28 "Etrange impression d'encombrement s'évanouissant avec le jour, qui alluma également le lustre, car j'avais laissé le contact." Beckett, *Molloy*, 49.

29 On the one hand, Elstir's painting mixes signs of the sea and the land to undercut both their literal meanings:

> Soit que les maisons cachassent une partie du port, un bassin de calfatage ou peut-être la mer même s'enfonçant en golfe dans les terres, ainsi que cela arrivait constamment dans ce pays de Balbec, de l'autre côté de la pointe avancée où était construite la ville, les toits étaient dépassés (comme ils l'eussent été par des cheminées ou par des clochers) par des mâts, lesquels avaient l'air de faire des vaisseaux auxquels ils appartenaient, quelque chose de citadin, de construit sur terre, impression qu'augmentaient d'autres bateaux, demeurés le long de la jetée, mais en rangs si pressés que les hommes y causaient d'un bâtiment à l'autre sans qu'on pût distinguer leur séparation et l'interstice de l'eau, et ainsi cette flottille de pêche avait moins l'air d'appartenir à la mer que, par exemple, les églises de Criquebec qui, au loin, entourées d'eau de tous côtés parce qu'on les voyait sans la ville, dans un poudroiement de soleil et de vagues, semblaient sortir des eaux, soufflées en albâtre ou en écume et, enfermées dans la ceinture d'un arc-en-ciel versicolore, former un tableau irréel et mystique.

On the other hand, the unreal impressions produced by this painting are constantly being "corrected" by the mind's return to the literal and realistic, as in the watercolors:

> C'était une belle matinée malgré l'orage qu'il avait fait. Et même on sentait encore les puissantes actions qu'avait à neutraliser le bel équilibre des barques immobiles, jouissant du soleil et de la fraîcheur, dans les parties où la mer était si calme que les reflets avaient presque plus de solidité et de réalité que les coques vaporisées par un effet de soleil et que la perspective faisait s'enjamber les unes les autres. Où plutôt on n'aurait pas dit d'autres parties de la mer. Car entre ces parties, il y avait autant de différence qu'entre l'une d'elles et l'église sortant des eaux, et les bateaux derrière la ville. L'intelligence faisait ensuite un même élément de ce qui était, ici noir dans un effet d'orage, plus loin tout d'une couleur avec le ciel et aussi verni que lui, et là si blanc de soleil, de brume et d'écume, si compact, si terrien, si circonvenu de maisons, qu'on pensait à quelque chaussée de pierres ou à un champ de neige, sur lequel on était effrayé de voir un navire s'élever en pente raide ou à sec comme une voiture qui s'ébroue en sortant d'un gué, mais qu'au bout d'un moment, en y voyant sur l'étendue haute et inégale du plateau solide des bateaux titubants, on comprenait, identique en tous ces aspects divers, être encore la mer. (*R*, 1: 836–38)

30 Beckett, *Molloy*, 49.
31 cf. J. D. O'Hara, "Jung and the 'Molloy' Narrative," *The Beckett Studies Reader*, ed. S. E. Gontarski (Gainesville: University Press of Florida, 1993), p. 135.
32 cf. Landa, *Samuel Beckett*, 75.
33 Nietzsche, *Will*, 265; Trezise, *Breach*, 131–34. Near the end of the *Recherche*, the narrator admits that he cannot escape the error of realist description because he cannot consistently replace it with an impressionist discourse: "[B]ien que l'erreur soit plus grave, [je pourrais] continuer, comme on fait, à mettre des traits dans le visage d'une passante, alors qu'à la place du nez, des joues et du menton, il ne devrait y avoir qu'un espace vide sur lequel jouerait tout au plus le reflet de nos désirs." (*R*, 3: 1045). Such a discourse can posit only ironically that it "remembers" past impressions, for it knows itself to be a repetition of realist error. Once again, Beckett's parody of Proust's narrator is the repetition

of an implicit self-parody of the narrator, who knows that he cannot avoid falling back into realist discourse.
34. Beckett, *Molloy*, 63. "Yes, there were times when I forgot not only who I was, but that I was, forgot to be" (*TN*, 49).
35. This failure to transcend language and be or not be is already coming about in so-called realist description, such as Flaubert's: "'Les petits faits vrais,' les célèbres 'détails,' les adjectifs, la multiplication des qualificatifs, le cercle toujours grandissant des descriptions du roman du dix-neuvième siècle ont leur origine dans le premier soupçon, celui qui allait devenir la hantise du siècle suivant, le soupçon que l'homme peut-être n'existe pas" (Bernal, *Langage*, 105); see also Trezise, *Breach*, 40 and Reid, *Narration*, 64–114. Just as Flaubert's and Proust's descriptions of impressions cannot distinguish trees from people (see Chapter 2), so the trilogy's descriptions blur being and non-being. The increasing collapse of the being/non-being distinction seems to culminate in Beckett's *The Unnamable*, but even there, the "I" ironically undercuts its status as a voice of silence.
36. See Trezise, *Breach*, 41: "[T]he physical deterioration suffered by Molloy and Moran both, but which, as I have noted, remains considerably less advanced in the case of Moran, coincides with an increasing discursiveness or errancy of language and, consequently, with an impoverishment of storytelling itself..."
37. I am not asserting that description represents space only and not time also. See Reid, *Narration*, 1–11.
38. Bernal, *Langage*, 40. Also see Trezise, *Breach*, 143–44.
39. Bernal, *Langage*, 37.
40. Beckett, *Molloy*, 115. "Fortunately it did no more than stress, the better to mock if you like, an innate velleity" (*TN*, 87).
41. The passage suggests, but does not develop, the liar's paradox, which Moran's entire discourse will play out. See also: "I say that night, but there was more than one perhaps. The lie, the lie, to lying thought" (*TN*, 28).
42. "[J]e ne sais plus très bien ce que je fais, ni pourquoi, ce sont là des choses que je comprends de moins en moins..." (Beckett, *Molloy*, 59).
43. Molloy once again resembles Tante Léonie, whose compulsions are compared by Proust to the effects of the current in the Vivonne river, which makes a waterlily alternate endlessly between its two banks (*R*, 1: 168–69). See Doubrovsky, "Writing," 66–87:

> Oui, cela m'arrive et cela m'arrivera encore d'oublier qui je suis et d'évoluer devant moi à la manière d'un étranger. C'est alors que je vois le ciel différent de ce qu'il est et que la terre aussi revêt de fausses couleurs. Cela a l'air d'un repos, mais il n'en est rien, je glisse content dans la lumière des autres, celle qui jadis devait être la mienne, je ne dis pas le contraire, puis c'est l'angoisse du retour, je ne dirai pas où, je ne peux pas, à l'absence peut-être, il faut y retourner, c'est tout ce que je sais, il ne fait pas bon y rester, il ne fait pas bon la quitter. (Beckett, *Molloy*, 55)

Forgetting, like lying, is a fundamental principle of transition in Molloy's discourse. It constantly defers his efforts to disclose who or what he is or what he is doing.

44 Beckett is associating Molloy's two fools with linguistic aspect, the imperfective aspect of reversibility that characterizes, for example, the imperfect tense, and the perfective aspect of irreversibility that characterizes, for example, the perfect tenses like the *passé composé*. For linguists, the imperfect and the *passé composé* are aspects rather than tenses, since they do not make a chronological distinction. For a discussion of the relation between the two aspects as expressions of irony and allegory, see Reid, *Narration*, 1–11.

6 MORAN'S WAY: THE FORGETFUL SPIRAL OF IRONY

1 See Wolfgang Iser, "The Pattern of Negativity in Beckett's Prose," in *Samuel Beckett*, ed. Harold Bloom (New York: Chelsea House, 1985), pp. 125–33, for an early reading of Beckett's discourse as a lie.
2 J. L. Austin, *How to Do Things with Words* (Cambridge: Harvard University Press, 1975), pp. 3–6.
3 In order to mark the son's inheritance of his father's talents in deceit, Moran gives his son his own name, Jacques, while his son names his teddy bear "Woolly Jack," as if he too were planning to give birth to an heir (*TN*, 98, 117, 123).
4 On Vautrin, signs, and power, see Reid, *Narration*, 57–63.
5 cf. Trezise, *Breach*, 143–44.
6 Moran questions the very existence of a central intention in referring to "the Obidil," an anagram, it would appear, for Freud's libido, desire: "I never saw him,... perhaps there is no such person" (*TN*, 162).
7 See also "The sky sinks in the morning... It stoops... Unless it is the earth that lifts itself up" (*TN*, 140).
8 Trezise, *Breach*, 137.
9 According to the increasingly impotent, unnamable, and impersonal narrator, all polarities describing a personal self break down and become parodic, as in Molloy's discourse. The narrator's point of view would thus be represented allegorically by his vision of his reflection in the water, which is dead and alive, male and female, young and old, or neither. It is a "face, with holes for the eyes and mouth and other wounds, and nothing to show if it was a man's face or a woman's face, a young face or an old face" (*TN*, 149).
10 cf. Paul Davies, *The Ideal Real: Beckett's Fiction and Imagination* (Rutherford: Fairleigh Dickinson University Press, 1994), pp. 63–81. See Beckett, *Proust*, 74 on the return of the question of truth. Beckett double scored a passage of his copy of the *Recherche* in which the narrator speaks of realism in allegorical painting as an effect, rather than an origin, of the text. See Pilling, "Beckett's *Proust*," 20.
11 "Moran's dispossession is essentially an allegory of the dispossession of Moran's story... Moran's belated awakening to the sense or senselessness of his quest (to the sense of his question *as* a quest of sense) [is] temporally indistinguishable from the substitution for Youdi of an anonymous voice" (Trezise, *Breach*, 56).

12 "Irony divides the flow of temporal experience into a past that is pure mystification and a future that remains harassed forever by relapse within the inauthentic. It can know this inauthenticity but can never overcome it. It can only restate and repeat it on an increasingly conscious level..." (de Man, "Rhetoric," 203).
13 Trezise, *Breach*, 48.
14 Moran's enormous ambivalence towards this new world and self is expressed by the ambiguity of "have done with," which signifies both a desire to have Molloy's face and a desire to get rid of it.
15 For a discussion of critics who see Moran as an earlier Molloy, which include Trezise, see Daniel Katz, *Saying I No More: Subjectivity and Consciousness in the Prose of Samuel Beckett* (Evanston: Northwestern University Press, 1999), p. 195 n.
16 cf. Katz, *Saying I*, 76.
17 Katz, *Saying I*, 72.
18 Chambers, *Mélancolie*, 168 states that Beckett "speaks ultimately *not* of the essence itself but only of the threshold," which he describes as "an existence endlessly excluded from while endlessly tending towards" the timeless essence of a self.

7 MALONE DIES AND THE IMPOSSIBILITY OF NOT SAYING I

1 Watson, *Paradox*, 22; H. Porter Abbott, "The Harpooned Notebook: *Malone Dies* and the Conventions of Intercalated Narrative," in *Samuel Beckett's Molloy, Malone Dies, The Unnamable*, ed. Harold Bloom (New York: Chelsea House, 1988), p. 123.
2 Fletcher, *Novels*, 153; Ben-Zvi, *Samuel*, 95.
3 Ben-Zvi, *Samuel*, 95.
4 cf. Trezise, *Breach*, 110; Ben-Zvi, *Samuel*, 92.
5 cf. Maurice Blanchot, "Where Now? Who Now?," in *Samuel Beckett's Molloy, Malone Dies, The Unnamable*, ed. Harold Bloom (New York: Chelsea House, 1988), p. 24.
6 Andrew Kennedy, *Samuel Beckett* (Cambridge: Cambridge University Press, 1989), pp. 105–6.
7 Ethel F. Cornwell, "Samuel Beckett: The Flight from Self," in *Critical Essays on Samuel Beckett*, ed. Lance St. John Butler (Aldershot: Scolar Press, 1993), p. 188; Eugene Combs, "Impotency and Ignorance: A Parody of Prerogatives in Samuel Beckett," in *Critical Essays on Samuel Beckett*, ed. Lance St. John Butler (Hants: Scolar Press, 1993), p. 176.
8 Fletcher, *Novels*, 170; Hesla, *Shape of Chaos*, 107–10; Porter H. Abbott, *The Fiction of Samuel Beckett: Form and Effect* (Berkeley: University of California Press, 1973), pp. 114–15.
9 Abbott, *Fiction*, 119.
10 D. P. Simpson, *Cassell's Latin Dictionary*, 5th ed. (New York: Macmillan, 1966), p. 534.
11 Cohn, *Return*, 93.

12 Samuel Beckett, *Malone meurt* (Paris: Minuit, 1951), p. 97.
13 cf. Connor, *Beckett*, 69–70.
14 See de Man, *Allegories*, 300.
15 "I have taken a long time to find him again, but I have found him. How did I know it was he, I don't know" (*TN*, 226).
16 cf. Trezise, *Breach*, 65.
17 With the sole exception of "when it came to doing some little thing for himself," giving himself some room to maneuver, whose basis will be discussed at the end of this chapter (*TN*, 244).
18 Beckett, *Proust*, 49.
19 Schopenhauer, *World as Will and Representation*, 1: 244; see Pilling, "Beckett's *Proust*," 12, for the argument that Beckett found the Calderón quotation and its interpretation in Schopenhauer's *World as Will and Representation*.
20 Here, as always, Proust is completely detached from all moral considerations. There is no right and wrong in Proust nor in his world... Tragedy is the statement of an expiation, but not the miserable expiation of a codified breach of a local arrangement organized by knaves for the fools. The tragic figure represents the expiation of original sin, of the original and eternal sin of him and all his 'soci malorum,' the sin of having been born.
> Pues el delito mayor
> Del hombre es haber nacido
> (Beckett, *Proust*, 49)
21 cf. Connor, *Samuel*, 72.
22 Blanchot, "Where Now?," 28: "Let us try to hear this voice that speaks knowing that it is lying, indifferent to what it says, too old perhaps and too humiliated to be able ever to say the words that would make it stop."
23 Maurice Blanchot, "The Narrative Voice or the Impersonal 'He'," in *The Siren's Song: Selected Essays*, ed. Gabriel Josipovici, trans. Sacha Rabinovitch (Bloomington: Indiana University Press, 1982), pp. 213–21.
24 Samuel Beckett, "Three Dialogues," 18.
25 Although Beckett's Lemuel gives death, rather than life, as does King Lemuel in Proverbs 31, the latter also gives death out of charity, an act that is not unlike Lemuel's production of physical pain in himself and his production of death in the prisoners he takes out to sea. King Lemuel's mother thus exhorts him to "[g]ive strong drink unto him that is ready to perish, and wine unto those that be of heavy hearts" (Proverbs 31:6); cf. Combs, "Impotency," 172.
26 See Slavoj Zizek, *The Fragile Absolute* (New York: Verso, 2002), pp. 92–107.
27 cf. Blanchot, "Where Now?," 28. See Brian T. Fitch, *Dimensions, structures et textualité dans la trilogie romanesque de Beckett* (Paris: Minard, 1977), p. 188. For a critique of Blanchot's impersonal narrator, see Abbott, *Fiction*, 126 concerning Beckett's questioning of the romantic belief that form and time can coincide.
28 cf. Trezise, *Breach*, 18–20, and Kern, *Existential*, 221–22.
29 Beckett, "Three Dialogues," 17.
30 Trezise (*Breach*, 75) appears at first glance to argue that all action in Beckett is linguistically determined. He states on the next page, however, that the

devalued term of an opposition comes to name the other of the opposition itself, suggesting that he uses the word "determination" to name that which is other than the necessity/possibility, determination/freedom oppositions. It would appear that, for Trezise's Beckett, we are not free to answer or to not ask the question of whether we are free, a statement that ironically deconstructs its own assertion of determinism.

31 Trezise, *Breach*, 77.

8 *THE UNNAMABLE*: THE DEATH OF THE IRONICAL SELF AND THE RETURN OF HISTORY

1 Blanchot, "Where Now?," 28.
2 Clearly, by saying "the text asserts" or "it asserts" rather than "the narrator asserts," my words once again create the fiction of a voice. It will argue, however, that, to the extent to which "the text" or "it" serves to question the notion of a narrator's voice, it indirectly puts the unity of "its" own voice into question as well.
3 "You think you are simply resting, the better to act when the time comes, or for no reason, and you soon find yourself powerless ever to do anything" (*TN*, 291).
4 *Webster's Revised Unabridged Dictionary* (online), Hypertext Webster Gateway (cited 9 January 2001), available from the World Wide Web: (http://smac.ucsd.edu:/cgi-bin/http_webster).
5 De Man, "Rhetoric," 207.
6 cf. Davies, *Ideal Real*, 88–89 on the move towards the present tense in the trilogy.
7 cf. Begam, *Samuel*, 9.
8 On Beckett's representation of language as a fall from an original but fictional godly intention, see James Reid, "Allegorizing Jameson's Postmodernist Space: *Waiting for Godot*," *Romanic Review* 84.1 (1993): 84–88.
9 For a passage in Proust to which Beckett may be alluding, see *R*, 1: 84–86, where the narrator praises the superiority of reading over life, because narrative allows readers to understand all of life's happiness and unhappiness by compressing into a few pages events that in reality take place over years and that we often do not perceive. *The Unnamable* interprets fiction's narrative compression of life, not as a means of better understanding real life, but of putting into question the continuity of a self and time in life or in art.
10 It is possible that in this passage Beckett is once again rereading the beginning of the *Recherche*. As Proust's narrator recounts his awakening, he compares dreaming to being away on a trip, self-consciousness to being home, and his mind, which alternately falls asleep and wakes up, to traveling between home and away: "Je me demandais quelle heure il pouvait être; j'entendais le sifflement des trains qui, plus ou moins éloigné, comme le chant d'un oiseau dans une forêt, relevant les distances, me décrivait l'étendue de la campagne déserte où le voyageur se hâte vers la station prochaine; et le petit chemin qu'il suit va être

gravé dans son souvenir par l'excitation qu'il doit à des lieux nouveaux, à des actes inaccoutumés, à la causerie récente et aux adieux sous la lampe étrangère qui le suivent encore dans le silence de la nuit, à la douceur prochaine du retour." (*R*, 1: 4). In this passage, it is time, the interval between a train's horn at different moments, that allows the narrator to imagine space by mentally reconstructing distances between himself and the two locations of the train. In Beckett's possible rereading of Proust in *The Unnamable*, by contrast, it is space that allows Mahood to figure time as linear intervals between being awake and dreaming, memory and imagination, self and other.

11 cf. Robert Champigny, "Adventures of the First Person," in *Samuel Beckett Now*, ed. Melvin J. Friedman (Chicago: Chicago University Press, 1970), p. 122.

12 cf. Martin Heidegger, *Being and Time*, trans. John Macquarrie and Edward Robinson (New York: Harper and Row, 1962), pp. 163–68, 296. At this point of the discourse, the "They" seems to resemble Heidegger's "they," "das man," the "they-self" defined by everyday, average speech, the idle talk of public discourse. The "they-self" belongs to Dasein. It disperses the "authentic Self," reducing it to "nobody," "nothing." However, in *The Unnamable*, Beckett's "they" turns outs, as in *Malone Dies*, to be a voice of language, not the voice of public, idle discourse. This voice of language states its own failure to say who, including itself, is speaking the text. It is a voice that proclaims the constitutive inauthenticity of all voices, including a voice of language.

13 The narrator at first proposes a narrative that is defined by his traveling on the island in irregular loops and parabolic sweeps, which are "unpredictable in direction" and "determined by the panic of the moment" (*TN*, 326–27). These unpredictable loops and parabolas replace a spatial representation of time as an itinerary between distinct poles on a globe with a spatial representation of time as directionless, in which one place in space and time does not differ from the next. This lack of differentiation explains Mahood's immobility in his next story.

14 Sarah Kofman, *Comment s'en sortir* (Paris: Galilée, 1983), p. 48.

15 See also "And they shall go forth, and look upon the carcasses of the men that have transgressed against me: for their worm shall not die, neither shall their fire be quenched; and they shall be an abhorring unto all flesh" (Isaiah 66:24).

16 cf. Fred Miller Robinson, "Samuel Beckett: *Watt*," in *Samuel Beckett*, ed. Harold Bloom (New York: Chelsea House, 1985), pp. 168 ff. For a discussion of Worm as the failed fiction of a pure negative, see Connor, *Samuel*, 76.

17 Beckett, *Molloy*, 16.

18 Writing becomes what Bataille calls a "parody of meaning" itself, where parody turns against all discourse in an infinite mise-en-abîme. See Bataille, "Molloy's Silence," in *Samuel Beckett's* Molloy, Malone Dies, The Unnamable, ed. Harold Bloom (New York: Chelsea House, 1988), pp. 13–22.

19 Raymond Federman, "Samuel Beckett: The Liar's Paradox," eds. Edouard Morot-Sir, Howard Harper, and Dougald McMillan III (Chapel Hill: University of North Carolina Department of Romance Languages, 1976), p. 125; Watson, *Paradox*, 35; Allen Thiher, "Wittgenstein, Heidegger, the Unnamable,

and Some Thoughts on the Status of Voice in Fiction," in *Samuel Beckett: Humanistic Perspectives*, eds. Morris Beja, S. E. Gontarski, and Pierre Astier (Columbus: Ohio State University Press, 1983), pp. 88–89.

20 The "here and now" appears to have always already taken the form of allegory, which makes "the past appear as a flight into the inauthenticity of a forgetting" (de Man, "Rhetoric," 205).

21 See Begam, *Samuel*, 176–77 on the both/neither interpretation of the spatial description of the narrator: "[Beckett] nonetheless continues to seek a third term that might serve as an alternative to the dualism he has been struggling to work beyond. He finds that alternative not so much beyond the binary terms of the Western tradition as within and between them, in that space of *différance* that separates – and ultimately subverts – subject and object, narrator and narrated." On the inside/outside interplay also see Trezise, *Breach*, 114–17.

Bibliography

Abbott, H. Porter. *The Fiction of Samuel Beckett: Form and Effect*. Berkeley: University of California Press, 1973.
Abbott, H. Porter. "The Harpooned Notebook: *Malone Dies* and the Conventions of Intercalated Narrative," in *Samuel Beckett's* Molloy, Malone Dies, The Unnamable, ed. Harold Bloom. New York: Chelsea House, 1988.
Acheson, James. *The American Heritage Dictionary of the English Language*, 1953. 3rd ed. New York: Houghton Mifflin, 1992.
Acheson, James. "The Art of Failure: Samuel Beckett's *Molloy*." *Southern Humanities Review* 17.1 (1983): 1–18.
Ames, Sanford S. "The Ruse of a Condemned Man: First Writing in *A la recherche*," in *Reading Proust Now*, ed. Mary Ann Caws and Eugène Nicole. New York: Peter Lang, 1990.
Austin, J. L. *How to Do Things with Words*. Cambridge: Harvard University Press, 1975.
Bataille, Georges. "Molloy's Silence," in *Samuel Beckett's* Molloy, Malone Dies, The Unnamable, ed. Harold Bloom. New York: Chelsea House, 1988. 13–21.
Bataille, Georges. "Proust and Evil," in *Marcel Proust's* Remembrance of Things Past, ed. Harold Bloom. New York: Chelsea House, 1987. 51–61.
Baudry, Jean-Louis. *Proust, Freud et l'autre*. Paris: Minuit, 1984.
Beckett, Samuel. *En attendant Godot*. Paris: Minuit, 1952.
Beckett, Samuel. *Malone meurt*. Paris: Minuit, 1951.
Beckett, Samuel. *Molloy*. Paris: 10/18, 1963.
Beckett, Samuel. *Three Novels by Samuel Beckett: Molloy, Malone Dies, and The Unnamable*. New York: Grove Press, 1958.
Beckett, Samuel. *Murphy*. New York: Grove Press, 1970.
Beckett, Samuel. *Proust*. New York: Grove Press, 1970.
Beckett, Samuel. "Proust in Pieces," in *Disjecta: Miscellaneous Writings and a Dramatic Fragment*, ed. Ruby Cohn. London: John Calder, 1983. 63–65.
Beckett, Samuel. "Three Dialogues," in *Samuel Beckett: A Collection of Critical Essays*, ed. Martin Esslin. Englewood Cliffs: Prentice Hall, 1965. 16–22.
Beckett, Samuel. *Watt*. New York: Grove Press, 1970.
Begam, Richard. *Samuel Beckett and the End of Modernity*. Stanford: Stanford University Press, 1996.

Benjamin, Walter. "The Image of Proust," in *Marcel Proust's* Remembrance of Things Past, ed. Harold Bloom. New York: Chelsea House, 1987. 37–49.
Benveniste, Emile. *Problèmes de linguistique générale*. Paris: Gallimard, 1966.
Ben-Zvi, Linda. *Samuel Beckett*. Boston: Twayne, 1986.
Ben-Zvi, Linda. "Samuel Beckett, Fritz Mauthner, and the Limits of Language," in *Samuel Beckett*, ed. Harold Bloom. New York: Chelsea House, 1985. 193–218.
Bernal, Olga. *Langage et fiction dans le roman de Beckett*. Paris: Gallimard, 1969.
Bernheimer, Charles. "*Watt's* in *The Castle*: The Aporetic Quest in Kafka and Beckett," in *Critical Essays on Samuel Beckett*, ed. Lance St. John Butler. Aldershot: Scolar Press, 1993. 278–81.
Bersani, Leo. "Beckett and the End of Literature," in *Samuel Beckett's* Molloy, Malone Dies, The Unnamable, ed. Harold Bloom. New York: Chelsea House, 1988. 51–70.
Bersani, Leo. "The Culture of Redemption: Marcel Proust and Melanie Klein." *Critical Inquiry* 12 (1986): 399–421.
Bersani, Leo. "Proust and the Art of Incompletion," in *Aspects of Narrative*, ed. J. Hillis Miller. New York: Columbia University Press, 1971.
Bessière, Jean. *L'Ordre du descriptif*. Paris: Presses Universitaires de France, 1988.
Bhabha, Homi K. "Cultural Diversity and Cultural Differences," in *The Post-Colonial Studies Reader*, ed. Bill Ashcroft, Gareth Griffiths and Helen Tiffin. New York: Routledge, 1995. 29–35.
Bhabha, Homi K. "Signs Taken for Wonders: Questions of Ambivalence and Authority Under a Tree Outside Delhi, May 1817," in *Europe and Its Others*, eds. Francis Barker et al. Vol. 1. Proceedings of the Essex Conference on the Sociology of Literature, July 1984. Colchester: University of Essex, 1985.
Bishop, Lloyd. *Romantic Irony in French Literature from Diderot to Beckett*. Nashville: Vanderbilt University Press, 1989.
Blanchot, Maurice. "The Narrative Voice or the Impersonal 'He'," in *The Siren's Song: Selected Essays*, ed. Gabriel Josipovici, trans. Sacha Rabinovitch. Bloomington: Indiana University Press, 1982. 213–21.
Blanchot, Maurice. "Where Now? Who Now?" in *Samuel Beckett's* Molloy, Malone Dies, The Unnamable, ed. Harold Bloom. New York: Chelsea House, 1988.
Bloom, Harold, ed. *Marcel Proust's* Remembrance of Things Past. New York: Chelsea House, 1987.
Bloom, Harold, ed. *Samuel Beckett*. New York: Chelsea House, 1985.
Bloom, Harold, ed. *Samuel Beckett's* Molloy, Malone Dies, The Unnamable. New York: Chelsea House, 1988.
Boucquey, Eliane. "Les Trois Arbres d'Hudimesnil: Souvenir retrouvé," in *Bulletin de la Société des Amis de Marcel Proust et des Amis de Combray* 38 (1988): 26.
Bourdieu, Pierre. *Les Règles de l'art*. Paris: Seuil, 1992.
Bové, Paul A. "Beckett's Dreadful Postmodern: The Deconstruction of Form in *Molloy*," in *De-structing the Novel*, ed. Leonard Orr. Troy: Whitston, 1982.
Bowie, Malcolm. *Freud, Proust and Lacan: Theory as Fiction*. Cambridge: Cambridge University Press, 1987.
Brodsky, Claudia. "Remembering Swann: Memory and Representation in Proust." *MLN* 102.5 (1987): 1014–42.

Brun, Bernard. "Sur le *Proust* de Beckett," in *Beckett avant Beckett*, ed. Jean-Michel Rabaté. Paris: P.E.N.S., 1984. 79–91.
Burroughs, William. "Beckett and Proust." *The Review of Contemporary Fiction* 7.2 (1987): 28–31.
Chambers, Ross. "Beckett's Brinkmanship," in *Samuel Beckett*, ed. Martin Esslin. Englewood Cliffs: Prentice Hall, 1965. 16–22.
Chambers, Ross. *Mélancolie et opposition: Les débuts du modernisme*. Paris: José Corti, 1987.
Champigny, Robert. "Adventures of the First Person," in *Samuel Beckett Now*, ed. Melvin J. Friedman. Chicago: Chicago University Press, 1970. 119–28.
Champigny, Robert. "Proust, Bergson and Other Philosophers," in *Proust: A Collection of Critical Essays*, ed. René Girard. Englewood Cliffs: Prentice Hall, 1962.
Cohn, Ruby. *Return to Beckett*. Princeton: Princeton University Press, 1976.
Combs, Eugene. "Impotency and Ignorance: A Parody of Prerogatives in Samuel Beckett," in *Critical Essays on Samuel Beckett*, ed. Lance St. John Butler. Aldershot: Scolar Press, 1993. 171–78.
Compagnon, Antoine. *Proust Between Two Centuries*, trans. Richard E. Goodkin. New York: Columbia University Press, 1992.
Compagnon, Antoine. *La Troisième République des lettres*. Paris: Seuil, 1983.
Connor, Steven. *Samuel Beckett: Repetition, Theory, and Text*. Oxford, New York: Basil Blackwell, 1988.
Cornwell, Ethel F. "Samuel Beckett: The Flight from Self," in *Critical Essays on Samuel Beckett*, ed. Lance St. John Butler. Aldershot: Scolar Press, 1993. 179–95.
Davies, Paul. *The Ideal Real: Beckett's Fiction and Imagination*. Rutherford: Fairleigh Dickinson University Press, 1994.
Deleuze, Gilles. *Proust et les signes*. Paris: Presses Universitaires de France, 1964.
de Man, Paul. *Allegories of Reading: Figural Language in Rousseau, Nietzsche, Rilke, and Proust*. New Haven: Yale University Press, 1979.
de Man, Paul. "Autobiography as De-Facement," in *The Rhetoric of Romanticism*. New York: Columbia University Press, 1984. 67–82.
de Man, Paul. *Blindness and Insight: Essays in the Rhetoric of Contemporary Criticism*. New York: Oxford, 1971.
de Man, Paul. "The Concept of Irony," in *Aesthetic Ideology*. Minneapolis: Minnesota University Press, 1996. 163–84.
de Man, Paul. "The Resistance to Theory," in *The Resistance to Theory*. Minneapolis: University of Minnesota Press, 1986. 3–20.
de Man, Paul. "The Rhetoric of Temporality," in *Interpretations*, ed. Charles Singleton. Baltimore: Johns Hopkins University Press, 1970. 173–209.
Descombes, Vincent. *Proust: Philosophie du roman*. Paris: Minuit, 1987.
Dettmar, Kevin J. H. "The Figure in Beckett's Carpet: *Molloy*," in *Rethinking Beckett: A Collection of Critical Essays*. ed. Lance St. John Butler and Robin J. Davis. New York: St. Martin's Press, 1990. 68–88.
Doubrovsky, Serge. *Writing and Fantasy in Proust: La place de la madeleine*, trans. Carol Mastrangelo Bové, with Paul Bové. Lincoln: University of Nebraska Press, 1986.

Edelman, Lee. "Homographesis." *Yale Journal of Criticism* 3.1 (1989): 189–207.
Ellison, David. "Beckett and the Ethics of Fabulation," in *Of Words and the World: Referential Anxiety in Contemporary French Fiction*. Princeton: Princeton University Press, 1993. 132–54.
Ellison, David. *The Reading of Proust*. Baltimore: Johns Hopkins University Press, 1984.
Federman, Raymond. "Samuel Beckett: The Liar's Paradox," in *Samuel Beckett: The Art of Rhetoric*, eds. Edouard Morot-Sir, Howard Harper, and Dougald McMillan III. Chapel Hill: University of North Carolina Department of Romance Languages, 1976. 119–41.
Federman, Raymond, and Angus Fletcher. *Samuel Beckett: His Works and His Critics, An Essay in Bibliography*. Berkeley: University of California Press, 1970.
Fitch, Brian T. *Dimensions, structures et textualité dans la trilogie romanesque de Beckett*. Paris: Minard, 1977.
Flam, Jack. "The New Painting." *New York Review of Books* 41.19 (1999).
Fletcher, John. "Beckett et Proust." *Caliban: Annales Publiées par la Faculté des Lettres de Toulouse* 1 (1964): 89–100.
Fletcher, John. *The Novels of Samuel Beckett*. New York: Barnes & Noble, 1964.
Flieger, Jerry Aline. "Proust, Freud, and the Art of Forgetting." *Sub-Stance* 29 (1981): 66–82.
Foucault, Michel. *Les Mots et les choses*. Paris: Gallimard, 1966.
Freud, Sigmund. *Beyond the Pleasure Principle*, trans. James Strachey. New York: W. W. Norton and Co., 1961. 8–11.
Frye, Northrop. "The Nightmare Life in Death," in *Critical Essays on Samuel Beckett*, ed. Lance St. John Butler. Aldershot: Scolar Press, 1993. 101–8.
Gaubert, Serge. "Marcel Proust: Le vieil homme et la peinture," in *Melanges offerts à Georges Couton*. Lyon: Presses Universitaires de Lyon, 1981. 577–81.
Girard, René. *Deceit, Desire, and the Novel*, trans. Yvonne Freccero. Baltimore: Johns Hopkins University Press, 1965.
Goethe, Johann Wolfgang von. *Selected Verse*. New York: Penguin, 1964.
Gontarski, S. E. "The Intent of Undoing in Samuel Beckett's Art," in *Samuel Beckett*, ed. Harold Bloom. New York: Chelsea House, 1985. 227–46.
Goodkin, Richard. *Around Proust*. Princeton: Princeton University Press, 1991.
Gray, Margaret E. "Beckett Backwards and Forwards: The Rhetoric of Retraction in *Molloy*." *French Forum* (May 1994): 161–74.
Gray, Margaret E. *Postmodern Proust*. Philadelphia: Pennsylvania University Press, 1992.
Harvey, Lawrence. *Samuel Beckett: Poet and Critic*. Princeton: Princeton University Press, 1970.
Hegel, G. W. F. *Phenomenology of Spirit*. Oxford: Clarendon Press, 1977.
Heidegger, Martin. *Being and Time*, trans. John Macquarrie and Edward Robinson. New York: Harper and Row, 1962.
Henry, Anne. "Quand une peinture métaphysique sert de propédeutique à l'écriture: Les Métaphores d'Elstir dans *A la recherche du temps perdu*," in *La Critique artistique: Un genre littéraire*. Paris: Presses Universitaires de France, 1983. 205–26.

Henry, Anne. *Marcel Proust: Théories pour une esthétique*. Paris: Klincksieck, 1981.
Henry, Anne. *Proust romancier: le tombeau égyptien*. Paris: Flammarion, 1983.
Hesla, David H. *The Shape of Chaos: An Interpretation of the Art of Samuel Beckett*. Minneapolis: University of Minnesota Press, 1971.
Hildebrandt, Hans-Hager. *Becketts Proust-Bilder: Erinnerung und Identität*. Stuttgart: J. B. Metzlersche Verlags Buchhandlung, 1980.
Hill, Leslie. "Fiction, Myth, and Identity in Samuel Beckett's Novel Trilogy," in *Samuel Beckett's* Molloy, Malone Dies, The Unnamable, ed. Harold Bloom. New York: Chelsea House, 1988. 85–94.
Hill, Leslie. *Beckett's Fiction: In Different Words*. Cambridge: Cambridge University Press, 1990.
Hutcheon, Linda. *A Poetics of Postmodernism: History, Theory, Fiction*. New York: Routledge, 1988.
Hutcheon, Linda. *A Theory of Parody*. New York: Methuen, 1985.
Iser, Wolfgang. "The Pattern of Negativity in Beckett's Prose," in *Samuel Beckett*, ed. Harold Bloom. New York: Chelsea House, 1985. 125–36.
Iser, Wolfgang. "Subjectivity as the Autogenous Cancellation of Its Own Manifestations," in *Samuel Beckett's* Molloy, Malone Dies, The Unnamable, ed. Harold Bloom. New York: Chelsea House, 1988. 71–83.
Jacobs, Carol. "Allegories of Reading Paul de Man," in *Reading de Man Reading*, eds. Lindsay Waters and Wlad Godzich. Minneapolis: Minnesota University Press, 1989. 105–20.
Jameson, Fredric. *Postmodernism: Or the Cultural Logic of Late Capitalism*. Durham: Duke University Press, 1991.
Jameson, Fredric. *The Prison-house of Language: A Critical Account of Structuralism and Russian Formalism*. Princeton: Princeton University Press, 1972.
Katz, Daniel. *Saying I No More: Subjectivity and Consciousness in the Prose of Samuel Beckett*. Evanston: Northwestern University Press, 1999.
Kawin, Bruce F. *The Mind of the Novel: Reflexive Fiction and the Ineffable*. Princeton: Princeton University Press, 1982.
Kennedy, Andrew. *Samuel Beckett*. Cambridge: Cambridge University Press, 1989.
Kenner, Hugh. *Samuel Beckett: A Critical Study*. New York: Grove Press, 1961.
Kenner, Hugh. "The Trilogy," in *Samuel Beckett's* Molloy, Malone Dies, The Unnamable. ed. Harold Bloom. New York: Chelsea House, 1988. 31–49.
Kern, Edith. "Moran-Molloy: The Hero as Author," in *Samuel Beckett*, ed. Harold Bloom. New York: Chelsea House, 1985.
Kern, Edith. *Existential Thought and Fictional Technique: Kierkegaard, Sartre, Beckett*. New Haven: Yale University Press, 1970.
Kierkegaard, Søren. *The Concept of Irony*, trans. Lee M. Capel. Bloomington: Indiana University Press, 1965.
Kierkegaard, Søren. *The Sickness Unto Death: A Christian Psychological Exposition for Upbuilding and Awakening*, trans. Howards V. Hong and Edna H. Hong. Princeton: Princeton University Press, 1980.
Klein, Melanie. "Mourning and its Relation to Manic-Depressive States," in *The Selected Melanie Klein*, ed. Juliet Mitchell. New York: Free Press, 1987.

Kofman, Sarah. *Comment s'en sortir*. Paris: Galilée, 1983.
Kristeva, Julia. *Proust: Questions d'identité*. Oxford: Legenda, 1998.
Kristeva, Julia. *Le Temps sensible: Proust et l'expérience littéraire*. Paris: Gallimard, 1994.
Landa, José Angel García. *Samuel Beckett y la narración reflexiva*. Zaragoza: Prensas Universitarias, 1992.
Leonard, Diane R. "Literary Evolution and the Principle of Perceptibility: The Case of Ruskin, Proust, and Modernism," in *Proceedings of the Xth Congress of the International Comparative Literature Association*, eds. Anna Balakian and James J. Wilhelm. New York: Garland, 1985. 132–42.
Lyotard, Jean-François. *Le Différend*. Paris: Minuit, 1983.
Lyotard, Jean-François. *The Postmodern Condition: A Report on Knowledge*, trans. Geoff Bennington and Brian Massumi. Foreword Fredric Jameson. Minneapolis: Minnesota University Press, 1984.
Macksey, Richard. "The Architecture of Time: Dialectics and Structure," in *Marcel Proust's Remembrance of Things Past*, ed. Harold Bloom. New York: Chelsea House, 1987. 89–97.
Mallarmé, Edouard. "Crise de vers." in *Mallarmé*, ed. Anthony Hartley. Baltimore: Penguin, 1965. 159–75.
McGinnis, Reginald. "L'Inconnaissable Gomorrhe: A propos d'*Albertine disparue*." *Romanic Review* 81.1 (1990): 92–104.
Mercier, Vivian. *Beckett-Beckett*. New York: Oxford University Press, 1977.
Moorjani, Angela. "Beckett's Devious Deictics," in *Rethinking Beckett*, ed. Lance St. John Butler and Robin J. Davis. New York: St. Martins Press, 1990. 20–30.
Moorjani, Angela. "A Cryptanalysis of Beckett's *Molloy*," in *The World of Samuel Beckett*, ed. Joseph H. Smith. Baltimore: Johns Hopkins University Press, 1991.
Morot-Sir, Edouard. "Grammatical Insincerity in *The Unnamable*," in *Samuel Beckett's* Molloy, Malone Dies, The Unnamable, ed. Harold Bloom. New York: Chelsea House, 1988. 131–44.
Morot-Sir, Edouard. "The PARADOX of the LIAR and the WRITING I IN PROUST," in *Reading Proust Now*, ed. Mary Ann Caws and Eugène Nicole. New York: Peter Lang, 1990. 23–46.
Morot-Sir, Edouard. "Samuel Beckett and Cartesian Emblems," in *Samuel Beckett and the Art of Rhetoric*, eds. Edouard Morot-Sir, Howard Harper, and Dougald McMillan III. Chapel Hill: University of North Carolina Department of Romance Languages, 1976. 25–104.
Morse, J. Mitchell. "The Ideal Core of the Onion: Samuel Beckett's Criticism." *French Review* 38 (1964): 23–29.
Murphy, P. J. "Beckett and the Philosophers," in *The Cambridge Companion to Beckett*, ed. John Pilling. Cambridge: Cambridge University Press, 1994. 222–40.
Newmark, Kevin. *Beyond Symbolism: Textual History and the Future of Reading*. Ithaca: Cornell University Press, 1991.
Nietzsche, Friedrich. "On the Uses and Disadvantages of History for Life," in *Untimely Meditations*, trans. R. J. Hollingdale. Cambridge: Cambridge University Press, 1983. 59–123.

Nietzsche, Friedrich. *The Will to Power*, trans. Walter Kaufmann and R. J. Hollingdale. New York: Vintage, 1968.
O'Hara, J. D. "Jung and the Molloy Narrative," in *The Beckett Studies Reader*, ed. S. E. Gontarski. Gainesville: University Press of Florida, 1993. 129–45.
Painter, George. *Marcel Proust: A Biography*. 2 vols. New York: Vintage, 1978.
Pilling, John. "Beckett's *Proust*." *Journal of Beckett Studies* 1 (1976): 8–29.
Poulet, Georges. *Etudes sur le temps humain*. Paris: Plon, 1950.
Poulet, Georges. *Proustian Space*, trans. Elliott Coleman. Baltimore: Johns Hopkins University Press, 1977.
Proust, Marcel. *A la recherche du temps perdu*. Bibliothèque de la Pléiade. 3 vols. Paris: Gallimard, 1954.
Proust, Marcel. *Albertine disparue*. Paris: Grasset, 1987.
Proust, Marcel. *Contre Sainte-Beuve*. Bibliothèque de la Pléiade. Paris: Gallimard, 1971.
Reid, James. "Allegorizing Jameson's Postmodernist Space: *Waiting for Godot*." *Romanic Review* 84.1 (1993): 84–88.
Reid, James. *Narration and Description in the French Realist Novel: The Temporality of Lying and Forgetting*. Cambridge: Cambridge University Press, 1993.
Renner, Charlotte. "The Self-Multiplying Narrators," in *Samuel Beckett's* Molloy, Malone Dies, The Unnamable, ed. Harold Bloom. New York: Chelsea House, 1988. 95–114.
Restrepo, Maria Cristina. *El Olvido en la obra de Marcel Proust*. Caracas: Universidad Pontificia Bolivariana, 1986.
Ricks, Christopher. *Beckett's Dying Words*. Oxford: Oxford University Press, 1993.
Ricoeur, Paul. *Temps et récit*. Vol. 2. Paris: Seuil, 1984.
Rivers, J. E. *Proust and the Art of Love: The Aesthetics of Sexuality in the Life, Times, and Art of Marcel Proust*. New York: Columbia University Press, 1980.
Robinson, Fred Miller. "Samuel Beckett: *Watt*," in *Samuel Beckett*, ed. Harold Bloom. New York: Chelsea House, 1985. 147–92.
Rosen, Steven J. *Samuel Beckett and the Pessimistic Tradition*. New Brunswick: Rutgers University Press, 1976.
Schopenhauer, Arthur. *The World as Will and Representation*. 2 vols. New York: Dover, 1958.
Shattuck, Roger. *Proust's Binoculars*. Princeton: Princeton University Press, 1962.
Sidorsky, David. "Modernism and the Emancipation of Literature from Morality: Teleology and Vocation in Joyce, Ford, and Proust." *New Literary History* 15.1 (1989): 137–53.
Simpson, D. P. *Cassell's Latin Dictionary*. 5th ed. New York: Macmillan, 1966.
Splitter, Randolph. *Proust's Recherche: A Psychoanalytic Interpretation*. Boston: Routledge, 1981.
Sprinker, Michael. *History and Ideology in Proust:* A la recherche du temps perdu *and the Third French Republic*. Cambridge and New York: Cambridge University Press, 1994.

Terdiman, Richard. "Deconstructing Memory: On Representing the Past and Theorizing Culture in France Since the Revolution." *Diacritics* (Winter 1985): 13–36.
Terdiman, Richard. *The Dialectics of Isolation: Self and Society in the French Novel from the Realists to Proust*. New Haven: Yale University Press, 1976.
Terdiman, Richard. *Present Past: Modernity and the Memory Crisis*. Ithaca: Cornell University Press, 1993.
Thiher, Allen. "Wittgenstein, Heidegger, the *Unnamable*, and Some Thoughts on the Status of Voice in Fiction," in *Samuel Beckett: Humanistic Perspectives*, eds. Morris Beja, S. E. Gontarski, and Pierre Astier. Columbus: Ohio State University Press, 1983. 80–90.
Trezise, Thomas. *Into the Breach*. Princeton: Princeton University Press, 1990.
Trieloff, Barbara. "'Babe of Silence': Beckett's Post-Trilogy Prose Articulated," in *Rethinking Beckett*, eds. Lance St. John Butler and Robin J. Davis. New York: St Martin's Press, 1990. 89–104.
Uenishi, Taeko. *Le Style de Proust et la peinture*. Paris: Sèdes, 1988.
Warning, Reiner. "Reading Irony in Flaubert." *Style* 19 (1985): 304–16.
Watson, David. *Paradox and Desire in Samuel Beckett's Fiction*. New York: St. Martin's, 1991.
Weber, Samuel. "Le Madrépore." *Poétique* 13 (1973): 28–54.
Willis, Sharon, "'Gilbertine' Apparue," *Romanic Review* 72.3 (1982): 331–45.
Winton, Alison. *Proust's Additions*. 2 vols. Cambridge: Cambridge University Press, 1977.
Zima, Pierre. *L'Ambivalence romanesque*. Frankfurt am Main: Peter Lang, 1988.
Zizek, Slavoj. *Enjoy your Symptom: Jacques Lacan in Hollywood and out*. 2nd ed. New York: Routledge, 2001.
Zizek, Slavoj. *The Fragile Absolute*. New York: Verso 2002.
Zizek, Slavoj. *The Ticklish Subject: The Absent Centre of Political Ontology*. London: Verso, 1999.
Zurbrugg, Nicholas. *Beckett and Proust*. Gerrards Cross: Colin Smythe, 1988.

Index

Abbott, H. Porter, 181
Abraham, 23–25
Acheson, James, 3, 174
allegory, 1–2, 3–5, 8, 18–19, 22–25, 26, 27, 28, 29–31, 32–38, 46, 64, 67, 70, 79, 83–94, 99, 109–10, 123
  allegory of allegory, 46, 69
allegory and irony, interplay between, 2, 3–5, 8–9, 22–25, 31, 44–45, 71–78, 82–98, 99, 104, 106–7, 112–16, 121, 122–23, 124, 125–26, 129–37, 138, 141–46, 150, 152–55, 161, 179

Balzac, Honoré de, 103–4
Bataille, Georges, 183
Baudelaire, Charles, 65, 66, 175
Beckett, Samuel
  En attendant Godot, 175
  Malone Dies, 1, 9, 20, 54, 117–37, 138, 145, 181, 183
  Molloy I, 1, 3, 9–10, 14, 79–98, 99, 100, 104, 105, 112, 113–16, 117, 118, 119, 125, 138, 174, 175, 176, 178, 179
  Molloy II, 94, 99–116, 117, 118, 179, 180
  Murphy, 176
  Proust, 1, 2, 14, 20, 27, 32, 35, 38, 46–47, 48, 54, 57, 74–75, 162, 164, 165, 166, 167, 168, 173, 176, 179, 181
  "Three Dialogues," 136, 159, 169–70
  The Unnamable, 1, 9, 10–12, 94, 138–55, 182, 183
  Watt, 89, 90, 93, 176
Begam, Richard, 158, 184
Benjamin, Walter, 14, 66, 163
Benveniste, Emile, 37
Ben-Zvi, Linda, 157
Bernal, Olga, 158, 178
Bersani, Leo, 173
Blanchot, Maurice, 132–33, 134–35, 138–39, 143, 155, 181
Bourdieu, Pierre, 65, 66, 163, 166, 171
Bowie, Malcolm, 167

Calderón de la Barca, Pedro, 20, 129
Camus, Albert (*L'Etranger*), 80
Chambers, Ross, 16, 162, 180
Connor, Samuel, 157, 158, 175, 176, 183
consciousness and self-consciousness, 1, 3, 5–8, 9–11, 18, 19, 26, 27–31, 32–42, 81, 85–97, 104–5, 108–9, 117–18, 165, 177

Davies, Paul, 182
Deleuze, Gilles, 28, 165, 167, 168, 169
de Man, Paul, 1, 4, 5, 36, 39, 72, 152–55, 156–57, 160, 161, 166, 172, 180, 184
Descombes, Vincent, 65, 66, 163, 164, 169, 170
Doubrovsky, Serge, 158, 159, 161, 165, 168, 174, 178

Ellison, David, 3, 23, 158, 160, 161, 169, 170, 174
ethical and moral readings, 19–22, 38, 77–78, 116, 121, 129–32, 133–36, 160, 162, 173, 181

father, 23–25, 50–55, 63, 101, 102–4, 109–10, 111, 115, 116, 121, 163, 179
Flaubert, Gustave, 30, 65
  L'Education sentimentale, 67
Flieger, Jerry Aline, 162, 165
forgetting, 2, 4, 6–8, 11, 13–15, 19, 24, 26–32, 34–39, 63, 80–82, 86–87, 93–97, 107–8, 112, 118, 120, 121, 123, 130, 134, 144, 150–51, 160, 162, 163, 165
  deliberate or artistic forgetting, 27, 28–31, 34, 36, 164
  questioning irony, 72–78, 153–55
  remembering forgetting, 44–45
forgetting and lying, interplay, 4, 79, 107, 116, 169
Foucault, Michel, 14
Freud, Sigmund, 14

Gaubert, Serge, 166
Goethe, Johann Wolfgang von, 49

Goodkin, Richard, 170
Gray, Margaret, 159, 161, 162, 166, 170, 171, 172, 174, 175

Hegel, Georg, 23, 109
Henri, Anne, 164, 165, 168, 172
Hill, Leslie, 158, 175
homosexuality, 46, 47, 52–54, 59–62, 63, 64, 85, 95, 163, 168, 169–70, 172, 174, 175, 176
Hutcheon, Linda, 173

impressions, 13–14, 27–38, 87–92, 108–9, 165, 177, 178
irony, 1–2, 3–4, 8, 9–12, 23–25, 39–45, 46–48, 49–68, 79, 99–104, 108, 112, 117, 120, 122–23, 125, 139, 146–50, 156, 167, 170, 171, 178
  irony of irony, 6, 24, 39, 41–44, 49–50, 70–78, 87–88, 98, 106–7, 109, 114, 130–31, 141–42, 151–54, 171, 173
  see also allegory and irony
Iser, Wolfgang, 179

Jameson, Fredric, 39, 43, 64–66, 67, 68, 163, 167, 171

Katz, Daniel, 180
Kern, Edith, 176
Kristeva, Julia, 169

literary historical interplays, 2–5, 9–12, 27, 78, 79, 85–88, 98, 116, 138, 153, 155, 161
lying, 4, 10, 17–18, 19, 39, 41–42, 44, 46–48, 49, 51, 53–57, 60–64, 70–78, 81, 96, 99, 106, 111, 114, 120, 121, 144, 149, 152–53, 168, 170, 171, 176, 179
  liar's paradox, 70–71, 178
  self-deception, 44, 60–62, 66, 106, 119
Lyotard, François, 171

Mallarmé, Stéphane, 164
McGinnis, Reginald, 169, 170
memory, 2, 3, 4, 13–24, 37, 76, 77, 80–87, 121, 173, 175, 176
  involuntary memory, 13–15, 26–30, 55, 64, 91–92, 131, 149, 164, 165, 166, 175, 176
Moorjani, Angela, 175
Morot-Sir, Edouard, 164
mother, 15–24, 53, 55, 63, 80–81, 83–87, 94, 113, 116, 131, 133, 149, 163, 165, 169, 174, 175

narrator
  remembering narrator, 5–11, 13–15, 19, 79, 80–81, 87–88, 90–92, 99, 100, 116, 123–24, 127, 128–29, 131–32, 174, 176

writing narrator, 5, 6–11, 14–15, 16–23, 56–68, 79–81, 84–86, 87, 91, 95, 97–98, 99–101, 102, 107–16, 117–37, 174
Newmark, Kevin, 162, 169, 173
Nietzsche, Friedrich, 14, 57–58, 62, 102, 104, 115, 120, 142, 171

parody, 10, 12, 79–82, 83–94, 95, 98, 115, 116, 127, 131, 171, 173, 175, 177, 179
Pascal, Blaise, 58
Pilling, John, 176, 181
Plato, 165
Poulet, Georges, 28
Proust, Marcel
  A l'Ombre des jeunes filles en fleurs II, 44, 75, 177
  Le Côté de Guermantes I, 175
  Le Côté de Guermantes II, 31–45, 70
  Combray, 5–8, 15–25, 80–81, 83–84, 85–88, 97, 100, 109, 114–15, 118, 140, 142, 182
  Contre Sainte-Beuve, 18, 173
  Jean Santeuil, 70
  La Fugitive (*Albertine disparue*), 47–48, 71
  La Prisonnière, 48–59, 71–74, 152–53, 176
  Sodome et Gomorrhe I, 175
  Sodome et Gomorrhe II, 59–61
  Le Temps retrouvé, 14, 21–22, 63–64, 67, 76, 77–78, 80, 127–29, 177

reading, 16–19, 23, 31
realist discourse, 39–44, 111, 167, 177, 178
Reid, James, 178, 179, 182
Ricoeur, Paul, 164

Sand, Georges (*François le Champi*), 16, 18, 23, 51
Schelling, Friedrich Wilhelm Joseph von, 35, 49, 164
Schopenhauer, Arthur, 20, 29, 129, 164, 165, 168, 181
Sidorsky, David, 170
social class, 33–36
social economy, 39
social history (influence or determinism), 34, 64–68, 161, 163, 167, 172, 175
social order (reproduction), 101–2, 103–4, 105, 106, 109
socially produced consciousness, 149
socially produced voices and words, 145–50, 151, 152, 155
speech acts, 100–1, 102–4, 106–9, 110–11, 117, 140–41
subject
  impersonal, 131–37, 138–55, 161, 179

personal, 1, 27–32, 35, 39–44, 48–55, 62, 63–64, 72, 79, 88, 90, 138, 139–50, 152, 154, 155, 163, 179, 180
socially produced, 39–44
split, 1–2, 3–4, 5, 6, 15, 17, 73–74, 81–83, 106, 116, 123–26, 139–55, 156

Terdiman, Richard, 14, 64–65, 66, 67, 157, 159, 163, 166, 170, 171, 175
"they" (*The Unnamable*), 145–46

Trezise, Thomas, 3, 158, 160, 161, 174, 179, 180, 181, 184

Wagner, Richard, 48, 57–59, 171
Weber, Samuel, 16, 18, 75, 163
Willis, Sharon, 170

Zima, Pierre, 172
Zurbrugg, Nicholas, 2–3, 174